PRAISE FOR

POSITIVE DISCIPLINE
TOOLS FOR TEACHERS

"To meet the social, emotional, and academic needs of the children in my classroom, I rely on Positive Discipline methods to inspire and motivate students to be active members of our classroom community. The easy-to-implement tools in *Positive Discipline Tools for Teachers* make an immediate impact, allow opportunities for engaged learning, as well as equip students with strategies to be solution seekers, creative thinkers, ethical decision makers, and collaborators who know how to communicate effectively and respectfully."

—Margaret Gunter, fourth-grade teacher at
Mount Vernon Presbyterian School, Atlanta, GA

"We have been using Positive Discipline in our school since we opened in 1999 because the respectful, holistic Positive Discipline approach fits so well with the Montessori philosophy. The clearly defined tools in this book, with real-life examples on how to effectively and realistically implement the tools when working with children, will help many teachers experience the success we have enjoyed."

—Karen Simon, director of Montessori School of Celebration

"This book should be in every guidance counselor's toolbox. Imagine the learning that could take place if the leadership in each school would implement this classroom management style. It would make their jobs a lot easier!"

—Nancy Page, director of Guidance at St. Johns Country Day School

ALSO IN THE POSITIVE DISCIPLINE SERIES

POSITIVE DISCIPLINE TOOLS FOR TEACHERS

EFFECTIVE CLASSROOM MANAGEMENT FOR
SOCIAL, EMOTIONAL, AND ACADEMIC SUCCESS

JANE NELSEN, ED.D., AND KELLY GFROERER, PH.D.

HARMONY

BOOKS · NEW YORK

Copyright © 2017 by Jane Nelsen and Kelly Gfroerer

All rights reserved.
Published in the United States by Harmony Books, an imprint of the Crown
Publishing Group, a division of Penguin Random House LLC, New York.
harmonybooks.com

Harmony Books is a registered trademark, and the Circle colophon is
a trademark of Penguin Random House LLC.

Library of Congress Cataloging-in-Publication data is available upon request.

ISBN 978-1-101-90539-5
Ebook ISBN 978-1-101-90540-1

Printed in the United States of America

All images are by Aaron Bacall with the exception of pages 81 and 112, by Bill
Schorr.

Cover photograph: GagliardiImages/Shutterstock

10 9 8 7 6 5 4 3 2 1

First Edition

Even though she is my coauthor, I have to dedicate this book to Kelly Gfroerer. It was her idea. She started with the idea that we create a deck of Positive Discipline Tools for Teachers *to complement the deck of* Positive Discipline Tools for Parents *and the deck of* Keeping the Joy in Marriage. *We had so much fun that we knew a book should follow. Then there is research. This book is so much richer because of her enthusiasm for adding "What the Research Says" for every tool. Then there is this—we had fun.*

—JN

This book is dedicated to my family: to my parents, who spent their entire careers in classrooms or as administrators supporting teachers. Thank you for providing lifelong role models for how to be quality, caring teachers. And, to my husband, Terry, and our three amazing children, Bryce, Riley, and Morgan. Thank you for the love, support, and patience you showed me throughout the many months I spent working on the tool cards for teachers and this book. I appreciate you giving up our dining room table for weeks at a time for all the stories and cartoons to be organized again and again.

And, finally to Jane, there is no way to express to you my gratitude. Your friendship means the world to me; I love writing with you and feel blessed for the time we have shared working and having so much fun. I look forward to our next project!

—KG

CONTENTS

FOREWORD

As a teacher and Positive Discipline Trainer, I have worked in a variety of difficult school settings. Teaching has been the most emotionally challenging and exhausting yet inspiring and rewarding experience of my life. I honor teachers for the heart and soul they put into their work. For me, it wasn't until I adopted Positive Discipline that I felt I became the educator I'd envisioned when I set out on this career path more than twenty years ago.

Adopting Positive Discipline did not come easily at first. I had to forget everything I had learned about "education" and rethink the role of the teacher as an encouragement facilitator. It was both scary and liberating. I no longer felt I had to be the behavioral motivator, using cheerleading, prize boxes, rewards, or competition to motivate students. With Positive Discipline tools, I no longer assumed the role of judge and jury, punishing students for bad behavior. I finally understood what democracy looked like in a classroom and turned the control over to students, who found the solutions to problems themselves once I allowed them to learn from their own mistakes.

Initially, I too wondered how my students' motivation to develop academically and grow socially could be improved by holding daily class meetings. Soon I discovered how taking time for class meetings positively affected my students and classroom community. Taking time to teach social skill activities, noticing the way I spoke to students, making wiser curriculum choices, and taking time to connect with my students all had an impact. After my first training, when I dared question whether Positive Discipline could actually work, Jody McVittie, M.D., a Positive Discipline Lead Trainer, replied with a confident smile: "Get curious and have faith in the process." So I did.

I didn't realize how much my efforts had paid off until Dr. Jane Nelsen came to visit my classroom several months later and declared, "This is what Positive Discipline looks like in a classroom." She said she heard my first-grade students using "I" messages and problem-solving language. They were intrinsically motivated to use the Wheel of Choice (page 178) to solve problems. She noticed how my students were emotionally articulate and capable of self-regulating. The cool-off spot was being used regularly and my students were initiating problem-solving. I was able to identify my own feelings about student behavior better as I used the steps from the Mistaken Goal Chart, and I found new ways of offering encouragement.

I am very grateful that over the years I have witnessed so many daily examples of Positive Discipline successes. It is an honor to share in this foreword my most heartbreaking and inspiring success story about Positive Discipline.

Innovations Academy, a charter school in San Diego, California, has been implementing Positive Discipline for seven years. As a consultant at the school, I have grown very close to the staff, so I was devastated when I learned that one of their beloved teachers, Alex, had been killed in a car accident on his way to school. Alex had been working at the school since it opened in 2008, and he had embraced Positive Discipline wholeheartedly.

Alex was a well-loved and highly dedicated teacher, a dear friend to his colleagues, and a joyful and beautiful spirit. Needless to say, the loss and sadness felt by all who knew him cannot be described, but the school's response to the events of that day illustrates in a beautiful way what children learn and experience in a Positive Discipline school community.

The school administrators were concerned that something serious might have happened that day, because they knew Alex would have reported if he was going to be late. They began calling the highway patrol and local hospitals. The most remarkable among the initial responses to his absence was the behavior of his own class. The morning of the accident, when Alex didn't show up for class, his sixth-grade students decided to start their morning classroom meeting without him. They circled together and started with compliments, while a parent went to the office to ask why Alex was not there. The students continued with their morning meeting, with another parent observing, until a substitute teacher arrived.

Later that morning, the school learned of the accident. The director, Christine Kuglen, had the presence of mind to bring in a crisis intervention team to help her share the news with the students and staff. What followed was a testament to the skills the students had learned through Positive Discipline. After being on campus for less than an hour, the crisis team shared with the administration their opinion that the students and staff were coping with the news with more skill and understanding than they had ever seen. The crisis team didn't feel they were even needed because everyone was already doing all they needed to do in response to the news. They were holding each other's pain; sharing their feelings, stories, and memories; and talking about how grateful they were for the time they had with Alex. Everyone recognized how deeply Alex would be missed. As each person processed the news in his or her own way, they all collectively supported each other. The way students articulated their pain made it clear they understood how to process their loss.

One concern the students shared was their worry about the future of the project they had been working on with Alex leading the way. They had been helping adults with Alzheimer's disease at a local care facility. They were studying how music could potentially help them bring back some of their memories. The students were worried that this project would be dropped now that Alex was gone. With some discussion and problem-solving, the students decided that with another teacher's support and help they could complete the project to honor Alex's memory.

Although Alex's death was an indescribable and terrible loss, the students and staff were left with the awareness that life is precious. They learned that no matter what we face in life and regardless of what unexpected event tests our resilience and faith, such trials can be met with courage and hope. I was in awe of the courage, compassion, and love this school community shared with one another. I was inspired by the powerful influence of Positive Discipline, which was clearly the foundational component that brought this school together as a community.

Now I am a principal of a private elementary school, Irvine Hebrew Day School, where we are employing Positive Discipline as our foundational approach to teaching and learning. I have an even deeper appreciation for the transformative nature of Positive Discipline in a school community and the impact this approach can have on staff, students, and families.

It is known that teacher-training programs, such as the one I experienced at Teachers College at Columbia University, are excellent at preparing teachers to be culturally proficient and skilled in developing strong curricula, understanding and using appropriate assessments, and implementing best practices. Yet even the strongest of programs doesn't focus on helping teachers develop the tools presented in this book, tools that help support the effective communication and relationship skills that teachers require to create mutually respectful classrooms, build intrinsic motivation, and develop cooperative learning communities.

Teachers will be encouraged and inspired by the tools and success stories in *Positive Discipline Tools for Teachers*. Its many examples are inspiring, and it is encouraging to know that there are other teachers implementing Positive Discipline all over the world. Their stories model the many ways Positive Discipline encourages and supports students' growth. Positive Discipline provides the very tools teachers require to be most successful, to respond to students with encouragement, to promote critical life skills so that students develop their full human potential, to model empathy and compassion, to show students the value of taking time to learn skills, and, most important, to develop in their students the ability to connect with their peers, teachers, and parents with the utmost respect.

Tammy Keces, M.A., principal at Irvine Hebrew Day School,
Certified Positive Discipline Lead Trainer

POSITIVE DISCIPLINE
TOOLS FOR TEACHERS

INTRODUCTION

The number one stressor for teachers who want to make a difference in the lives of their students is the time they spend dealing with misbehavior. Teachers from around the world have shared how the tools in this book can save them time and stress—and make discipline encouraging and helpful instead of discouraging and stressful.

This book will help educators to better understand the downside of using a reward and punishment system, and what to do instead to inspire and motivate students. Research (including neurological research) shows that using rewards and punishment actually decreases internal motivation, cooperation, self-control, and independent problem-solving.[1] Positive Discipline increases all of these important characteristics.

Most educators would prefer not to use punishment if they had other tools that were not only respectful but also more effective. In this book we share decades of research demonstrating that punishment is not effective long term, and we provide many Positive Discipline tools (again based on research studies) that are respectful as well as helpful long term.

The following is a list of long-term beliefs and behaviors that are likely to be created by punishment.

THE FOUR R'S OF PUNISHMENT
1. Resentment: "This is unfair. I can't trust adults."
2. Rebellion: "I'll do just the opposite to prove I don't have to do it their way."

3. Revenge: "They are winning now, but I'll get even."
4. Retreat:
   a. Sneakiness: "I won't get caught next time."
   b. Reduced self-esteem: "I am a bad person."

Some teachers conclude that if punishment is not helpful, they are left with only one alternative in dealing with a student's misbehavior—permissiveness. This choice, however, can be just as damaging as punishment. Permissiveness invites students to develop such mistaken beliefs as "I should be able to do whatever I want," "I need you to take care of me because I'm not capable of responsibility," or even "I'm depressed because you don't cater to my every demand."

"So," you may ask, "if not punishment, and not permissiveness, then what?" The Positive Discipline tools in this book help show how many possibilities there are that do not include rewards and punishment. Positive Discipline tools address the belief behind the behavior, as well as the behavior itself, and follow these criteria:

THE FIVE CRITERIA FOR POSITIVE DISCIPLINE
1. Helps children feel a sense of connection, belonging, and significance
2. Is kind and firm at the same time
3. Is effective in the long term
4. Teaches valuable social and life skills for good character: fostering respect, concern for others, problem-solving skills, cooperation
5. Invites children to discover how capable they are and to use their power constructively to contribute in social settings

Even though the Positive Discipline tools are designed to meet these criteria, it is essential to understand that they are based on the principles and philosophies of Alfred Adler and Rudolf Dreikurs. These tools are not effective if used as "techniques," that is, based on a memorized script. When you understand the principle upon which the tool is based, you can use your own wisdom to apply these tools in many different situations in ways that are genuine and caring from your heart.

In contrast to behaviorists who advocated for external rewards and punishment in the classroom to motivate change, Adler believed the best way to change behavior is from the inside out, by using encouragement to help people experience deep belonging and connection, which is balanced by contribution in their social settings. *A sense of belonging without contribution equals a feeling of entitlement.* Positive Discipline includes many tools that balance the needs for belonging and for contribution by involving students in many ways, including problem-solving, which is a necessary skill in all aspects of life.

Forbes magazine recently reported that businesses could learn from school programs that base their discipline on mutual respect and dignity, rather than punishment.[2] Positive Discipline is specifically acknowledged in this article, along with astounding reports from one high school that stopped using punishment. Lincoln Alternative High School in Walla Walla, Washington, has received a lot of press since principal Jim Sporleder, inspired by the Adverse Childhood Experiences Study by Dr. Vincent Felitti and Centers for Disease Control epidemiologist Robert Anda, decided to use love and respect instead of punishment with "misbehaving" students. The results were telling:

2009–2010 (BEFORE NEW APPROACH)
- 798 suspensions (days students were out of school)
- 50 expulsions
- 600 written referrals

2010–2011 (AFTER NEW APPROACH)
- 135 suspensions (days students were out of school)
- 30 expulsions
- 320 written referrals

Three years later, the number of fights at Lincoln Alternative High School had gone down by 75 percent and the graduation rate had increased fivefold.[3]

Alfred Adler and Rudolf Dreikurs advocated avoiding rewards and punishments because of the negative effects. They were leaders in the development of the field of psychiatry, as well as the first to focus on psychology in the classroom, and long ago recommended democratic leadership focused on kind and firm classroom management.

This can require a big paradigm shift for many teachers and school administrators, since historically schools have relied on the use of rewards and punishment. However, making this shift will change your classroom for the better and make your job as a teacher a whole lot easier. You will help your students develop internal motivation to learn as well as the skills to work with others cooperatively. As a result, your students will learn to manage themselves. No more wasted time with sticker charts, red/yellow/green lights, or ClassDojo boards. All of these teaching aids publicly shame students.

Not only are these reward and punishment systems ineffective in the long term, they are exhausting and time-consuming. On the other hand, Positive Discipline emphasizes tools such as Class Meetings, the Wheel of Choice, Four Problem-Solving Steps, Classroom Jobs, Positive Time-Out (for self-regulation), and Mistakes as Opportunities for Learning to help your students learn and thrive at school and in life. They will be learning the skills they need for success in the twenty-first century, instead of only learning how to please their teacher, scrape by in school, or drop out.

We hear your next argument: "How can I find time to teach social-emotional skills when I'm being asked to focus on an academic curriculum, both to get my students to pass tests and because there's the pressure of knowing that everyone will see scores and school rankings printed in newspapers and discussed on national TV?" We agree that this is extremely discouraging and hope that someday it will be changed. Meanwhile, we can provide tools for teaching social-emotional skills that are fun and effective. Think of the time you'll save when you have a classroom full of trained problem-solvers and self-regulators instead of having to constantly punish or reward for good behavior.

Also consider this question: How will students use their academic learning if they don't have social-emotional skills? You may be thinking, "Obviously, students need social-emotional learning, but that's the parent's job; my job is academics." We don't want to diminish the responsibility of parents, but students spend more of their waking hours in classrooms than in their homes. Schools are social environments—the perfect place to practice social-emotional skills. And students who have strong social-emotional skills are more cooperative in the classroom and take more responsibility for their learning environment.

Positive Discipline is not about allowing students to "get away" with anything. It is about understanding why students make mistakes in the first place (the beliefs behind their behavior) and using tools that encourage them to change their beliefs and thus their behavior. It means teaching skills for focusing on solutions to challenging behavior instead of making them "pay" for challenging behavior. It means providing a place where they will feel belonging (connection), a strong sense of capability, and the value of contribution.

THE ICEBERG ANALOGY

We have found the analogy of an iceberg to be an excellent way to convey the philosophy of Adler and Dreikurs. A student's behavior, like the visible tip of the iceberg shown here, is what you see. However, the hidden base of the iceberg, which is much larger than the tip, represents the *belief* behind the behavior and the real motivation for the behavior, which is the student's deep need for belonging and contribution. Most classroom management models address only the behavior. Positive Discipline addresses the behavior, the belief behind the behavior, and skills to help students create healthier beliefs.

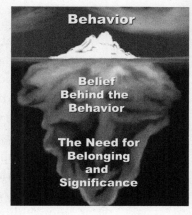

When students misbehave, they usually have a *mistaken belief* about how to gain a sense of belonging. The belief generates what teachers see as misbehavior. Without recognizing the belief behind the behavior, some adults react to the behavior with some kind of punishment, such as blaming, shaming, or inflicting physical pain. This kind of response only confirms a student's belief that he or she doesn't belong, creating a vicious cycle that leads to more misbehavior. In this cycle the student's deep need for belonging, contribution, and skills is not being addressed at all.

Adler and Dreikurs taught that "a misbehaving child is a discouraged child." The discouragement comes from the child's belief that "I don't belong." This conclusion often leads to misbehavior because it is based on beliefs such as "I will belong only if I get lots of attention" (or "if I am the boss," or "if I hurt others like I feel hurt," or "if I give up"). These beliefs and behaviors do not produce the desired results of belonging and contribution. This is why Adler called them "*mistaken* beliefs." Rudolf Dreikurs, a Viennese psychiatrist and protégé of Adler, further developed these four major beliefs and called them the "four mistaken goals" of behavior—"mistaken" because the true goal is to belong, and the "mistake" is faulty ways to achieve belonging. Adler and Dreikurs asserted the only way to change behavior is to help individuals change the belief behind the behavior. (See "Understand the Mistaken Goal" tools beginning on page 23.)

CREATING A RESULTS ROAD MAP

In our workshops we do an activity called The Two Lists: Challenges and Characteristics and Life Skills to create a visual guide for what teachers hope to accomplish with their students. During this process we have discovered that teachers all over the world share the same challenges and hope to influence their students to develop the same characteristics and life skills. For the "Challenges" list, teachers struggle with the same misbehaviors such as talking back, lack of motivation, entitlement, interrupting, fighting, lying, and not listening. For the "Characteristics and Life Skills" list, teachers worldwide list responsibility, honesty, self-control, problem-solving, independence, resilience, cooperation, and compassion, just to name a few. What is unique about Positive Discipline is that every challenge is viewed as an opportunity to teach characteristics and life skills. As impossible as it sometimes seems, Positive Discipline will help you handle misbehavior and teach life skills and contribution at the same time.

PUTTING YOURSELF IN THEIR SHOES

During our Positive Discipline workshops and classes, we teach through experiential activities, where teachers have the opportunity to step into the shoes of their students by role-playing. These role-playing activities help teachers gain a sense of what works with students and what doesn't. This process helps teachers understand how their words, behaviors, and teaching methods may have a part in creating or re-inforcing the very misbehaviors they want to change. When teachers experience what it is like to be the student through role-playing, they better appreciate how effective the Positive Discipline tools can be in helping their students develop the characteristics and life skills they hope for them.

Dreikurs pointed out that change can be difficult when students are accustomed to strict autocratic rule. There can be a period of chaos when students enter a democratic classroom because they are not used to taking responsibility or contributing. However, this period is short, and teaching students the skills for cooperation has far-reaching, long-term benefits. Adler and Dreikurs recognized that respectful discipline is the only way to teach problem-solving and other important life skills.

Will *Positive Discipline Tools for Teachers* take care of all your classroom management challenges? We can't promise that, but we can promise that Positive Discipline tools will help your students feel a greater sense of belonging and contribution, as well as a stronger belief in their personal capability. And every time your students test limits, you will have tools to help them learn from their misbehavior instead of being punished for it.

To encourage you along your Positive Discipline journey, this book offers explanations and examples of many Positive Discipline tools for teachers. To emphasize the volumes of research that support the original ideas of Adler and Dreikurs (and are accepted as best practices for classroom management), each Positive Discipline Teacher tool ends with a section called "What the Research Says." Most important, we feature stories from teachers all over the world who are using these tools in their classrooms. While all the teachers and their stories are real, we have changed the names and identifying information of all students to protect student privacy. We hope the successes these teachers share will inspire you as you learn about each of these tools and begin to put Positive Discipline into practice in your own classroom.

CHAPTER ONE

UNDERSTANDING YOUR STUDENTS

BECOME A MISTAKEN GOAL DETECTIVE

When we know the goal of a person, we know approximately what will follow.

—*Alfred Adler*

As stated in the Introduction, a unique and most important insight of Positive Discipline is the understanding that there is a belief behind every behavior. Students have a reason for doing what they do. Adler called it "private logic." A student's behavior may not make sense to us, but it makes sense to him or her. In Positive Discipline we teach adults to be "behavior detectives" by trying to understand the belief behind the behavior.

"I *do* respect your learning style, but not the part where you crumple paper and throw it around the classroom."

It's time to channel your inner detective and start reading the signals that your students are sending you. This means that you will be a teacher whose energy is focused on following clues to discover the belief behind a student's behavior, rather than a teacher focused on needlessly punishing unacceptable behavior. It means you will use your best teaching skills to encourage a student to develop a new belief and a new behavior.

The Mistaken Goal Chart (page 12) and the Mistaken Goal Detective Clue Form (page 11) help you become a master behavior detective. Use them to solve the mystery of how to encourage a challenging student.

MISTAKEN GOAL DETECTIVE CLUE FORM

1. Think of a recent challenge you had with a student. Write it down. Describe what occurred as though you are writing a script: What did your student do? How did you react? What happened next?

2. What were you feeling when you were in the middle of this challenge? (Choose a feeling from Column 2 of the Mistaken Goal Chart.) Write it down.

3. Now move your finger over to Column 3 of the Mistaken Goal Chart to see if your behavior, as you described it in your challenge, comes close to any of these typical adult responses. If what you did is described better in a different row, double-check to see if there is a feeling in another row in Column 2 that better represents how you were feeling at a deeper level. (For example, we often say we are feeling annoyed when, at a deeper level, we are feeling challenged or hurt, or we might say we feel hopeless and helpless when we really feel challenged or defeated in a power struggle.) How you react is a clue to your deeper feelings.

4. Move your finger across to Column 4. Do any of these descriptions come close to what the child did in response to your reaction?

5. Now move your finger back to Column 1 of the Mistaken Goal Chart. It is likely that this is your student's mistaken goal. Write it down.

6. Move your finger to the right, to Column 5. You have just discovered what may be the discouraging belief that is the basis for the student's mistaken goal. Write it down.

7. Move your finger to Column 6. Does this come close to a belief you have that may contribute to the student's misbehavior? (Remember, this is not about blame, only about awareness.) While you are learning skills to encourage the student, you will also change your own belief! Try it now by writing down a response that would be more encouraging to your student. You'll find clues in the last two columns.

MISTAKEN GOAL CHART

1	2	3	4	5
THE STUDENT'S GOAL IS:	IF THE PARENT/ TEACHER FEELS:	AND TENDS TO REACT BY:	AND IF THE STUDENT'S RESPONSE IS:	THE BELIEF BEHIND THE STUDENT'S BEHAVIOR IS:
Undue attention (to keep others busy or get special service)	Annoyed Irritated Worried Guilty	Reminding Coaxing Doing things for the student that the student could do for him- or herself	Stops temporarily, but later resumes the same or another disturbing behavior Stops when given one-on-one attention	"I count [belong] only when I'm being noticed or getting special service." "I'm important only when I'm keeping you busy with me."
Misguided power (to be the boss)	Angry Challenged Threatened Defeated	Fighting Giving in Thinking, "You can't get away with it" or "I'll make you" Wanting to be right	Intensifies the behavior Defiant compliance Feels he or she has won when the parent or teacher is upset Passive power	"I belong only when I'm the boss, in control, or proving no one can boss me." "You can't make me."

6	7	8
HOW ADULTS MAY CONTRIBUTE TO THE PROBLEM:	**THE STUDENT'S CODED MESSAGES:**	**PARENT/TEACHER PROACTIVE AND EMPOWERING RESPONSES INCLUDE:**
"I don't have faith in you to deal with disappointment." "I feel guilty if you aren't happy."	"Notice me. Involve me usefully."	Redirect by involving student in a useful task to gain useful attention. Tell your child you care, and then say what you will do: "I love you and _____" (for example, "I care about you and will spend time with you later"). Avoid special services. Say it only once and then act. Have faith in the student's ability to deal with his or her feelings (don't fix the problem or rescue the student). Plan special time. Set up routines. Engage the student in problem solving. Use family or class meetings. Ignore (touch without words). Set up nonverbal signals.
"I'm in control and you must do what I say." "I believe that telling you what to do, and lecturing or punishing you when you don't do it, is the best way to motivate you to do better."	"Let me help. Give me choices."	Acknowledge that you can't make the student do something, and redirect to positive power by asking for help. Offer a limited choice. Don't fight and don't give in. Withdraw from conflict and calm down. Be firm and kind. Act, don't talk. Decide what you will do. Let routines be the boss. Develop mutual respect. Get help from the student to set a few reasonable limits. Practice follow-through. Use family or class meetings.

1	2	3	4	5
THE STUDENT'S GOAL IS:	**IF THE PARENT/ TEACHER FEELS:**	**AND TENDS TO REACT BY:**	**AND IF THE STUDENT'S RESPONSE IS:**	**THE BELIEF BEHIND THE STUDENT'S BEHAVIOR IS:**
Revenge (to get even)	Hurt Disappointed Disbelieving Disgusted	Retaliating Getting even Thinking, "How could you do this to me?" Taking the student's behavior personally	Retaliates Hurts others Damages property Gets even Intensifies Escalates the same behavior or chooses another negative behavior	"I don't think I belong, so I'll hurt others in the way I feel hurt." "I can't be liked or loved."
Assumed inadequacy (to give up and be left alone)	Despairing Hopeless Helpless Inadequate	Giving up Doing the task for the student Helping too much Showing a lack of faith in the student	Retreats further Passive No improvement No response Avoids trying	"I don't believe I can belong, so I'll convince others not to expect anything of me." "I am helpless and unable; it's no use trying because I won't do it right."

6	7	8
HOW ADULTS MAY CONTRIBUTE TO THE PROBLEM:	**THE STUDENT'S CODED MESSAGES:**	**PARENT/TEACHER PROACTIVE AND EMPOWERING RESPONSES INCLUDE:**
"I give advice (without listening to you) because I think I'm helping." "I worry more about what the neighbors think than what you need."	"I'm hurting. Validate my feelings."	Validate the student's hurt feelings (you might have to guess what they are). Don't take the student's behavior personally. Step out of the revenge cycle by avoiding punishment and retaliation. Suggest Positive Time-Out for both of you, then focus on solutions. Use reflective listening. Share your feelings using an "I" message. Apologize and make amends. Encourage strengths. Put kids in the same boat. Use family and class meetings.
"I expect you to live up to my high expectations." "I thought it was my job to do things for you."	"Don't give up on me. Show me a small step."	Break tasks down into small steps. Make the task easier until the student experiences success. Set up opportunities for success. Take time for training. Teach skills and show how, but don't do the task for the student. Stop all criticism. Encourage any positive attempt, no matter how small. Show faith in the student's abilities. Focus on the student's assets. Don't pity the student. Don't give up. Enjoy the student. Build on the student's interests. Use family or class meetings.

8. Move your finger to Column 7, where you will find the coded message the child is sending about what he or she needs in order to feel encouraged.

9. Move once more to Column 8, the last one, to find some ideas you could try the next time the student presents this challenging behavior. You can also use your own wisdom to think of what to do or say that would speak to the coded message in Column 7. Write down your plan.

10. How did it go? Record in your journal exactly what you discovered and what happened. Did the student's behavior change? Did yours? If your plan isn't successful the first time, try another tool. Make certain that in every effort you begin by making a connection before you attempt a correction.

Another way to discern mistaken goals is to use what Dreikurs called "goal disclosure." The Mistaken Goal Chart may not include a particular student's belief, but it can help you make informed and helpful guesses about what the motivating belief may be. The goal disclosure process can help you confirm your guesses in a way that creates a connection with the student, because it provides the deepest form of empathy: helping the student feel deeply understood.

GOAL DISCLOSURE

Wait for a calm time (not during conflict) to talk with a student in private. A friendly atmosphere is essential. Ask the student for permission to make guesses about why he or she is behaving in a certain way. Let the student know that he or she can tell you if you have guessed correctly or not. (This is usually an intriguing challenge to the student.) Ask the questions below, one at a time. If after any question you get a yes or a recognition reflex (for example, a spontaneous smile even while saying no—the no is an automatic denial, while the smile suggests that the student has subconsciously gained a deeper understanding of herself), you can follow up with plans for the student to get her needs met in ways that are positive and empowering. If no clarifying response to a question occurs, go on to the next question.

1. "Could it be that you do this particular behavior to get my attention?" (Undue Attention)
2. "Could it be that you want to show me I can't make you do as I ask?" (Misguided Power)
3. "Could it be that you feel hurt and want to hurt back?" (Revenge)
4. "Could it be that you believe you can't succeed and want to be left alone?" (Assumed Inadequacy)

Here are some effective responses if the student responds with a yes (or a recognition reflex) to a question indicating a specific goal.

1. Undue Attention: "Everyone wants attention. There are encouraging ways and discouraging ways to get attention. Would you be willing to work with me on a plan for you to get attention in ways that are positive and encouraging to others as well as yourself, such as a morning greeter?"
2. Misguided Power: "Power can be used in encouraging ways or discouraging ways. I would appreciate your help in using your power in ways that are useful to yourself and the whole class. Would you be willing to lead our class meeting tomorrow, or would you like to be a tutor in one of the lower grades for a student who needs some help?"
3. Revenge: "I can see that you are feeling hurt. I'm so sorry. Is there anything I can do to help?" When the mistaken goal is Revenge, validating hurt feelings is often enough to invite behavior change. If it doesn't seem that validation is enough, follow up by saying, "Would you like to get together again tomorrow to see if we can figure out some ways to find a solution to this challenge?"
4. Assumed Inadequacy: "I won't give up on you. I care too much. We'll do whatever it takes to help you succeed. Let me show

you some small steps to help you get started." (For example, if the child is having trouble drawing a circle, say, "I'll draw the first half of the circle, and you can draw the second half." This technique can be effective with whatever learning task the student is struggling with.)

Goal disclosure can be a powerful tool. When the teacher's empathy is genuine, the student experiences a connection with the teacher that is deeply caring. Goal disclosure will help you better understand your student, and your student will gain valuable insights about his or her deeper needs and motivations.

A teacher's friendly demeanor during goal disclosure demonstrates how much he or she cares. Because effective goal disclosure includes authentic empathy from the teacher and a new sense of connection for the student, the process will increase the student's feeling of belonging and contribution. Remember, when belonging and contribution increase, misbehavior decreases.

TOOL IN ACTION FROM KOWLOON, HONG KONG

Alex is an eight-year-old boy. He is very intelligent, but he cannot make friends at school. Most of the girls just walk away from him. Most of the boys fight with him. Refusing to follow instructions from teachers or parents is a big issue for Alex. He will avoid participation when he has no interest in a subject. The PE teacher has a very hard time calming him down when he interrupts the class because he wants to avoid group participation. He is very good at math and science, but when he finishes assigned tasks early and is bored, he becomes disruptive. He told me that he understands his behaviors are not acceptable sometimes, but he cannot control his emotions.

Most of our teachers feel challenged, defeated, and angry with Alex. They prefer dealing with Alex through methods that exclude him from the group. They ask him to calm himself down by standing outside the classroom, or they send him to time-out when he interrupts the learning of others in class.

I feel upset about his behaviors. He is smart enough to understand what he is doing. He knows what is right and wrong, but he chooses not to do what is right. He makes trouble for himself in his classes. Given his misbehavior, it was inevitable that eventually nobody wanted to be his friend.

When I follow the Mistaken Goal Chart, I see that his goal is Misguided Power. He wants to have power, "to be the boss." Alex may be thinking, "The teacher cannot make me follow her instructions. I feel safe and happy if I can control this situation. I am the boss and nobody can tell me what to do."

Using the Coded Messages column ("Let me help. Give me choices") and suggestions in the last column, we decided to create more responsibilities for Alex and to encourage him to help others. I had a meeting with Alex in which we discussed the issues, and I invited him to choose a few reasonable options to try over a period of at least one month. I created the chart on page 20 to keep track of the existing behavior and two options of new behaviors for Alex to choose.

During the next few weeks, Alex might slip into his old behaviors, and I would ask, "What did you decide you would do when you are bored?" He would remember his choice and would do it. Alex's behavior did not become perfect, but he improved dramatically. He shared that he feels good and strong when he takes this responsibility.

ISSUE IN THE CLASSROOM	EXISTING BEHAVIORS	NEW OPTION 1	NEW OPTION 2	DECISION AND RESULT
Alex is bored when he completes his work in the classroom.	He walks around and interrupts or distracts other classmates.	He can ask his teacher to give him more work to do to keep him busy until the class completes the activity.	He can ask the teacher's permission to help other classmates who can benefit from his knowledge.	Alex chose option 1. It keeps him busy focusing on his own work, and he has no time to interrupt others.
He dislikes the group activities in PE class.	He argues with the PE teacher or runs away, leaving the classroom or group.	He can ask the PE teacher if he can take a rest and sit down outside the group. (Positive Time-Out)	He can ask the PE teacher if he can observe the activity first and try it himself only when he feels he is ready to do so.	Alex chose option 1. The PE teacher gave me feedback that it is easier to help him calm down when he chooses "Positive time-out." The PE teacher was able to focus on his teaching by not spending time correcting or arguing with Alex during the activity.
He always fights with others.	When classmates disagree with his ideas during teamwork, he has a strong intention to prove that he is right and ends up fighting with others.	Alex can write down the ideas or opinions of group members first, and then take his turn to share his own ideas.		Alex realized that when he wrote down his classmates' opinions and focused on common points between them, he could vote with the majority. He enjoyed serving the group rather than spending time fighting over right or wrong.

—Ms. Siu Mei (Veronica) Ho, school counselor, Certified Positive Discipline Educator

After over thirty years of teaching children from different backgrounds and with different abilities, I have found that the program that works for all children in a positive, encouraging, respectful way is Positive Discipline. Positive Discipline has helped me redirect my discipline methods toward a more child-focused approach. I am more effective at helping my students find new, more appropriate behaviors, along with a sense of belonging and significance in my classroom.

The tool I use during each and every school day is the Mistaken Goal Chart. This tool has made the biggest difference in my understanding of a child's purposeful, although at times misguided, behavior. By recognizing the child's belief behind his behavior of choice, I have been able to redirect behavior so that positive outcomes can occur for the child, myself, and the whole class.

Instead of being irritated by a child who consistently needs undue attention, I now see the purpose behind his behavior and understand the child's private logic and misguided goal. Instead of reacting out of my own stress when I feel irritated, I become a goal detective and look for the coded message in the child's misbehavior. I realize the child's behavior is his way of saying "notice me, connect with me." I have a game plan that immediately brings into play the tools that will help the student connect in positive, constructive ways, rather than continuing to seek this connection in negative ways. I know that giving the student a job, involving the student in a cooperative learning group, and simply taking a moment to check in with him individually are all ways to meet his goal in a positive way and facilitate change. Knowing there is always a goal behind a student's behavior keeps me from simply reacting emotionally and becoming a part of the child's misguided behavior. Instead, I can think rationally and focus on the clues that reveal the student's actual need as opposed to the mistaken belief that is motivating his negative behavior.

—Meg Frederick, kindergarten teacher

TOOL TIPS

1. It takes a paradigm shift to remember to deal with the belief behind the behavior instead of just the behavior.

2. Using the Mistaken Goal Detective Clue Form and goal disclosure takes time that will be saved tenfold when it helps a student experience the kind of encouragement that invites behavior change.

WHAT THE RESEARCH SAYS

Studies indicate that students who perceive their teacher as empathetic and caring are more attentive and engaged in the learning process. When goal disclosure is done with genuine empathy, the process will communicate understanding and help the student connect with the teacher in a lasting way. Students from different cultural backgrounds particularly benefit from teachers who demonstrate understanding and are open to discussing diverse perspectives with empathy.[4]

Researchers Beaty-O'Ferrall, Green, and Hanna identify the importance of empathy, which provides support for how the disclosure of the goal behind misbehavior can be a useful strategy for connecting with and redirecting difficult students.[5] They point out that empathy in the classroom is a concept largely misunderstood and difficult to practice for many educators. They define empathy as distinctly different from caring or affection and highlight that Adler defined empathy as "seeing with the eyes of another, hearing with the ears of another, and feeling with the heart of another." The end result of having been shown empathy is that the person "feels understood." This sense of being understood is crucial in reaching and relating to students. Showing empathy when a student tries to engage in power struggles is effective in communicating your understanding and acceptance of the student. Feeling understood increases one's sense of belonging, which directly impacts school performance.

UNDERSTAND THE MISTAKEN GOAL: UNDUE ATTENTION

Once we are aware of the mistaken goal of the child, we are in a position to realize the purpose of his behavior.

—Rudolf Dreikurs

Everyone wants attention. It is part of the need for belonging and contribution. The problems begin when a student (or anyone) seeks attention in pointless and annoying ways because they have the belief that "I'm okay *only if* I get attention."

Adding to the challenge is that there are so many useless ways to seek attention. Being the class clown, acting helpless and demanding undue service, and having temper tantrums are just a few of the annoying ways to get attention that are motivated by beliefs that come from discouragement and lead to getting attention in all the wrong ways.

Using the analogy of the iceberg, we provide a synopsis of the mistaken goal of Undue Attention.

For Undue Attention, the belief behind the misbehavior is "I belong only when you pay constant attention to me, and/or give me special service." The coded message that provides clues for encouragement is "Notice me. Involve me usefully." You can go to the Mistaken Goal Chart (page 12) and look at Column 2 to identify feelings that are your first clue in understanding a student's mistaken goal.

GUIDANCE COUNSELOR

BACALL

"Just because everyone applauded when you dropped you lunch try in the cafeteria doesn't mean that you should purse a career in show business."

In the "Tool in Action" section below, the teacher, Joy, felt annoyed, irritated, and worried, which indicates the mistaken goal of Undue Attention. Seeing this on the Mistaken Goal Chart helped her to understand the belief behind the behavior and then find ways to encourage a very disruptive student.

TOOL IN ACTION FROM LONDON, ENGLAND

I first discovered Positive Discipline in 2007 when I was running an educational nonprofit organization in New York City. That year I vividly remember walking into a fourth-grade classroom for the first time in Brownsville, Brooklyn, as a chair came flying past my head.

The room was in complete chaos, most of which was created by one little boy. My initial reaction was to send him out of the room for his own safety and for the safety of others. However, I was reminded of an important lesson that Rudolf Dreikurs taught: "A misbehaving child is a discouraged child."

I thought about the vision of the iceberg and remembered that the behavior is just the tip of the iceberg. I was determined to understand this boy's belief behind his behavior. By tapping into my own feelings of being annoyed, irritated, and worried, I realized that what this boy was really saying was "I belong only when you are paying attention to me."

Whenever he misbehaved I imagined him wearing a T-shirt that said, "Notice me, involve me usefully." That shifted my entire perspective and my response to his behavior. Instead of sending him out of the classroom, I did the exact opposite—I asked for his help.

He became my helper and passed out papers, distributed the snacks, and monitored the supplies. Not only did his behavior improve, but also his attendance became more consistent and he would even show up to school early and ask if there was anything he could do to help. He now felt a sense of belonging and significance in the classroom and did not need to misbehave in order to try to have those needs met.

When I changed my perspective as well as my response, the entire climate in the classroom changed. The Mistaken Goal Chart was life-changing for me as an educator and the one tool that I would not let any teacher enter a classroom without.

—Joy Marchese, tenth-grade teacher, American School of London,
Certified Positive Discipline Trainer

TOOL TIPS

1. Speak to the coded message by guiding your students to gain attention usefully. The following are a few examples:
   - "Will you please hand out these papers for me?"
   - "Let's make a deal. You sit quietly and get your work done, and we'll have time to hang out for a few minutes at recess."
   - "Tomorrow you can take a whole minute at the start of class to lead the class in making funny faces and jokes."
   - "Today you can be the monitor to let me know when someone needs help."

2. The last column of the Mistaken Goal Chart includes other ways to respond to the coded message "Notice me. Involve me usefully."

WHAT THE RESEARCH SAYS

Researcher Robert Blum summarizes extensive research showing that "second only to family, school is the most important stabilizing force in the lives of young people."[6] The value of feeling significant at school is supported by strong scientific evidence demonstrating that increased student connection at school decreases absenteeism, fighting, bullying, and vandalism. On the other hand, when students experience feelings of connection at school, it increases motivation, engagement in the classroom, academic performance, and attendance.

UNDERSTAND THE MISTAKEN GOAL: MISGUIDED POWER

By doing nothing in a power contest, you defeat the child's power.

—*Rudolf Dreikurs*

What does Dreikurs mean when he suggests "doing nothing" in a power contest? The answer lies in how many people it takes to engage in a power struggle, which is at least two. If one person decides to disengage, there cannot be a power struggle.

Notice that Dreikurs didn't say "defeat the child"; he said "defeat the child's power." We also know that he did not mean all of the child's power—just misguided power.

There are many ways to disengage. One example is to simply validate the feelings of the student. Another example is to name what is going on: "It looks like we are in a power struggle. Let's wait until we calm down." Another way is to say, "Tell me more about what is going on for you."

It is important to keep being encouraging once the power struggle is eliminated. However, since encouragement may not be helpful when a student is upset, the first thing to do is to wait for a cooling-off period. (See

"This isn't a good time. I'm in trouble with the Dean for using a cell phone in class. I'll call you back."

the Understanding the Brain tool, page 172, and the Positive Time-Out tool, page 185.)

Dreikurs had a powerful way of describing how to defuse a power struggle: "Remove your sails from their wind." If you don't acknowledge or validate the child's misguided power by reacting negatively, he or she will eventually run out of wind.

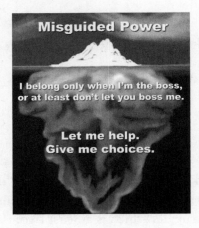

Again, the iceberg provides a graphic illustration for understanding this mistaken goal. For Misguided Power, the belief is "I belong only when I'm the boss; or, at least, I don't let you boss me." The coded message that provides clues for encouragement is "Let me help. Give me choices." The coded message provides two examples for guiding students to use their power in useful ways. There are several other examples in the last column of the Mistaken Goal Chart. When you add your heart and wisdom to any of these ideas, it will unlock additional unique ways to productively address their hidden belief, which then leads to helping them use their power in useful ways.

TOOL IN ACTION FROM PARIS, FRANCE

Virginie, a four-year-old in my class of thirty kids, started singing during quiet time. With a smile, I showed her the guidelines we had decided upon in the class.

She looked back at me with a provocative smile and sang louder.

I put my finger against my lips to show her to be quiet. It didn't work.

I felt defied, which gave me the clue that her mistaken goal is Misguided Power. I decided to give her some power, as it seemed that was what she was asking for with her behavior. I went to her and asked, "Virginie, what would help you be quiet now?"

She showed interest in my question, took a superior attitude, and said, "I would need you to draw a mouth and cross it."

I felt relieved that she was actually taking the power I was offering her. I decided to give her more power by asking her what color she wanted me to draw the mouth.

She said, "Red."

I asked if she wanted to get the pen or if I should get it. She decided to get the pen. I kept giving her more power by asking what to do with the sheet of paper. She wanted to fold it, so I passed it to her.

When I felt that I had given her enough choices, I asked, "Are you going to be able to be quiet now?"

She nodded and never disturbed the quiet time again.

—Nadine Gaudin, preschool and elementary teacher,
Certified Positive Discipline Trainer

TOOL IN ACTION FROM GUAYAQUIL, ECUADOR

I am the principal of a large preschool, and we try hard to practice Positive Discipline tools in our classes. The other day Marta, who is one of our best teachers (and a Certified Positive Discipline Teacher Educator), came to me upset. She teaches five-year-old children. It was only the second week of the school year and she was unable to connect with one little boy. He was playing around all the time, making fun of her, and inviting the other kids to misbehave. She thought he was ruining her class activities and she felt sad for the other kids. She had tried being nice to him, giving him special responsibilities. This worked for a while, and then the bad behavior started again. She didn't know what to do.

I was worried but eager to trust the process, so I asked her if she had read the Mistaken Goal Chart. Her face fell, and she said, "No. I just assumed his goal was Undue Attention." So I invited her to look at the Mistaken Goal Chart with me and to find the feeling that *she* had. Immediately she said: "It is not Undue Attention. His mistaken goal is Misguided Power! I don't feel irritated, I feel angry and challenged!" Then she discovered that her strategies were not effective because she did not give the boy the opportunity to make decisions. She told me she was going to engage him in some helpful activities but let him have a choice about them.

Three days later she came to my office, beaming. She had the Mistaken Goal Chart in her hand and said, "This stuff really works! Now things are getting better. I feel confident and my boy is happy. Now I want to talk you about a girl. . . ."

I liked this experience so much that I asked her permission to share it with other teachers in a meeting about Positive Discipline. I think it will help teachers to take their time to use the chart before jumping to conclusions!

—Gabriela Ottati, principal, Preescolar Delta-Torremar,
Certified Positive Discipline Classroom Educator

TOOL TIPS

1. It takes two to engage in a power struggle. Take responsibility for your part and then speak to the coded message of "Let me help. Give me choices." For children under the age of four, this might mean focusing on limited choices to engage the child in helping. For older children, try any of the following:

   - "I need your help. What ideas do you have to fix this problem?"
   - "I think we are in a power struggle. Let's take some time to calm down and then try again."
   - "What is your understanding of our agreement?"
   - "What would help us the most right now, putting this on the class meeting agenda or brainstorming for a solution that works for both of us?"

2. Use the Mistaken Goal Detective Clue Form (page 11) to practice becoming more familiar with the mistaken goal of Misguided Power.

WHAT THE RESEARCH SAYS

Studies have examined the physiological reactions associated with feeling a lack of belonging and have found evidence that one of them is the secretion of cortisol, which is the hormone best known for its involvement in our physiological stress response.[7] This research shows that students actually have a fight, flight, or freeze reaction when they do not feel belonging and significance in the classroom, thus increasing the likelihood of fighting or engaging in power struggles. Research also shows that class meetings can facilitate a sense of belonging, and therefore serve as a proactive means of helping to increase belonging and decrease students' stress levels. When students experience lower levels of stress, they are less likely to engage in power struggles and more likely to engage in positive group problem-solving. Class meetings have been shown to create a positive, inclusive classroom atmosphere that has an impact on students' social and emotional well-being, including academic success. Furthermore, class meetings help avoid power struggles because they provide a controlled venue for problem-solving and conflict resolution. When problems arise and are placed on the class meeting agenda, this allows for a cooling-off period.[8] Also, class meetings encourage teachers and students to resolve conflicts without getting into power struggles, which easily occur in moments when stress levels are high. Browning, Davis, and Resta used classroom meetings with twenty first-grade students to teach them positive forms of conflict resolution and decrease acts of verbal and physical aggression.[9] These researchers reported that prior to the introduction of the class meeting, acts of aggression were common. However, after repeated classroom meetings, the number of aggressive acts was significantly reduced.

UNDERSTAND THE MISTAKEN GOAL: REVENGE

Children misbehave and sacrifice peace, happiness, and relaxation for the dubious value of mischief because they are discouraged.

—*Rudolf Dreikurs*

It can be tricky to understand revenge because too often we don't know where it starts. A student may be hurt by something that happened at home, or with his or her peers, and then take it out on you. Many students have experienced serious trauma that you don't know about. It could be that a student feels hurt by something you did unintentionally—something that would make no sense to you even if you learned about it. For example, a third-grade teacher was baffled when a student she had felt close to started ignoring her. This was especially hurtful because their families were friends. This teacher volunteered to participate in the Teachers Helping Teachers Problem-Solving Steps (page 265). During the process she discovered that her student felt hurt because she had gone on vacation. Who could have guessed? When she talked with him, he became teary as he shared that he felt hurt because she hadn't told him she was going to be away or when she would be back. Remember, beliefs usually don't make sense to anyone except the believer.

"Okay, so I failed all the tests and never handed in an assignment. So what's your point?"

When Jane was an elementary school teacher, there was one second-grade class where all the kids complained about a troubled boy named Phillip. She asked Phillip to sit in the library while she talked with the class. Jane asked all the students why they were so mad at Phillip. They shared all the mean and hurtful things he did, such as stomping on the sand castles they made, grabbing the soccer ball and running away with it so they couldn't play, and calling them hurtful names.

She asked, "Why do you think he does these things?"

They came up with all kinds of ideas, hypothesizing that he was mean and a bully. Finally one little boy said, "Maybe it is because he is a foster child."

She asked, "What do you think it feels like to be a foster child?"

The atmosphere changed as they started empathizing and sharing how bad it might feel to not be with your family anymore, to move, to change schools, and to not have friends.

"How many of you would be willing to help by encouraging Phillip?"

They all raised their hands.

Jane invited the class to share exactly what they would do to help and wrote their ideas on the board. Their ideas included playing with him at recess, walking to school with him, eating lunch with him, complimenting him, et cetera. She wrote down the name of each student who volunteered to do each of these things.

She then sat down with Phillip and told him, "Your classmates told me about some of the problems you have been having. Do you know how many of them would like to help you?"

He looked glum and said, "Probably none of them."

She said, "Every one of them wants to help."

He looked incredulous and said, "Every one?"

The students followed through with their encouragement ideas, and Phillip's behavior changed dramatically. As a group, they were able to accomplish more than what one teacher could.

As Dreikurs said, "A child needs encouragement like a plant needs water." Knowing that there is a belief behind every behavior, and finding out what it is, can be so helpful in providing clues about how to encourage.

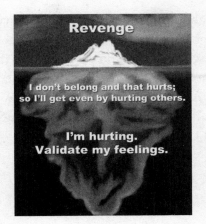

For the mistaken goal of Revenge, the belief is "I don't belong, and that hurts, so I'll get even by hurting others." The coded message that provides clues for encouragement is "I'm hurting. Validate my feelings."

Of course, validating a revengeful student's feelings is not the end of it. It is just the beginning. The basic need to belong must be addressed, followed by finding solutions to problems.

Bullying is a common behavior of the revengeful student. The following "Tool in Action" provides an excellent example of addressing bullying with students during a class meeting—one of the best ways to focus on solutions while creating a sense of belonging.

TOOL IN ACTION FROM CUERNAVACA, MEXICO

We have been working with Positive Discipline at our school for more than five years now. As the assistant principal, I am in charge of the social-emotional character development program. A couple of months ago, we observed some incidents between some fifth graders that could grow to become bullying if we didn't address them properly.

These students have been living the Positive Discipline principles in school for a while, but we knew that bullying can happen in any community when students don't feel belonging. So we decided to talk to them to make sure they understood that bullying is not only about the bully, but it is also about the bullied and the observers. We had a small talk about understanding that everyone might be a victim and that anyone can feel discouraged or powerless, even the bully. We asked them to brainstorm ideas for three lists with the following headers: "What to Do If I Am Bullied," "What to Do When I Know I Am Doing the Bullying," and "What to Do When I See Someone Bullying." They came up with the following ideas:

WHAT TO DO IF I AM BULLIED

Tell them to stop.
Run away.
Ask a friend for help.
Ask an adult for help.
Tell the bully in a strong voice: "I don't like what you are doing to me and I won't allow you to do it!"

WHAT TO DO WHEN I KNOW I AM DOING THE BULLYING

Go to therapy.
Hit a punching bag or a pillow.
Ask the teacher for help.
Ask a friend to help me.
Take deep breaths.

WHAT TO DO WHEN I SEE SOMEONE BULLYING

Tell them to stop.
Ask the bullied person to come with us.
Ask for help.
Invite the bully to play with us.

The ideas the students came up with were so powerful that the incidents diminished. And the students felt so empowered and engaged that they decided to do an anti-bullying campaign in all the elementary grades with the motto "We are the solution to bullying." We learned again to not underestimate the power of students and to never forget that they are our best resource for solving problems.

—Ari Hurtado de Molina, assistant principal, Colegio Róndine

TOOL IN ACTION FROM AUGUSTA, GEORGIA

For my first job in a school, I was the counselor and middle school social studies teacher. The school was a small program specifically for students with learning disabilities. Many students at this relatively new school had experienced lots of discouragement in their previous schools because those programs simply did not have the resources in place to adequately serve students with disabilities. When the appropriate strategies and accommodations are not in place, students with learning disabilities are at risk for experiencing great frustration and discouragement. When students perceive teachers as frustrated or overwhelmed by the student's need, it can be really discouraging and hurtful. I saw the result of this firsthand. Understanding the goals of misbehavior helped me quickly decode the hidden message and provide the support and encouragement needed.

It was just the first week of school, and every time I passed the bulletin board in the front hall I noticed either that something on it had been torn or that random pen marks had been made on it. As students shuffled to carpool one afternoon, I noticed one sixth-grade student taking his pen and marking a horizontal black line as he walked past. Hmmm. Well, my first response (since I was very proud of my first bulletin board ever) was, "Huh—I can't believe he just did that." I felt hurt. My hurt feelings were an immediate clue to the student's belief: he was hurting and wanted to hurt back. As a school counselor/teacher in my first job, I can't tell you how helpful it was to have this insight into the student's mistaken goal.

The next day at lunch I asked the sixth graders for some help. I said, "I noticed that the bulletin board in the front hallway is already looking a bit worn. I need your help in coming up with a bulletin board idea that will be more durable in such a high-traffic area. Also, I am noticing that some students aren't treating the bulletin board with respect. I am hoping we can work together to come up with a plan for taking care of our school and replacing the bulletin board so the entrance to our school looks nice." I also mentioned that the week before school the other teachers and I had brainstormed a bulletin board with a "welcome" theme to brighten the front hall and welcome everyone at the start of school. I used an "I" message to share how I felt: disappointed and surprised that it was already looking like a mess.

The students loved the idea of coming up with an idea for the bulletin board and worked together to actually make it. The sixth graders decided to put up pictures of students in each grade at recess, carpool, and lunch—anywhere they could find students having fun. The students used disposable cameras donated by parents in each class and took pictures. I wish I had a picture of the final product; it was a fantastic face of the school, much better than what I had made, and made 100 percent by students. The students felt capable and connected!

You can see several tools in action in this story. First, when I noticed my own feelings, I immediately understood the belief behind the behavior, and I was able to identify what was really going on. Students who had experienced hurt in school were hurting back. Rather than respond with punishment, shame, or blame, Positive Discipline tools helped me be an encourager. I used "I" messages to share my feelings about what was happening to the bulletin board. I used the Classroom Jobs tool to help students feel capable and connected through working together to plan and make a new bulletin board. Finally, we developed guidelines and agreements about how to respect school property and others' hard work. Because the students had the opportunity to make the bulletin board themselves, they now understood from experience how discouraging it would be if it was damaged. Making the bulletin board also helped them feel capable and connected, because they contributed by working together and doing it themselves. This also modeled teamwork and cooperation for the younger students in the school.

—Kelly Gfroerer, Ph.D., school counselor, Positive Discipline Trainer

TOOL TIPS

1. Our gut reaction (even for adults) is to strike back when we feel hurt.

2. Break the revenge cycle and speak to the coded message. Examples:
   - "I'm guessing you feel hurt by something and want to hurt back."
   - "No wonder you feel upset when it seems you always get in trouble while others don't get caught."
   - "Looks like you are having a bad day. Want to talk about it?"
   - "I care about you. Why don't we take a break and try again later?"

WHAT THE RESEARCH SAYS

Gere and MacDonald's article "Update of the Empirical Case for the Need to Belong" summarizes research showing that when people feel disconnected and rejected, they tend to retaliate and are less likely to seek connection.[10] This line of research has important implications for the classroom and explains the mistaken goal behind some misbehaviors—a desire for revenge. For example, one research team gave research participants the option to use "noise blasts" to express their hurt feelings. The researchers report that when participants were rejected by being told that others did not want to work with them and then were given the opportunity to use their noise blasts, the rejected research participants subsequently delivered more intense noise blasts to others in the group.[11]

Studies show that decreased feelings of belonging impact one's efforts to manage emotional responses, causing a decrease in one's resources for successful intrapersonal interactions. This has a nega-tive impact on task-oriented behaviors as well as one's ability to learn. Adler and Dreikurs long ago identified the mistaken goal of Revenge, and research now supports the conclusion that following perceived re-jection or hurt, a person may retaliate with revenge rather than with more useful, prosocial behavior.

UNDERSTAND THE MISTAKEN GOAL: ASSUMED INADEQUACY

The fourth goal is the deficiency, which is found in children who are so discouraged that they do not expect to succeed.

—Rudolf Dreikurs

The student whose mistaken goal is Assumed Inadequacy may not gain your attention during the school day. It is easy to ignore this student because he or she is usually not overtly involved in misbehavior. However, this student may haunt you at night because you know he or she needs help, and you wish you had more time to provide individual support.

Dreikurs called it "assumed" inadequacy because he did not believe any child is inadequate, but the child might believe it to be so and would thus avoid even trying. The student who has adopted the goal of Assumed Inadequacy could be the most discouraged of all—believing it is not possible to belong or to contribute.

This is also the mistaken goal that can be the least challenging for teachers during the day but the most discouraging when they feel hopeless about the possibility of encouraging this student. It can turn into a vicious cycle: the student gives up and won't try; the teacher gives up on trying to be encouraging; the student sees this as evidence that he doesn't belong and further

"I can't convince my teacher to give up on me."

withdraws. Often it takes a village (in the form of class meetings or a whole staff pitching in) to encourage a student with the mistaken goal of Assumed Inadequacy, as you will see in the "Tool in Action" story below.

For Assumed Inadequacy, the belief is "I give up. Leave me alone." The coded message that provides clues for encouragement is "Don't give up on me. Show me a small step."

TOOL IN ACTION FROM MORRISTOWN, NEW JERSEY

One wintry February, a new seventh-grade student named Stephen arrived at a school where Positive Discipline had been adopted as a school-wide philosophy. It was apparent from the beginning, though, that Stephen was struggling both socially and academically. Several students tried to welcome Stephen and help him feel comfortable, but his reactions caused everyone concern.

Stephen often annoyed his classmates. They were uncomfortable with the things he said and weren't sure how to respond. Stephen frequently fell asleep in class. He rarely did his homework. He would speak out at inappropriate times, making comments that weren't relevant to what was happening in the classroom. He regularly complained, "I can't do that" and "I don't understand." He often seemed to be in a world all his own.

Stephen said he never did his homework because he had no place at home quiet enough to work. He rejected efforts to help solve his problems: even the offers of a small desk for his room and a trip to buy supplies were rejected. He resisted any attempts at friendship.

As time passed, the staff learned from Stephen that his home environment was far from stable. Stephen had a difficult relationship with his nineteen-year-old sister, who in many ways was his acting parent. Stephen was slightly overweight; most of his clothes were too small and out of style. Stephen didn't look right; he didn't act right. Stephen didn't fit in, and he knew it.

The teachers and staff gave Stephen a great deal of extra help and support. They tried various methods to reach him, hoping they could get him to do his work. The special education teacher began to work with him directly and to coach the staff.

At this school, the staff held a Positive Discipline meeting every three weeks. Several weeks passed before Stephen's name came up as part of the Teachers Helping Teachers Problem-Solving Steps. After hearing about Stephen, the staff reviewed the Mistaken Goal Chart. It was painfully clear that Stephen was living the goal of Assumed Inadequacy. The belief behind his behavior was "I don't believe I can belong, so I'll convince others not to expect anything of me. I am helpless and unable; it's no use trying because I won't ever do it right."

The staff discussed what they believed Stephen needed and what they believed he was really saying with his behavior, which was "Don't give up on me!" Everyone agreed that his academics and homework were not important when he was so thoroughly discouraged about himself, his world, and whether or not he belonged. Together, the staff brainstormed a plan that everyone agreed to try, including the principal, teachers, kitchen staff, office secretary, and after-care workers. The plan was as follows:

1. From the moment Stephen exited the bus in the morning until the time he got back on the bus in the afternoon, he would receive encouragement. (Encouragement is a key principle of Positive

Discipline; the English term comes from a French word meaning "to give heart to.")

2. Everyone who encountered Stephen would acknowledge him and find something positive to say.

3. The staff would make an effort to learn about his personal interests.

4. Arrangements were made for Stephen to stay after school until 6:00 pm in the after-care program two days a week, at no cost to his family. There he would have a quiet place to work and could receive help with his homework. He would also be invited to help younger students.

5. The special education teacher would talk with him privately and let him know the staff cared and would not give up on helping him.

The staff committed to following this plan for one month and planned to check in on Stephen's progress at the next Positive Discipline meeting. Less than two weeks later, the principal discovered that the staff couldn't wait for the next meeting to share their stories about Stephen. Together, they learned just how effective their encouragement plan had been.

The change in Stephen was remarkable. Not only was he staying awake in class, but he was also participating. He smiled. His homework was being turned in, and he had even asked for some extra-credit assignments. He dressed differently and took better care of himself. At lunch he sat with his classmates (he sat at the end of the table, but he was there). In class, during the acknowledgment portion of class meetings, his classmates offered appreciation for his acts of kindness. They too had noticed the change in Stephen and were responding.

During the staff meeting, Stephen's mother happened to call the principal. She had noticed the changes in her son and wanted to know if arrangements could be made for Stephen to attend the after-care program *five* days a week.

Stephen is now an eighth-grade student. The reports on his progress continue to be positive. He is reaching out, shows responsibility in his work, and engages in lunchtime activities with the other students. Soon Stephen will move on to another school and on with his life. He will certainly experience setbacks and challenges. However, encouragement has changed forever the lives of Stephen and his teachers. Encouragement, feelings of value and significance, and belief in our own potential are essential in life. Never miss an opportunity to reach out and encourage someone!

—Teresa LaSala, Certified Positive Discipline Trainer

TOOL IN ACTION FROM CAIRO, EGYPT

I had a child in class who was extremely violent; he used to hit and bite everyone in the class, including his teachers. He would run out of the classroom or leave the garden if we were outside. Teachers would run after him to bring him back before he did anything that might hurt him.

I was very emotionally attached to him—when calm, he was kind and caring, and one of the most brilliant students in class.

He used to hit and then draw me pictures to tell me that he loves me. Sometimes, after hitting or biting, he would come running quickly to me and hug me tightly. Sometimes he would help other students fix things. He was full of contradictions.

I talked with him to understand what exactly bothered him. I told him that he was my friend, and he could tell me whatever he felt or wanted. But it made no difference.

I felt helpless. This let me know that he might be feeling Assumed Inadequacy about how to find belonging and significance. His belief was "I can't belong because I'm not perfect, so I'll convince others not to expect anything of me; I am helpless and unable; it's no use trying because I won't do it right."

After several meetings with his parents, I discovered that his father was a perfectionist and always sought perfection in all his family members. If they didn't do things the way he wanted, he would shout and tell them that they couldn't do anything right.

The son's coded message was "Don't give up on me. Show me a small step."

I decided to create more of a connection by telling this boy more about myself. I wanted him to feel comfortable and to understand that I would always be there for him. I started giving him challenging tasks to do and telling him that I had full confidence that he could do them. I kept him busy as much as I could. Some of the other teachers even felt that I was helping him too much.

Sometimes, no matter what I did, there was no improvement at all. It always helped to start the day with a feelings game, so he could continue to avoid challenging behaviors by telling me what he was feeling instead.

I encouraged any positive attempts he made, focused only on his assets, and encouraged the other teachers and his father to do the same. I didn't give up on him.

After I tried the Positive Discipline methods in class, especially the Encouragement tool, he surprised me with amazing results. He became calmer and began to feel proud of himself. When his father tried to change even a little, this made a big difference in the boy's behavior. Consequently, his father began to use Positive Discipline tools at home in earnest.

By the end of the year, we saw significant change in this lovely boy. We were all amazed. Some challenging behaviors still occur, but they can be resolved quickly.

—Noha Abdelkhabir, preschool teacher

TOOL TIPS

1. The following examples are encouraging ways to use the coded message to help change the child's belief and behavior:
   - "Try a small step. I'll be here to help."
   - "I'll do one math problem, and you can do the next one."
   - "It's okay to make mistakes. That's how we learn."
   - "Remember how hard it was when you first tried? Now you have mastered it."

2. Sometimes it is best to forget about academic achievement until a student feels a strong sense of belonging and significance.

WHAT THE RESEARCH SAYS

Research shows that when students do not feel belonging and significance in the classroom, it affects their learning. In one study when research participants felt left out, cognitive processing and ability to focus were negatively impacted. Specifically, participants performed less well on intelligence tests, recall of complex passages, and complex analytical questions compared to participants who experienced acceptance.[12]

Furthermore, researchers at Yale University report that teachers who create a positive emotional climate for learning have students who feel more connected and engaged and, therefore, become more successful academically. Studies show that when students do not feel a sense of belonging and connection, they are less likely to be engaged in learning, and as a result academic performance decreases.[13]

CHAPTER TWO

FOUNDATIONAL PRINCIPLES

ENCOURAGEMENT

A misbehaving child is a discouraged child.

—*Rudolf Dreikurs*

This chapter begins with one of our favorite Dreikurs quotations. We also love his related quote: "A child needs encouragement like a plant needs water." Encouragement is one of the foundational principles upon which all the Positive Discipline tools are based. Because this is such a basic principle, we refer to Positive Discipline as an "encouragement model."

It is important to note that encouragement is very different from praise. Praise puts the spotlight on the student and communicates adult approval or recognition. The child soon learns, "I'm okay if you tell me I am." Even though students may love praise, over time it can promote insecurity and dependency. Praise leads students to wonder "How do I compare to others?" rather than "How can I use my strengths to help others?" On the other hand, encouragement teaches self-evaluation: "How do I feel about myself and my actions?" Encouragement means turning over control to young people as soon as possible so that they have power over their own lives. It means allowing them to figure things out for themselves and having faith in them to learn and recover from their

"Remember, Edward, inside every 'F' student is an 'A' student trying to get out."

mistakes. Your encouragement will help your students look inward to discover their own strengths and find the courage to handle difficulties in school and in life.

One of the best ways to understand the difference between praise and encouragement is through an experiential activity. Pretend you are a student, and notice what you are thinking, feeling, and deciding when you hear the first set of statements below, as opposed to what you are thinking, feeling, and deciding as you listen to the second set of statements. It will be even more effective if you ask someone else to read these statements to you so you can concentrate on being the student. (Notice that some of the statements are exaggerations to emphasize the point.)

PRAISE STATEMENTS

> All A's—you get a big reward.
> I'm so proud of you.
> I'm glad you listened to me.
> I like what you did!
> I'm glad you followed my advice.
> Great! That's what I expected.
> You are such a good student.

ENCOURAGEMENT STATEMENTS

> You worked hard. You deserve it.
> You must be so proud of yourself.
> How do you feel about it?
> I trust your judgment.
> I have faith in you to learn from mistakes.
> You figured it out for yourself.
> I care about you no matter what.

Which of these statements felt the most encouraging to you? What do you think the long-term effects of these statements would be for students?

If you do this activity with others, don't be surprised if some of them prefer the praise statements. They may have learned to be "approval junkies." More often, however, the person who receives the praise statements will make comments such as "I felt conditionally loved," or "It was all about you," or "I felt pressured to live up to adult expectations."

The person who receives the encouragement statements usually makes comments such as "I felt empowered to be myself and to improve myself. I felt unconditionally accepted and encouraged to do even better."

This exercise is not meant to make you feel paranoid about giving praise once in a while. Praise, like candy, can be enjoyable on occasion, but too much can be unhealthy and addictive. Encouragement, however, should be the staple that you give to yourself and your students every day. Encouragement allows your students to see themselves as being capable, and it values their effort and improvement rather than focusing on perfection or pleasing others.

Your tone of voice and the specificity of your words as you notice students' efforts and progress will show that you have faith in them. Encouragement is especially important for discouraged students. When you show faith in students through the encouragement process it helps them develop internal self-talk that says, "I can do this, my effort counts, and it feels good to keep trying."

TOOL IN ACTION FROM MOUNTAIN VIEW, CALIFORNIA

Too often children are suspended for misbehavior in school, instead of encouraged in ways that change their behavior. In one of the schools where I worked as a psychological consultant, a third-grade student was in the process of being assessed for ADHD. He was very disruptive in the classroom and on the verge of suspension.

When he disrupted class again, the teacher (who was just starting to learn how to utilize Positive Discipline in the classroom) sent him to the office, and his mother was called to school. Talking to her taught me a lot about this student, and I wanted to empower him. I suggested that instead of suspension, this student needed to be given more responsibilities so he could practice leadership skills.

With his mother's permission, I asked him to volunteer and assist me in the kindergarten class. He was thrilled. There he got to supervise play, read books to the younger children, and lead the cleanup that came after free play. This activity enhanced his self-worth, sense of responsibility, and feeling of capability. His parents were grateful for our efforts to work with their son in a nonjudgmental manner, and we all worked together to assist the child.

—Keren Shemesh, Ph.D., clinical psychologist

TOOL IN ACTION FROM ATLANTA, GEORGIA

John is a five-year-old boy in my class. Puzzle assembly has been very challenging for this youngster. While attempting to complete a twenty-five-piece puzzle, he declared in frustration, "I can't do this!"

We discussed why it was difficult, reviewed strategies for completion, and shared the work, and I used words of encouragement such as "You continued to turn the piece around until you learned if it fit. You are sticking with a hard job. You're working hard."

When he finished, I asked, "How do you feel about finishing the puzzle?"

He answered with a big smile, "Can I do this again?"

—Barb Postich, preschool teacher, Kingswood School

TOOL TIPS

1. Encouragement focuses on effort and progress, not perfection.

2. Encouragement teaches an inner locus of control for self-evaluation. Examples:
   - "I see that you studied hard and feel ready."
   - "This is hard for you, but you are sticking with it."
   - "You trusted yourself and came up with a solution."
   - "I appreciate your help."

3. When you catch yourself using praise statements, shift to words of encouragement instead.

WHAT THE RESEARCH SAYS

A teacher's expression of faith in students and willingness to provide genuine, thoughtful, and encouraging feedback directly increases students' self-efficacy and motivation. Dr. Carol Dweck, a professor at Stanford University, released research that shows how important teacher feedback is in relation to a student's motivation and willingness to grow and learn from success and failure.[14] For example, Dweck reports that students who were praised for being smart when they accomplished a task later chose easier tasks. To hold on to that praise, these students were unwilling to take the risk of making a mistake and their motivation decreased. On the other hand, students who were encouraged for their efforts chose more challenging tasks when given choices and were not afraid to fail. The encouraging teachers focused on effort, improvements, contribution, enjoyment, and confidence.

Dweck's extensive research also shows how praise undermines student motivation and performance.[15] Dweck's research validates what Adler and Dreikurs taught about encouragement versus praise as far back as the early 1900s.[16] Unfortunately, praise is a common response to work well done in the school setting. However, research supports the use of process-oriented feedback that provides encouragement for students' hard work and effort.

CARING

An educator's most important task, one might say his holy duty, is to see to it that no child is discouraged at school, and that a child who enters school already discouraged regains his self-confidence through his school and his teacher.

—*Alfred Adler*

Alfred Adler coined the German word *Gemeinschaftsgefühl*. It is not easy to provide an English definition for this word because it means so much. Some have tried to summarize it as "social interest" or "social feeling." We would like to define it as "caring" in the broadest sense possible: teachers caring about students, students caring about teachers, students caring about each other, caring about their classroom, caring about making contributions wherever possible, caring about peace in the world. Then comes the important part of showing all this caring through actions. These actions could be referred to as "contributions" in all social settings. (See page 155 for the Contributions tool.)

Maya Angelou once said, "I have learned that people will forget what you said, people will forget what you did, but people will never forget how you made them feel." Taking time

"Your heart is slightly bigger than the average human heart, but that's because you're a teacher."

to purposefully show students you care helps them thrive socially, emotionally, and academically because their basic need for belonging is being met. Teachers find that when they take time to connect in meaningful ways, there are fewer discipline issues and a greater sense of cohesiveness in the classroom.

We know you care, but do your students know? You might be surprised if you asked. Making sure the message of caring gets through is another way of creating a connection—an important factor in predicting success in schools (as indicated by research) and a basic concept of Positive Discipline. Since the primary goal of children is to belong and contribute, you could call caring a basic need that must be provided by the adults in their lives if children are to thrive.

The first "Tool in Action" vignette below provides a beautiful example of how a school counselor and teacher created an atmosphere where a student could share something very personal because of the caring environment that had been created through the use of many Positive Discipline tools, including class meetings.

TOOL IN ACTION FROM SEATTLE, WASHINGTON

On Monday C. told me he found out he has autism. I asked him if he wanted to share this information with classmates at this time or keep it private. He said he'd like to keep it private for now.

During the following week there were a few incidents involving classmates that frustrated C. significantly. Julietta, our counselor, and I talked about how sharing C.'s diagnosis with the class could be incredibly powerful and important for C.

Julietta and C. discussed this during their private time together. When he returned to the classroom the next day, he told me, "You know how I told you I wanted to keep the news of my autism private? I've changed my mind." I told him how brave he was and asked when he'd like to do it. He said he wanted me to be the one to tell the class.

At the end of the day, we sat around our rug like we usually do for our Friday Gratitude Circle. This is what I told the class: "C. has some news that he has asked me to share with all of you. He recently found out that he has autism. Autism is a brain difference that presents itself in different ways. I read recently that people with autism are like snowflakes—no two are alike. For C., his autism means that he sometimes has challenges with communication, strong reactions to others, and difficulty expressing himself. I want to commend C. for sharing his difference with us. We all know that our differences are our superpowers and that C. has many incredible superpowers. Let's pass the talking stone around and let C. know the superpowers we see in him." To which C. said with a smile, "I wasn't expecting this."

I wish you could have been here to hear the phenomenal words of compassion, appreciation, and truth. C. was just beaming and sitting up super straight the whole time. The bell rang to end school, but the students ignored it and continued until everyone had a chance to acknowledge C.'s superpowers. I couldn't have been prouder of the class and of C.

—Julie Colando, fourth-grade teacher, Queen Anne Elementary,
and Julietta Skoog, school psychologist

TOOL IN ACTION FROM SALT LAKE CITY, UTAH

Robert Rasmussen, called "Ras" by his students, was voted the high school's Teacher of the Year five years in a row by juniors and seniors. The Granite School District also honored him as Teacher of the Year. While Ras was out of the room, we asked his students why they thought he received these honors. Their answers could be divided into three categories: (1) "He respects us," (2) "He listens to us," and (3) "He enjoys his job."

"What does enjoying the job have to do with anything?" we asked. One of the students explained: "Many teachers come to work with an attitude problem. They hate us. They hate their jobs. They seem to hate life. They take it out on us. Ras is always up. He seems to enjoy us, his job, life in general—and us."

Ras has a unique way of making sure the message of caring

(connection) gets through. He has a teddy bear in his classroom. He introduces the bear to his students and says, "This is our care bear. If any of you feel discouraged or a little down, come get the bear. He'll make you feel better." At first the students think Ras is bonkers. After all, they are high school juniors and seniors, young adults. But it doesn't take long for them to catch the spirit. Every day several students, including the big football players, go to Ras's desk and say, "I need the bear."

The bear concept became so popular that Ras had to provide more bears to keep up with the demand. Sometimes the kids carry them around all day, but they always bring them back. Sometimes when Ras sees a student who looks a little down, he tosses a bear to the student. This is his symbolic way of saying, "I care. I don't have time to spend with you personally right now, but I care."[17]

TOOL IN ACTION FROM ATLANTA, GEORGIA

Children who are not achieving academic benchmarks in school often come to the classroom environment withdrawn and defensive. These children seem to lack a sense of belonging to the learning community. Working with the lowest-achieving first- and second-grade reading students in an independent school setting has provided me the opportunity not only to remediate their reading skills but also to address the underlying social and emotional concerns that are vital to learning. These children are most often very capable but suffer from learning differences that cause traditional reading development to be challenging. When they receive appropriate instruction for their learning needs along with a sense of belonging and support that the Positive Discipline program promotes, the results can be impressive.

Even though I am with my students for only a small portion of the school day, I make class meetings a priority during our time together as a way to show caring. Gathering in a circle for these meetings is so important because the circle represents equality and space for all.

I believe that two components of our time together in this circle have directly contributed to my students' success in reading. First, we greet one another, focusing on eye contact and smiling as we welcome each other to the group. We also shake hands when greeting one another, incorporating the sense of touch into our connections.

This simple act of greeting has increased the sense of belonging and connection for my children in ways that I never expected. Greeting one another centers both the children and myself and allows learning to occur. Second, we practice giving each other compliments during our class meetings. Some examples of compliments my children have offered are "Sam is very kind to others. He likes to learn a lot, and he helps people when they have trouble" and "Meg is always nice, always has a smile on her face, and always helps people who are struggling." The genuine nature of the children's compliments for one another only helps to create connection, belonging, and trust within our group. From this positive beginning, teaching my students to read flows naturally in a way I believe it would not without this building of each child's sense of self.

—Rosalyn Devine, first- and second-grade reading teacher

TOOL TIPS

1. During a faculty meeting, brainstorm ways to show students you care. Examples include smiling, greeting students at the door, spending special time with students, asking students for help, and complimenting them often.

2. Create a copy of this list for each teacher to keep on his or her desk.

3. Check the list often for ways to show you care on a daily basis.

4. Have your students create a list of ways they can show they care about each other.

5. Ask students to create an illustrated Caring Chart to hang in the classroom.

WHAT THE RESEARCH SAYS

The Centers for Disease Control reports that a strong sense of connection at school is directly related to increased academic performance, a decrease in dropout rates, and regular school attendance. In addition, students who feel connected at school are less likely to smoke cigarettes, drink alcohol, have sexual intercourse, carry a weapon, become involved in violence, develop eating disorders or emotional distress, or consider/attempt suicide.[18] When teachers take time to show they care and to build a meaningful relationship with students, it's clear that there are far-reaching benefits. Dr. Kathryn Wentzel at the University of Maryland examined adolescents' relationships with their teachers, parents, and peers. In her sample of 167 sixth-grade students, teacher support was a positive predictor of motivation at school and class-related interest. Social responsibility and goal pursuit were also positively related to a caring teacher-student relationship.[19]

Other studies show similar findings, supporting the importance of teachers forming caring relationships based on trust with their students.[20] Tschannen-Moran reports that the teacher-student relationship is key in preventing disruptive behavior and that students who perceive their teachers as caring exerted greater effort in their work and demonstrated an increase in social responsibility. Finally, students in low-income, unsafe schools identified the teachers who were most effective at dealing with difficult situations as the most caring.[21]

Positive Discipline Tools for Teachers can help teachers find ways to connect and show they care on a daily basis. Research shows that students' sense of belonging in school decreases as they progress to higher grade levels.[22] Class meetings, giving individual students a few minutes after school (special time), and many other Positive Discipline tools can help students in all grade levels feel a sense of belonging, which is crucial to overall student success.

FOCUS ON SOLUTIONS

Sometimes the problem can be solved by discussing it with the children and seeing what they have to offer.

—*Rudolf Dreikurs*

Y̲ou may have heard the story about the man who left his home and traveled all over the world in search of wealth. Finally, with a feeling of failure and despair, he returned to his home. One day, while planting a garden, he discovered gold in his own backyard.

Many teachers do not know they have such wealth in their own classrooms. All they have to do is recognize this fact and then "dig for the gold." That "gold" is a room full of problem-solvers. All that is needed is to recognize this fact, teach a few problem-solving skills, and then watch the "solutions" flow.

Focusing on solutions is an important life skill, and is another foundational principle of Positive Discipline. A great question that helps students and teachers remember this principle is: *Are you looking for blame, or are you looking for solutions?* Students enjoy creating a poster with this motto to hang in a prominent place in the classroom. Then they love reminding each other, and especially teachers, whenever anyone

"They were out of red crayons."

focuses on blame: "Are you looking for blame, or are you looking for solutions?"

Instead of focusing on solutions, it is very common for some to ask, "What punishment should be applied for this behavior?" This is the wrong question. Punishment is designed to make kids pay for what they have done in the past. "What is the solution that will solve this problem?" is a better question. Focusing on solutions helps students learn for the future instead of requiring that they pay for a past event that can never be changed.

Be ready for initial resistance when you first start "digging for the gold." It is normal for students not to know how capable they are when they haven't been provided with training and with opportunities to discover and practice their problem-solving skills. If you ask your students to think of solutions and they say, "I don't know," you can respond with encouragement: "Take time to think about it. You can tell me what you come up with when we meet again."

Of course, it helps if you are having regular class meetings where your students are practicing their problem-solving skills on a regular basis. And if you are asking curiosity questions (pages 112 and 117) routinely, you will invite students to think for themselves and search for solutions.

A set of criteria for evaluating solutions can be summed up as "the three R's and an H." A solution should be:

Related
Respectful
Reasonable
Helpful

After brainstorming for solutions, go over each idea and ask your students if their solutions fit the above criteria. Even better, involve students in taking turns evaluating each brainstormed solution to determine which ideas match the three R's and an H and which don't. Cross off any proposed solutions that don't meet all the criteria. Soon it will be second nature for your students to evaluate solutions and identify the most useful to try.

We received the following question from someone who represents the beliefs of many: "I need to ask a question regarding punishing kids who hit their classmates. At the school where I work, they cannot accept that kids who hit other kids go without punishment. Please give me examples of school policies to deal with hitting that are not punitive and that are kind and firm at the same time."

The answer to this dilemma is very simple, but it can be very hard for some to understand if they haven't made the paradigm shift necessary to understand that punishment may seem effective immediately but does not have long-term positive results. It doesn't make sense to model the opposite of what you want to teach. Punishing a student who has hurt another student is humiliating. Rather than "making him pay," it's much better to have a student repair the damage he has done to another by focusing together on a solution.

Have you ever thought about how ironic it is that some adults want to hurt kids as their means of teaching children not to hurt others? Those same adults are likely to agree that modeling by example is the best teacher. Yet when they use punishment, they model the opposite of what they want to teach.

As we often say in this book, punishment is designed to make children pay for what they have done in the past. Positive Discipline, on the other hand, uses encouragement. What would Positive Discipline's approach look like in comparison to punishment? Here are several possibilities:

1. Validate the hitter's feelings: "You must have been very angry." We know it may seem more logical to first take care of the student who has been hit. Why this may not be the best approach is explained later.
2. Ask curiosity questions (page 117) in a kind and friendly manner to find out what happened.
3. Next, turn to the student who was hit, and ask for his or her

version of what happened. You may discover that the student who appears to be the innocent victim may have actually provoked the hitting.

4. If it turns out the hitting was not provoked, ask the hitter, "What could you do to make amends?"

5. If both students were responsible, focus on solutions: "What ideas do both of you have to solve this problem?" (Review the Same Boat tool on page 237.)

6. Another possibility is to ask the students involved to put the problem on the class meeting agenda so they can get help from everyone about how to make amends and solve the problem.

Those who are convinced that children must be punished will continue to punish. The punished student will continue to get more and more discouraged, and will become even more likely to hit others in the future. Punishment inevitably creates a "revenge cycle."

Understanding that encouragement is the best way to change future behavior will keep teachers and students focused on the search for real solutions. Focusing on solutions rather than on punishment and revenge will help create peace, and not just in the classroom!

TOOL IN ACTION FROM ST. CATHARINE, KENTUCKY

As the college instructor for our Classroom Management: Positive Discipline in the Classroom course during both the fall and spring semesters, I observe my college-level education students as they volunteer in the local public schools. The students assist in classrooms, choosing the grades they hope to teach. In return, the teachers agreed that the college students could teach both the foundation Positive Discipline activities and the Eight Essential Skills for Successful Class Meetings in their classrooms.

One morning I passed the middle school principal as he left the eighth-grade classroom. When I arrived, the students' faces looked pretty grim. Quickly the students began on their own to move their desks and form their circle to begin their class meeting. After appreciations and compliments, the meeting leader reviewed the previous meeting's suggestions and then asked if anyone had something to discuss.

The room went silent. After a few moments my college student raised her hand and asked if there were any problems that needed solutions. Again the room was quiet. I waited a bit longer and then finally said, "May I ask a question?"

"Sure," was the response.

"I noticed the principal had just walked out of your classroom as I came in. Does anyone wish to share what he had to say?"

"He was upset because we're 'out of uniform' when we have our shirttails out, or we don't wear our belts," one student offered.

"Well," I asked, "does anyone have an idea how we can solve those problems?"

The students quickly went into solution mode. Hands were raised, and the scribe quickly wrote out on the board the suggestions for solving both of these issues. Then the students voted on the three possible solutions to try:

1. Have two students standing at the door while the class files in and remind those of us who have our shirttails out to tuck them in.
2. Those students who have extra belts can bring them to school and put them in a box to store extra belts. Again, the two students at the door can remind everyone to put on a belt for the school day. (The belts would be returned to the box at the end of the day.)
3. Two students volunteered to make a poster with reminders to "be in uniform with shirttails in and belts on."

There were smiles all around after this class meeting. The students not only took responsibility for their school's dress code but also worked together to find a solution that was related, reasonable, respectful, and helpful.

—Mary Hogan Jones, professor at St. Catharine College,
Certified Positive Discipline Trainer

One of the nine-year-old boys in my special education class is really learning and absorbing the Positive Discipline lessons. Positive Discipline seems to strongly appeal to his sense of justice. Today this student was very upset because the teacher was going to punish him for being disrespectful by limiting where he could play at recess. When I asked the teacher about this, she said she was willing to make a change if he could come up with a solution for his disrespectful behavior in class.

I sat with him, and we brainstormed together, and fifteen minutes later this student had solutions written down. All his solutions were related, respectful, and reasonable, and so we talked about which one he wanted to try first. He decided that if his toy car was too noisy, the teacher could take it away from him for three minutes. If he caused a distraction again, he'd have to put the car in his backpack. He presented his solution to the teacher, and she agreed to give it a try. He was very proud of himself. The car did not become an issue again.

—Jackie Freedman, special ed instructional assistant,
fourth- and fifth-grade classroom, Certified Positive Discipline Educator

I am a high school special education English teacher. This year I teach both ninth and tenth graders. Unfortunately, at the beginning of the school year there are always many handouts for my class. The problem I had in my classroom was that students were misplacing handouts or not taking handouts when they were first distributed, and so they did not have the handouts they needed in class. Consequently, I put this problem on the agenda for a class meeting. I titled it "Missing Handouts and Templates" and explained that when students don't have the handouts needed for class instruction their learning can be negatively impacted. This was a concern for me, their teacher. When students do not have what they need, it interrupts instruction time. I asked, "How can students best get duplicate copies of handouts that were passed out but which they don't have with them for class? I need your help so everyone has what they need."

During a class meeting we discussed solutions: (1) students could go to the file cabinet and grab what they needed, provided there were extra copies; (2) students could share with their neighbor; and (3) we could keep track of handouts when first distributed, and if a student did receive a copy but was unable to find it later, that student would be responsible for copying another student's.

What we decided on was that once a handout was distributed to the class, a student would have the job of storing the remaining copies in a single handout binder kept at the back of the classroom. If a student realized that he didn't have a needed handout, he would go quietly to the binder and get the one needed. If a student went to the binder and found that she was taking the last copy, she would write a note. It would be a class job to copy extra handouts and templates to keep in the binder.

This simple system has changed my class dynamics. Students are getting what they need independently, and I can focus on my lesson without being interrupted by students who are missing the necessary handouts!

—Diana Loiewski, high school teacher, Certified Positive Discipline Educator

TOOL TIPS

1. Teach your students to focus on solutions, not only during class meetings but all day long.

2. Invite some students to make a poster of the following steps for focusing on solutions:
   - Identify a problem.
   - Brainstorm for as many solutions as possible.
   - Pick one solution that works for everyone.
   - Try the solution for a week.
   - In a week, evaluate. If the solution chosen didn't work, start the process again and keep trying.

WHAT THE RESEARCH SAYS

The negative effects of punishment are well documented, but the studies addressing this are mostly hidden in academic journals.[23] Punishment, by design, is focused on making students "pay" for what they have done rather than on solutions. Learning theory shows how punishment is not beneficial for learning and may lead to avoiding the punisher, a shift to a more negative behavior, and even an emotional response of fear. Additionally, researchers have found that the use of punishment to gain control in the classroom leads to lower levels of internal motivation. Punishment, a key component in autocratic teaching, has been shown to decrease self-regulation while increasing problem behavior.[24]

On the other hand, there are many long-term benefits to developing social and emotional skills for problem-solving and focusing on solutions. Research shows that students who are learning skills in self-regulation, emotional expression, cooperation, sharing, and problem-solving are more likely to transition well in school and achieve greater academic success.[25]

KIND *AND* FIRM

Firmness refers to your behavior in a conflict situation: domination means forcing your decision on the child.

—*Rudolf Dreikurs*

As a teacher, do you have a tendency toward being a little too kind, and have difficulty being firm? (You don't want to be one of those mean, autocratic teachers.) Or are you a little too firm because you think kindness can be wishy-washy? (You don't want to be one of those permissive teachers.) Is it your tendency to be kind until misbehavior occurs, and then too firm? A cycle of vacillating between too kind and too firm is easy to fall into, especially when you teach large class sizes with challenging classroom dynamics. Or maybe you have so many individual student challenges that you feel overwhelmed.

Your reaction to student behavior does not have to be either too kind or too firm. Rudolf Dreikurs promoted the respectful method of kind *and* firm at the same time. Students thrive when they trust that they will consistently be met with kindness, even when they make mistakes. At the same time, they learn order when

"My name is Mrs. Clawson and I have a graduate degree in early childhood education . . . and a black belt in karate."

they know that established rules and expectations are firmly in place. Being kind *and* firm communicates "I care and understand, *and* you are still accountable." This congruent response expresses a sense of faith in your students' ability to handle tough situations and challenges at school.

While most teachers readily recognize the benefits of democratic leadership (cooperative problem-solving) as opposed to autocratic leadership ("I am the boss, do as I say") and laissez-faire leadership (no structure and often too permissive), it can be difficult to be consistently kind *and* firm in the classroom if there is no plan in place. To avoid an inconsistent and ineffective back-and-forth between kindness and firmness, Positive Discipline teaches specific language that is both kind *and* firm. Some teachers find it helpful to write phrases on Post-it notes to serve as a visible reminder. Teachers report that memorizing even a few key phrases helps as they walk the difficult walk of consistently implementing kind *and* firm democratic leadership in the classroom. Here are some examples of sentences that will help. Notice there are many ways to show kindness before setting a firm limit.

- Validate feelings: "I can tell you are upset about something, *and* it is time to be working on your project. I'm available after school if you would like to talk about why you're upset."

- Show understanding: "I can understand why you would rather be doing something else right now, *and* your assignment needs to be done first."

- "I" message: "You don't want to do your homework, *and* I don't want you to fail. Let's find time to talk about what you need to succeed."

- Follow through on a previously made agreement: "I noticed you didn't hand in your assignment on time, *and* what was our agreement about when it would be done?" Kindly and quietly wait for the answer.

- Provide a choice: "I know you would prefer to play games now, *and* it is quiet work time. Do you want me to hold your phone until after class, or can you keep it in your backpack?"

Even though these are scripts, remember that tools are effective only when based on sound principles and when you then add your heart and wisdom to use your words to fit the situation. If using kindness *and* firmness is not effective, it could be that you are involved in a power struggle or not understanding some other discouraging belief behind a student's behavior. It may be time for relationship building through other Positive Discipline tools such as Special Time or Curiosity Questions, or through joint problem-solving during class meetings.

TOOL IN ACTION FROM LIMA, PERU

The philosophy of Positive Discipline—which intends to apply firmness and kindness at the same time, understand emotions, empower children in the search for solutions, and assume that mistakes are great opportunities to learn—opened my eyes to new ways of managing classroom behaviors.

I have been applying Positive Discipline for two years. The first year, my fellow teachers told me, "Of course, it worked for you because you had a high-quality group." The second year, I was assigned a very difficult group of students, and my colleagues said, "Let us see now if you will be able to apply Positive Discipline." That made me even more eager to strive to be respectful and firm at the same time.

At the end of the year, my colleagues observed how much my group had advanced, and they appreciated the work I had done with my students. They realized that what I had done (and what I had proposed to them for their own classrooms) could be successful because they saw the positive changes in the children. In addition, the teacher who received my students from last year found that the children established routines easily without being told, that they had the ability to resolve problem situations and self-regulate, and that they could hear each other with respect and empathy.

She asked me how to continue the work I had begun, and I was able to convey my understanding and experiences to her. Now she is encouraging her fourth-grade partners to apply the Positive Discipline tools.

—Sandra Colmenares, third-grade teacher, Certified Positive Discipline Educator

TOOL IN ACTION FROM CAIRO, EGYPT

There is a student in the second year of middle school (grade seven) who since primary school refused to follow the school rule requiring close-cropped hair for boys. The fact that he intentionally refused to comply with this rule set a very bad example for other students, especially the younger students, who are always watching older students and following the models they set with their behaviors.

This year we decided to try other ways to work with him about this school rule. We first tried the Connection Before Correction tool and validated his feelings. We asked curiosity questions to explore what he was feeling about this request from the school and why he did not want to respect this school policy. After listening to him, we expressed our feelings about the policy and why his disregarding the policy was a problem. After this private discussion, we gave him limited choices: we let him choose when he would come back to school with short hair.

Unfortunately, we were not successful on the first try, but we decided to remain kind *and* firm. We told him very clearly and calmly that we were frustrated by the situation and explained to him what we would do: if he did not come to school with short hair, he would no longer be able to have access to the school. The following day he came to school again with his long hair, so we asked him again what he understood about his choice. He recognized that we had told him he could not come to school without short hair.

The next day he came to school with short hair. He was very proud to show us his hair, and we encouraged him for his choice. Since then we have been meeting with him periodically to check if everything is fine with him. More than three months later, we haven't received any complaints about his behavior.

—May El Yamani, students affairs and guidance coordinator, and Fabienne Labouré, Positive Discipline Coordinator at Oasis International School

TOOL TIPS

1. Being too kind is the language of permissiveness and being too firm is the language of excessive control.

2. It takes thought and self-control to be both kind *and* firm at the same time. For example:
   - "It is easy to look for blame, *and* we are focusing on solutions."
   - "I know you would prefer to spend time on the computer, *and* it is time for reading."

3. Let kids know it is okay to feel what they feel, but what they do is not always okay: "You can feel angry *and* you cannot hurt others." (Also see " 'I' Messages" on page 193.)

WHAT THE RESEARCH SAYS

Dreikurs used Lewin's classic group dynamics research to help teachers develop effective leadership skills for the classroom.[26] Dreikurs developed effective techniques for kind and firm leadership in the classroom based on Lewin's findings that democratic group leadership (characterized by freedom and order) was optimal compared to either the autocratic (blind obedience) or laissez-faire (permissive) style.[27] Lewin's study was conducted in an all-boys camp in Iowa. The camp counselors were specifically trained in each of the three leadership styles for the purposes of the study. The children in the democratic leadership style group showed cooperation and sharing. Their group work was well done. In the autocratic group, the children interacted in ways the leaders prescribed, with their actions controlled by the leaders of the group. The children in the laissez-faire group demonstrated relatively little interaction or cooperation; over time they were observed behaving in isolated, disconnected ways.

TAKE TIME FOR TRAINING

Security comes from a feeling of being able to deal effectively with anything life may have to offer.

—*Rudolf Dreikurs*

In the Introduction, we shared that students can learn the characteristics and life skills you hope for them by using the Positive Discipline tools. The question is, how long does it take? There isn't an exact answer to this question. Every student is different and there are so many different circumstances. However, some tools seem to work in seconds, like magic, while some may take more training. Think about any academic subject, such as reading. We don't get disappointed if students don't become fourth-grade-level readers when they are in the first grade. We know it takes time—and lots of practice. Just as students don't master reading or math after one lesson, one week, or even one year, it takes time to learn valuable social and life skills.

We have known some teachers to try a Positive Discipline tool, such as Class Meetings, and say, "Well, that didn't work. Forget about that tool." These same teachers would never

"The school computers are six months old. How can I be expected to be competitive in the job market if I'm trained on obsolete equipment?"

say, "My students didn't learn to read the first day or even the first week. Forget about teaching reading."

When Jane first tried to teach class meetings, she told teachers to "prepare for a month of hell," since the kids weren't used to the responsibility and skills required for class meetings. Then she discovered the importance of taking time for training in the Eight Essential Skills for Successful Class Meetings (page 125) before inviting students to use these skills to solve real problems. "It wasn't that the kids weren't ready; I had to change my teaching methods," she reported. These new methods eliminated the "month of hell" and helped students learn the skills for success. In fact, taking time for training is important to use with many of the Positive Discipline tools. In the next "Tool in Action" section, you'll see how role-playing was used to take time for training.

TOOL IN ACTION FROM CAIRO, EGYPT

In September 2015, we adopted the Positive Discipline approach in our school, from the kindergarten classes up to the diploma. As in most schools, we face some pretty challenging situations. We try to solve these problems using Positive Discipline.

I would like to share a situation that happened last November (one day before holiday departure) in one middle-school biology class with one of our ninth-grade students. One student was moving around the classroom, disturbing the class. The teacher asked him to go back to his seat, but he refused in front of the entire class.

In order to avoid a power struggle, the teacher decided to ignore the situation and continue her class. At the end of the class, she asked to have a meeting with the student. I attended as well. During the meeting, we used curiosity questions to ask the student exactly what happened. Then we invited him to participate in a role-play where he was the teacher and his teacher was the student. After role-playing, we asked what he had been thinking and feeling when he was in the role of his teacher. His teacher also shared her feelings when she was playing the role of student.

He was very affected by the role-play and the discussion with his teacher, because it helped him to understand what had happened in class from someone else's perspective (his teacher and his peers). Next, we invited him to think about how he could recover from the mistake he made, interrupting during instruction time. He first acknowledged exactly what he had done wrong and decided to present his apology to the teacher during our meeting. He also decided to send an email to the entire class, explaining the situation and apologizing. (He preferred to send the email immediately rather than waiting until we were back at school after the holiday.) To resolve the situation, he agreed to have a respectful attitude in the biology class, and if he needed to move during class, he would respectfully communicate with his teacher rather than disrupt instruction time.

We have been doing regular feedback with the teacher about this student's behavior, and the student is really working in class and not disturbing others.

—May El Yamani, students affairs and guidance coordinator, and Fabienne Labouré, Positive Discipline Coordinator at Oasis International School

TOOL IN ACTION FROM ATLANTA, GEORGIA

Having a well-developed plan for a smoothly running classroom is a goal for many teachers. In order to develop this kind of well-oiled machine where student learning is the central focus, it is important to take time for training. In my experience, the children want to be in charge, in some way, of their learning. Since there are so many working parts to running a classroom effectively, I often prioritize my goals based on the needs of my current class.

To keep the chaos at bay, I ask the kids to raise their hand and wait their turn when answering a question. This is a great practice and minimizes the noise level. But what about the student who is wildly raising/waving his hand but has no intention of answering the question? I am referring to the student who needs a restroom break. This child and his need may be lost in the sea of raised hands.

To alleviate such a situation and the emergency it entails, I ask the children to put a thumb up if they need an immediate bathroom break. This is a silent and direct signal to me that a break for that student is necessary. It also may be a comfort to them to know that we are not so regimented that breaks can only occur at midmorning and after lunch.

Because I take time for lessons on this silent signal of a thumb up, I have not seen this plan abused. At first, some may want to try the "magic signal." But after taking time for training and practice, it just becomes another part of our classroom protocol that adds to the students' sense of ownership and responsibility.

—Patty Spall, first-grade teacher, St. Jude the Apostle Catholic School,
Atlanta, Georgia

TOOL TIPS

1. Class meetings provide an excellent example of a situation in which Positive Discipline might fail because of a lack of training. The Eight Essential Skills for Successful Class Meetings (page 125) provide students with the training needed for success.

2. Take time to practice each skill with students before tackling real challenges.

3. Use fictional but typical problems to role-play as a fun way to practice.

4. Some skills may take several days or weeks for proficiency. Other skills may take only a day or two.

5. Encourage learning from mistakes whenever things don't go well.

WHAT THE RESEARCH SAYS

Emmer and Stough have reviewed extensive research on the principles of effective teaching.[28] These studies include highly heterogeneous classrooms and classes with many students from lower socioeconomic strata. Findings indicate that at the beginning of the school year, effective teachers take time to teach expectations and classroom procedures to their students in very specific ways. They carefully plan and teach routines and procedures for class activities, even if training takes several weeks. Effective teachers monitor students' behavior and take additional time as needed to work closely with each student on expectations and classroom procedures. This emphasis on taking time for training results in a more positive climate and increases student cooperation throughout the entire school year.

MISTAKES AS OPPORTUNITIES FOR LEARNING

Making mistakes is human. Regard your mistakes as inevitable instead of feeling guilty, and you'll learn better.

—*Rudolf Dreikurs*

Mistakes are not nearly as important as what we do about it afterwards.

—*Rudolf Dreikurs*

Students can be taught to feel shame when they make a mistake, or they can be taught to be excited about the opportunities to learn that mistakes present. The former leads to low self-esteem and a fear of learning. The latter leads to a sense of confidence, capability, and resilience.

Too many of us grew up believing that mistakes were shameful, so we decided we should do one or all of the following:

1. Don't take risks for fear of making mistakes.
2. If you make a mistake, try to hide it—even if that means lying about it.
3. Find excuses or, even better, blame someone else.
4. Become a perfectionist and compulsive about not making mistakes.
5. Decide you are "not good enough" because you aren't perfect.

Imagine a classroom where mistakes are celebrated and welcomed as learning opportunities. In this classroom students feel safe (and even encouraged) to share their mistakes and what they learned from them.

When the mistake creates a problem, students are encouraged to focus on solutions. When the mistake involves hurt feelings, students (and teachers) can use the four R's of Recovery to make amends:

1. Recognize that you made a mistake. Feel the embarrassment and then let it go.
2. Take responsibility for your mistake without blame or shame.
3. Reconcile by apologizing. (Students are so forgiving when others, including adults, are willing to apologize. The universal response is "That's okay.")
4. Resolve by focusing on solutions for the future.

"WELL, AM I WITHIN THE MARGIN OF ERROR ?"

Teachers who take time to celebrate mistakes and share their own mistakes help students develop a healthy attitude and skills that will serve them throughout their lives.

TOOL IN ACTION FROM YANGPYEONG, KOREA

One day one of my students bumped into a desk by mistake and a lot of school supplies fell all over the floor. I was about to get annoyed and scold him. But before I spoke, several students came to his desk and helped him to clean up what had spilled. This student thanked his friends for their help.

One of my students told me, "Our class doesn't condemn or shame, but we help one another when a friend makes a mistake."

My students were teaching me what I had been teaching them, and I regretted I had been about to condemn a student for a simple and honest mishap.

—Seonghwan Kim, sixth-grade teacher, Johyeon Elementary School

TOOL IN ACTION FROM PARIS, FRANCE

I was helping a teacher implement Positive Discipline in her class of nine-year-olds. When I arrived in the school that day, all the little girls came to me in the playground (it was recess time) like little birds, all talking at the same time and telling me that there was a thief in the classroom. I suggested we discuss it during a class meeting.

During the class meeting, they explained that a thief had stolen the ball from the Positive Time-Out place. So I ask them, "When we make a mistake, do we become the mistake we make?"

All at the same time they replied, "No, we do not!"

Then I said, "When you say there is a thief, you are saying that the person is the mistake they made. But the mistake is what the person did, not who they are. If someone stole the ball, how do you think they feel?"

They answered that the person must feel just awful and must totally regret having done that.

I was starting to suggest that the child could give back the ball at a time when no one was looking when, surprising everyone, a boy raised his hand with the ball in it and said, "I took it. I'm sorry."

All the other children looked at him and said, "Wow, this is really courageous of you. Thank you for giving it back."

He said, "I really liked it, and now I realize that it was not okay to do that."

I was in awe to see that the child felt safe enough in the classroom to admit his mistake. He knew that making a mistake was an opportunity to learn and that he could recover from it.

—Nadine Gaudin, preschool and elementary teacher,
Positive Discipline Certified Trainer

TOOL IN ACTION FROM SEATTLE, WASHINGTON

I wanted to share a story about apologizing for a mistake. In our Positive Discipline in the Classroom class we teachers had talked about apologizing and showing our students that we make mistakes too and can't always keep it together. I had a fourth- and fifth-grade African drumming concert that night and had been spending music class practicing with the students. One of my most talented fourth-grade boys, who is also a leader on the drums, was not taking our practice seriously. He was goofing off, being silly, and ended up distracting the entire group. Being on my last nerve before the performance, I called him out in front of the entire class. As soon as I humiliated him in front of the group, I saw that he was devastated. I knew I had made a mistake. We finished practice, and he did a great job. At the end of class I pulled him aside and said, "I just wanted to apologize for calling you out in front of the entire class. You always work really hard, and I lost my patience and should not have done that."

He immediately smiled and said, "No, I was not following directions, and I can do better."

I replied with, "Yes, you can, but I am still sorry for how I handled the situation."

At that moment everything we had been discussing and practicing finally clicked—not only with this fourth grader but also with many other students. I stop myself or breathe and think about the child before I get upset.

—Tricia Hill, music teacher at Woodside Elementary, after taking a
Positive Discipline in the Classroom class with Casey O'Roarty,
Certified Positive Discipline Trainer

TOOL TIPS

1. True discipline helps children learn from their mistakes. Punishment makes children pay for their mistakes.

2. Post the four R's of Recovery (page 81) where students can use them to practice learning from mistakes in ways that are respectful and encouraging.

3. Share stories with your students where you followed the four R's of Recovery after a mistake.

4. If the student's mistake requires amends or finding a solution, engage the student (or the whole class) in a plan for the best way to make amends or to brainstorm for solutions.

5. Share inspirational stories about great men and women who have made mistakes and learned from them, such as Thomas Edison, who is widely reported to have said, "I haven't failed. I found ten thousand ways that won't work."

6. Once a week, during class meetings, pass the talking stick around the circle and invite students to share a mistake they made and what they learned from it.

WHAT THE RESEARCH SAYS

Carol Dweck, a professor and researcher at Stanford University, has extensively studied learning as related to processing mistakes and failure.[29] In her research, Dweck found that students who perceive mistakes as opportunities to learn and grow are more successful in the long term compared to students who avoid difficult tasks because they fear making mistakes. Dweck points out that students who are taught to embrace mistakes as opportunities develop strategies that lead to greater academic and personal success. These students seem to have a higher sense of self-efficacy and motivation for taking on more difficult tasks.

Kornell, Hays, and Bjork reported that students who made mistakes on tests demonstrated enhanced learning when errors are evaluated as opportunities for learning.[30] Their findings show that taking on more challenging tasks—and making errors—actually provides a deeper opportunity for learning. Other researchers identify the important role of mistakes in developing self-discipline.[31] Students need to be allowed to make mistakes in order to grow and learn.

CHAPTER THREE

FORMING A BOND

CONNECTION BEFORE CORRECTION

The beneficial effects of building morale, providing a feeling of togetherness, and considering difficulties as projects for understanding and improvement, rather than as objects of scorn, outweigh any possible harm.

—*Rudolf Dreikurs*

Where did we ever get the crazy idea that in order to motivate children to do better, first we have to make them feel worse? Unfortunately, it is still the approach used by far too many parents and teachers in their attempts to motivate students to improve their behavior and their learning.

"I channeled John Dewey. He says if you want to be a good teacher, don't teach reading and writing. Teach students."

Making children feel worse creates distance and hostility, not improved behavior. The research is very clear that connection creates closeness and trust as well as a platform for kind and firm correction that will motivate change. It is well known that children do better when they feel better! When students feel a sense of connection and capability, then they can learn. Alfred Adler called it the need for a sense of belonging—the primary goal of all people.

Some argue that helping students feel good after they have misbehaved will just "give them what they want" and reinforce the misbehavior. That is because they misunderstand what it means to "help them feel good." Helping them feel good does not mean giving in or pampering. It does not mean losing a power struggle. It means understanding how the brain works and understanding that students need to feel safe and respected before they can access the prefrontal cortex for rational thinking. It is about "winning students over" instead of "winning over students."

Connection, to help students feel safe and respected, is a Positive Discipline foundation tool, and thus is the basis of many of the tools. We want to start with some examples of using hugs to create a connection. Hugs may not seem appropriate for older students, but a fist bump, a high-five, or simply validating feelings can convey the same message; other methods for connecting with older students are conveyed in later success stories.

TOOL IN ACTION FROM PORTLAND, OREGON

Steven Foster, a special education teacher, shared these two stories about hugs.[32]

Hug Story No. 1

Today a four-year-old boy stormed away from the art table, screaming that he was "mad, frustrated, and not happy." My assistant followed him over to our comfy cushion, where he had wrapped himself in a blanket and was now just screaming wordlessly and kicking the cushion. He refused to talk to the assistant, just continuing to scream.

I sat next to him and whispered, "I need a hug."

He continued screaming and writhing.

After about fifteen seconds I repeated, "I need a hug."

He stopped screaming and flailing but kept his back to me.

Ten more seconds. "I need a hug."

After a long pause he turned over, climbed into my lap, and hugged me. I asked him if he wanted to go back to the art table by himself or if he wanted me to go with him. He asked me to go with him. He went back, finished his project happily, and left the table.

Hug Story No. 2

During my social skills class for preschoolers, Ryan was having an awful morning: hitting kids repeatedly, telling adults to shut up, running off, et cetera.

Near the end of the day I pulled him aside and told him it looked like he was having a very hard day: kids were mad at him, he was telling grown-ups to shut up. Predictably, he told me to shut up . . . again.

I wondered aloud whether something had happened at home that was bothering him.

"Shut up!"

I said that I really wanted to help him but didn't know what to do.

"Shut up!"

I asked him if he wanted a hug.

"No!"

I said. "Hmm. You're feeling pretty icky, and you don't want a hug. You know what? I could use a hug. Will you give me one?"

Long stare.

I said nothing.

He launched himself at me and squeezed.

"Wow, that's a nice hug! I could use another one like that."

He gave me another one, and we went to go have a snack. His life might still have been in chaos, but his last ten minutes of class went smoothly. Hugs can be a powerful tool, even in non-tantrum moments.

—Steven Foster, special ed teacher, Certified Positive Discipline Lead Trainer, and coauthor of *Positive Discipline for Children with Special Needs*

TOOL IN ACTION FROM SAN RAMON, CALIFORNIA

A student was having a difficult time staying focused in class. He was often disrespectful and off-task.

I made an effort to connect with him on a daily basis. I greeted him at the door, did a check-in to see how he was doing, and talked with him about non-class-related topics. I was gradually able to build a relationship with him that enabled me to have an objective discussion about his attitude in class without my coming across as threatening or negative.

—Shanin McKavish, high school teacher

TOOL IN ACTION FROM SAN DIEGO, CALIFORNIA

I have found the concept of "connection before correction" to be particularly powerful and have many memories of times when this concept has helped me keep my cool so I could successfully help a child keep his or her cool too.

For example, one of my special day students, a ten-year-old girl, decided one day that she didn't want to line up after recess. Not only was she refusing to line up, she had decided to sit in the hallway, which was out of bounds.

I could have yelled and threatened her. Instead, I chose to bend down, get at her eye level, uncross my arms, and smile. Then I asked her why she was not lining up with the other children. She responded that she didn't "feel like it."

When I asked if she was mad at a friend, she confirmed my guess.

I validated her feelings, telling her that I had fought with my friends too when I was her age. Then I asked her what she needed to do to feel better.

She said she wished she could talk to her friend and make up.

I comforted her by telling her that they could discuss the situation when we got back to class.

When we returned to the classroom, she and her friend went outside the room to talk. Within five minutes they came back in ready to learn.

—Jackie Freedman, special ed instructional assistant,
fourth- and fifth-grade classroom, Certified Positive Discipline Educator

A student came to school with a shirt that was very low under the arms—an inappropriate blouse for school. The principal was notified and came to the class.

STUDENT: Oh, am I in trouble?

PRINCIPAL: No, you are not in trouble. You look so cute today.

STUDENT: Thanks.

PRINCIPAL: That top you are wearing is adorable. Just a little naked for school.

STUDENT: Oh. I could put on my tennis shirt.

PRINCIPAL: That would be great.

Instead of scolding the student, the principal made a lovely connection with her, and then gently let her know the blouse was inappropriate for school. This normally rebellious student came to her own conclusion about how to correct the problem and did so willingly and with a positive spirit.

—Sheri Johnson, principal, Health Sciences High and Middle College

TOOL TIPS

1. Connection before correction is the best way to motivate behavior change. Examples:

   Connection: I see you are frustrated and angry.

   Correction: It is okay to feel what you feel, but it is not okay to hit. What else could you do?

   Connection: I care about what you have to say.

   Correction: Let's find time to sit together and brainstorm for solutions that are respectful to everyone.

2. See the Class Meetings tool (page 124) for one of the best ways to help kids achieve a sense of overall connection and belonging.

WHAT THE RESEARCH SAYS

School connectedness research has spanned several decades, demonstrating that having a positive connection at school is a primary factor in academic achievement. Studies related to school connectedness specifically identify the importance of the teacher and student relationship. The National Longitudinal Study of Adolescent Health reported that school connectedness was the strongest factor in protecting students from negative behaviors.[33] This longitudinal research included more than thirty-six thousand middle and high school students. Findings indicate school connectedness is linked to decreased drug and alcohol use, decreases in early sexual behavior, and less violence, as well as decreases in many other risky behaviors. Other studies show that school connectedness is positively related to healthy self-esteem, self-efficacy, optimism, and positive peer relationships.[34] In one related study 476 adolescents in the sixth and seventh grades were evaluated based on level of school connectedness across one year. Results showed that high levels of school connectedness offset the adverse effects of negative family relations for boys as well as girls. Also, school connectedness lessened the occurrence sometimes observed in girls of lower effort in school. That is, girls who had a tendency not to put forth effort in academics actually put forth more effort when they felt a sense of school connectedness. When teachers take time for connection before correction, the benefits are far-reaching. Motivation, self-regulation, and student attitude toward school all improve.[35]

GREETINGS

The teacher has a chance of winning the student over the first day of school if she stands by the door and greets each student personally.

—*Rudolf Dreikurs*

Greeting students as they enter the classroom is an opportunity for connection that should not be wasted. We heard from one sixth-grade student who told us she could vividly remember the teachers between kindergarten and sixth grade who greeted her and those who didn't.

You'll notice that many of the Positive Discipline tools work well when combined with others. The Greeting tool ties into the same foundational purpose that is behind the Connection Before Correction tool, and the Special Time tool because it helps students immediately feel how much you care. For some students, your morning greeting may make all the difference in how they approach their entire school day.

Greeting your students can be contagious—following your lead, students will begin greeting each other. Actually, being a morning greeter can be one of the classroom jobs that rotate among students. Modeling positive, caring ways to greet each other in the morning (and even role-playing if students need practice) may be an important step, depending on grade level.

"Hip, Hip Horray, you're all here today!"

Research shows that students become more engaged in learning when teachers take just a few minutes to connect.

TOOL IN ACTION FROM RALEIGH, NORTH CAROLINA

Each morning, for about twenty minutes before the school day begins, I hold open the front door of the school for students and visitors. I have a chance to greet students with a smile and a look in the eyes. Sometimes we speak: "Good morning." "Thank you." "You're welcome." Sometimes we simply nod to each other. But holding the door is a regular event, one that is recalled by many alumni. It is time well spent for the principal to be out, viewing the front of the campus including the carpool lane.

More and more, I have noticed that students hold the doors open for their peers and for guests. Occasionally students will hold the door open for me with a smile and awareness that they too enjoy being in the business of being kind and connecting.

—Thomas Humble, Ph.D., principal, Raleigh Charter High School

TOOL IN ACTION FROM EUREKA, ILLINOIS

I had a wonderful experience recently while doing a follow-up training with a small Catholic school with whom I had done some training last year. I had a pretty busy August going to lots of schools for teacher in-service training, and St. Mary's was my last program. I felt a bit low on energy, and that morning had been rough at home.

When I arrived at St. Mary's, Father greeted me warmly, asking me how I was, and I told him I was fine but admitted that I'd gotten a bit of a rough start that morning. People gathered around the table and he opened, as he always does, with a prayer, and then he said, "I think we'll start this morning's session with a Car Wash, and we're going to Car Wash Dina."

Now, for those of you who have never heard of a Car Wash, it's something we did at my old school when someone was in need of some encouragement. We put that person in the center of the circle (only figuratively), and we "washed" them with compliments and appreciations. The idea is that, just as the big brushes and sudsy soap leave your dusty and dirty car all shiny and clean like new, a human car wash of compliments leaves you feeling hopeful and encouraged to keep trying.

I had shared the idea with them the previous year and had completely forgotten that I had told them about it. So Father began by giving me a beautiful compliment about all he had learned from me and how much he appreciated my presentation style. Then every person in the circle gave me a compliment. Even the three new people on the staff who had never met me and didn't know anything about Positive Discipline gave me a compliment. I just stood there and took them all in, still a bit in shock! When everyone had spoken, I thanked them again, and we began our morning.

I felt so different, like I had literally been transformed. I noticed how relaxed I was all morning, and how easily the information that I wanted to share came out of my mouth. I felt very present to the group and was able to respond to their questions in a very confident and positive way.

—Dina Emser, former director of Blooming Grove Academy,
Certified Positive Discipline Lead Trainer

TOOL IN ACTION FROM ATLANTA, GEORGIA

One of the highlights of my day is to stand at the door each morning and engage in a short dialogue with each of my students. Goodwill is contagious! It benefits the giver and the receiver. Whether it's about last night's baseball game, their favorite lunch item, new earrings, a cute hairstyle, or an infectious smile, each comment binds us as much more than a class.

Greetings also spur conversation among each other, and the kids

Norcross Branch

GWINNETT COUNTY
PUBLIC LIBRARY

Customer ID: **********9542

Items that you checked out

Title: Positive discipline tools for teachers :
effective classroom management for
social, emotional, and academic success
ID: 34158108479771
Due: Saturday, September 2, 2023
Messages:
Item checkout ok. You just saved $17.00 by
using your library.

Total items: 1
Account balance: $0.00
8/12/2023 11:06 AM
Checked out: 10
Overdue: 0

Library Hours

Monday - Thursday 10 am - 8 pm
Friday - Saturday 10 am - 5 pm
Sunday 12 pm - 5 pm

770-978-5154
http://www.gwinnettpl.org

Total items: 1
Account balance: $0.00
8/12/2023 11:06 AM
Checked out: 10
Overdue: 0

Library Hours
Monday - Thursday: 10 am - 8 pm
Friday - Saturday: 10 am - 5 pm
Sunday: 12 pm - 5 pm

770-978-5154
http://www.gwinnettpl.org

notice details about their classmates that might have gone unrecognized before seeing positive behavior modeled. Compliments, nods of agreement, and expressions of empathy start our morning. It is very powerful to see the children become connected and carry that spirit throughout the day.

—Patty Spall, first-grade teacher, St. Jude the Apostle Catholic School

TOOL TIPS

1. Greet each student at the door with "Good morning."

2. You might want to add a handshake or a high-five.

3. If you notice anything specific (such as a hairstyle change or a happy smile), mention it.

4. Morning greetings could also be a job that rotates—a student standing with you to add his or her welcome to classmates.

5. Students could also take turns at the end of the day saying "Goodbye" or "Have a nice day."

WHAT THE RESEARCH SAYS

Allday and Pakurar systematically studied the effect of teacher greetings on student behavior.[36] In this study teachers were instructed to greet the students at the door by using the student's name and a positive statement. No specific scripts were given because of the need for this interaction to be perceived by students as sincere and consistent with the setting. Results showed that greetings increased students' on-task behavior in class from 45 percent to 72 percent during the greeting "intervention" phase. Teacher greetings can easily be implemented in classrooms to improve students' on-task behavior.

Marzano and Marzano report research that shows teachers' actions impact student achievement more than curriculum, assessment, staff collegiality, or community involvement do. Furthermore, studies show that the quality of the student-teacher relationship is the keystone for effective classroom management.[37]

SPECIAL TIME

The greatest stimulation for the development of the child is exposing him to experiences which seem to be beyond his reach but are not.

—*Rudolf Dreikurs*

As a school counselor, Kelly had thirty-minute lessons in each classroom every week. It is common, especially for the younger students, to need structure and a routine as they transition from their teacher leaving the classroom to Kelly entering to start the lesson. For one kindergarten class, this transition seemed particularly challenging because they came in from the playground. Spending even a few seconds connecting with students helped. Kelly identified students who might seem restless or wound up after recess and went over for a quick hello as the other students hung up coats and settled back in the classroom.

One student in particular seemed to struggle with coming in because he would have his mind on the soccer game that came to a quick close at the end of recess. This student often had feelings to share about something not being fair about the game (from his perspective). Taking a few seconds to greet him with eye contact and validate

"I want you to sit up front right by my desk. It's not because I want to keep an eye on you. It's a feng shui thing."

his feelings with just a sentence or two facilitated a smooth transition. Once Kelly connected with this student, he felt heard, and he was more easily able to focus on the next classroom activity, a group lesson. When it was time to brainstorm, this student always had some of the best solutions. The few seconds of special time made all the difference.

Many teachers have reported that simply spending a few minutes after school (or any other time alone) with a student for special time has helped the student feel encouraged enough to stop misbehaving, even though the misbehavior is not mentioned during this time.

One of the most important foundational principles of Positive Discipline, if not *the* most important, is connection, which often takes just a few minutes. (This is one reason the principle is repeated so often.) Connection is the key to helping students feel belonging and significance.

Research shows that the greatest predictor of student success is the degree to which students feel a connection at school.[38] The Centers for Disease Control report that when students perceive their teachers as caring about them, this serves as a significant protective factor. Studies show that when students feel connected to their school, they are less likely to engage in high-risk behaviors. Furthermore, students who feel a sense of belonging and significance at school are more likely to have higher grades and test scores as well as better school attendance records. This demonstrates that connection often *is* the correction.

To make sure you spend some special time with every student, use a copy of your student roster and put a check mark next to the student's name once you have spent some scheduled special time.

Robert Rasmussen, the high school teacher in Salt Lake City, Utah, that we mentioned in Chapter Two, had four history classes. He decided to test this theory that special time makes a difference by spending special time with every student in two of his classes, with half of the students in one of his classes, and with none of the students in the fourth class. To accomplish this task, he set up two desks at the back of the room. While the students were doing assignments at their desks, he called one student at a time to come sit with him for about five minutes. During this time he would ask questions such as "What are your hobbies or your favorite things to do when not in school?" and "Do you have any questions, or is there anything you need help with?" He made notes on what he learned, and later made short comments to the students about their interests or made sure they got the help they asked for.

It took several weeks to get to every student in the two classes, but he spoke with each and every one. He noticed a distinct difference in cooperation and camaraderie in the two classes where he spent special time with every student in comparison to the class where he didn't spend special time with any of his students. He thought it was particularly interesting that, even though he hadn't announced what he was doing, just about every student who didn't get special time in the class where he purposely spent time with just half of the students came to him and asked, "When do I get my interview?"

Special time does not always need to be planned in advance. In the story below, a teacher shares how valuable it can be to use special time spontaneously whenever it is needed. The time used for discussing a problem one-on-one with the student created a sense of trust and connection so that he could realize the teacher's purpose was to support his learning, not punish him.

TOOL IN ACTION FROM CAIRO, EGYPT

I had a very talkative student in my tenth-grade class. He took longer than usual to complete assigned tasks and was very easily distracted. One day when students were working individually on a task in class, he was distracted by others at his table and was disruptive. According to class guidelines, I used a verbal redirection and a nonverbal (silent) signal to help him refocus. When this didn't work, I decided to try Positive Time-Out. However, when I asked him to move to a quiet table for Positive Time-Out, with the intention of working with him and redirecting his focus, he refused to move. Instead, he stood up and challenged me using hand gestures and an elevated voice to tell me that I was not being fair and he was not moving. He continued to stare at me and only went back to work when I looked away.

I recognized that this student was not willing to compromise at that moment and that the situation had become a power struggle. I decided it was up to me to end the power struggle, so I let it go.

It took me a couple of minutes to decide what I would do. I quietly asked the two other students at his table to move to another table to minimize distraction, and they did so. Then I kindly asked if the student would agree to meet with me after class, but I did not push the issue further during the lesson. He worked quietly for the remainder of the class.

After class, I met with him and started the conversation by asking about his feelings, about why he was so frustrated. He said he felt "picked on" because he was the one who was asked to move to time-out. There seemed to be a lack of trust and understanding as to what Positive Time-Out meant. He had perceived it as a punishment instead of time to redirect and focus on the task at hand. I validated his feelings and acknowledged my mistake when I had directed him to leave the table instead of asking him if it would help him to go to the Positive Time-Out area.

We ended the meeting with an agreement about some verbal and nonverbal signals I would use to get his attention, and we agreed that he could choose when he needed a time-out. Since our conversation he has never repeated this disruptive behavior. Instead, he now recognizes my verbal and nonverbal signals calling his attention to potential misbehavior. In another incident he even recognized his inability to sustain his focus and opted for time-out himself.

—Heba Hefni, tenth-grade teacher, Oasis International School

TOOL IN ACTION FROM CHICAGO, ILLINOIS

Building individual connections with high school students isn't always easy, especially when your semester roster includes over 150 students. However, it is possible! I make it my mission to know all of my students' names and something about them as quickly as possible. During the first day of class, students fill out a form that includes some of their special interests, and they share some of that information during introductions. Some teachers do similar activities but never use the information after the first day. I keep these forms in a folder and jot down information as it arises that may be helpful in building connections, such as if I find out that they become active in a sports team or join one of the academic clubs.

As the semester continues, special time occurs both formally and informally. During passing periods, I stand at the door and greet each student. As I practice remembering each student's name, I make a point of recalling one of their special interests from the first-day activity or strike up a short conversation about an activity they may be involved in at school. If I don't get a chance to engage with a student at the door, I make a point of at least briefly engaging with the student one-on-one during bell work or during a class activity. Each student has some kind of interaction with me each and every day, and if for some reason that doesn't happen, I make a point of making it happen the next time we see each other as they enter the classroom. As a former mentor teacher, I recall observing a student in a classroom behaving defiantly toward a teacher I was mentoring. I asked the student to take a walk with me one-on-one. I didn't mention the behavior I witnessed, but instead engaged with the student about his day and interests. When I brought the student back to class, he discontinued the behaviors that were disruptive. He just needed an outlet for some frustrations he was facing, and the special time we shared allowed him that opportunity.

I no longer teach at a high school, but have found that the college students I teach now are more engaged and feel more connected because

I make a point of meeting with each student formally to discuss his or her career path and interests. In both high school and college-level courses, students are more engaged when they feel connected. The information obtained from special time with students contributes to student engagement, because I can provide examples as I lecture or activities that are based on their individual interests.

—Sarah Moses, doctoral student, Adler University

TOOL TIPS

1. Ask a student to join you for lunch or at another identified time. Keep a roster to make sure all of your students have this opportunity.

2. During special time, students love to hear you share your interests too.

3. Use special time spontaneously whenever you notice that a student needs it, and/or that you need it to connect with a student who is particularly challenging.

WHAT THE RESEARCH SAYS

As we've previously established, decades of attachment studies show children's fundamental need for belonging and connection.[39] Classroom management research identifies the importance of developing relationships with individual students through personal interactions such as spending special time one-on-one with students. Research shows that teachers who take time to develop relationships with students report fewer behavior problems and an increase in academic performance.[40] Teachers who have high-quality relationships with their students report significantly fewer discipline problems.[41] McCombs and Whisler report that students appreciate personal attention from their teachers.[42]

While extensive interaction with individual students may be difficult, teachers can communicate personal interest without taking up much time. Talking to students in the lunchroom one-on-one, commenting on extracurricular activities, and complimenting students are simple strategies that work well to connect with students.

VALIDATE FEELINGS

Since no two children are alike, the teacher will need to be sensitive to the feelings of each member of her class in order to know when and how to encourage.

—*Rudolf Dreikurs*

When students are discouraged (and misbehaving students are discouraged students), they do not need punishment in any form. They need encouragement. One of the best ways to help students feel encouraged is to listen until you understand their point of view and then validate their feelings.

"My teacher and my computer were both down today."

If you are listening carefully (or watching closely), you can probably guess what the student is feeling. As Rudolf Dreikurs explained, it is okay to be wrong when you make guesses, because the student will let you know if you have guessed correctly or not, and that gives you more information about how to be helpful.

Students also appreciate knowing how you are feeling when you share in a heartfelt way instead of making an accusation. It does not help to say, "*You* made me feel terrible." Not only will this accusation invite defensiveness, but the statement also isn't true. Students can't *make* us feel anything. However, they can certainly push our buttons in ways that *invite* us to experience thoughts and feelings that stem from old belief patterns. When we change our thoughts, we change our feelings. For example, when a student is misbehaving and we remember that his behavior is a sign of discouragement, we will respond with different feelings and actions. The kind of sharing students appreciate is "I remember when something like that happened to me, and how terrible I felt."

Validating students' feelings and sharing your own builds connection and helps students feel understood and more open to cooperation. It is a powerful way to create a connection that often invites correction at the same time.

TOOL IN ACTION FROM OCEANSIDE, CALIFORNIA

Five-year-old Albert started kindergarten being disruptive, aggressive toward peers, and defiant toward the teacher. He would not sit on his carpet square without bumping into others, and if he did not want to do something, he would hide under a table and refuse to come out. He would even run out of the classroom. One time Albert ran off campus, and the principal had to chase after him. He would also cry and throw himself on the ground during recess. The teacher or playground supervisor would threaten him with going to the principal's office if he did not stop crying and get up, and he usually wound up visiting the office.

One day I witnessed this on the playground. The other students had just gone to recess. I asked the adults to let me speak with Albert. Since he was lying on the ground crying, I kneeled close to him and said, "Albert, you are really sad right now." (Sadness was his way of describing being upset.)

He nodded.

I said, "Do you want to be sad here or in the counseling office?"

He gave no response but became slightly calmer. I said, "I see you want to be sad right here. That's fine. How long would you like to be sad here on the ground: for one minute or five?"

He stopped crying. I waited.

After a few seconds he got up and with a smile said, "I'm finished being sad. I'm going to recess now." He got up and ran off to the playground.

—Lois Ingber, counselor, Certified Positive Discipline Lead Trainer

TOOL IN ACTION FROM CAIRO, EGYPT

I am a teacher in fifth grade with a class of twenty-five students. I have used many techniques from the Positive Discipline approach and, in particular, with a student who had a habit of disrupting the class by speaking in Arabic. His purpose was to make his classmates laugh. I teach in French and do not understand Arabic, so this was a difficult situation for me.

To address this problem, I decided to share my feelings with him in an individual meeting so that he might understand how his behavior was disturbing to me. I also asked him to think about why he interrupted class. Then I invited him to search for solutions with me. He proposed two things: he made an agreement to try to refrain from making his classmates laugh, and he also suggested that he would sit alone if he was having difficulty respecting our agreement, to avoid being tempted by the attention of his friends.

I noticed that he changed his behavior quickly; he did not need to sit alone. Sometimes he needs a reminder about the agreement. After this change, I took time to point out to him how much I appreciated this change, and I encouraged him to continue. He was very proud. I can also see that he feels better in class. This way of addressing the problem was a big success, especially since everything was managed calmly and without conflict. On my side, I also feel better because I can teach the class without being frequently interrupted.

—Pierre Sudre, fifth-grade teacher, Oasis International School

TOOL TIPS

1. Make a guess about what the student is feeling so you can be empathetic.

2. Verbalize your guess: for example, "Looks like you are really angry right now" or "Are you feeling sad?"

3. If the student says no, try another guess.

4. Be genuine: "I care about you and would like to know what is going on for you if you want to talk about it."

5. Use your intuition about what to do next. It may tell you to offer a choice, or to ask what the student or you could do to help solve the problem. Or it may tell you to just listen and validate feelings.

WHAT THE RESEARCH SAYS

Adler defined empathy as "seeing with the eyes of another, hearing with the ears of another, and feeling with the heart of another."[43] Hanna, Hanna, and Keys report that empathy is a crucial component in relating to students, especially high-risk students, who may be harder to reach, as well as students who are entering adolescence.[44] A study conducted in urban schools addressing early adolescents' perspectives on motivation and achievement found that teacher empathy is a key practice in promoting academic motivation and achievement.[45]

LISTEN

Stimulate children to find solutions. Don't tell them.

—*Rudolf Dreikurs*

Have you ever complained that your students don't listen to you? If so, ask yourself how well you model listening. Is it possible you make some of the following mistakes?

- React and correct: "Don't talk to me that way. Why can't you be more respectful?"
- Dismiss: "You shouldn't feel that way. Don't feel bad."
- Lecture: "Maybe if you would do ___, then___" (for example, "Maybe if you would be friendlier, then you would have more friends").

Avoiding these mistakes could provide room for you to adopt some of the following listening skills:

- Listen closely so that you have a sense not only of what your students say but also of what they mean.
- Validate the feelings and point of view of your students before sharing your own.
- Listen with your lips closed, so all that comes out is "Hmmm" or "Umm."

"Before you continue your emotional tirade, let me know if you're picking up on my nonevaluative and empathetic listening."

Students will listen to you *after* they feel listened to. As you master the art of listening, your students will too. Example is the best teacher. Practice being a good listener and model the behavior you want to see. You can then teach your students about listening mistakes and listening skills, and provide them opportunities to role-play and practice.

TOOL IN ACTION FROM POWAY, CALIFORNIA

As someone who runs a Positive Discipline classroom, I have noticed that I am spending time helping students grow not only academically but also emotionally. After giving it some thought, I am slowly coming to the realization that treating students equally means meeting their needs no matter where they are.

Most recently in a class meeting, we had a conversation about how we treat others. The golden rule came up, and together we discussed treating others the way we would want to be treated. We realized that if we followed the golden rule, none of us would be happy because most people have a certain expectation for the way they want to be treated. One of my students provided the following example: "If I treated you the way that I want to be treated, I would bring you a new snake every day because reptiles are my favorite animals." Instead, we decided it would be best to discover how others want to be treated and treat them that way, respectfully.

—Diana Loiewski, teacher

TOOL IN ACTION FROM SOUTHERN CALIFORNIA

In class I had the students copying from the overhead projector to make a map of the United States. One of my students didn't understand why he and his friend couldn't use the atlas in the class to create the map. He was also upset that, as a teacher, I didn't know all of the states myself. Afterward my student and I privately discussed why he was upset and refusing to follow my directions.

Because he was clearly not listening to me, I calmly put my fist over his head and said, "My brain is on you. I will listen now." We have used this action to symbolize that I am listening to him and vice versa. I gave him my full attention. I repeated back what he said and confirmed that I heard him correctly.

Then I made eye contact with him, gently held his fist over my head, and said, "You are frustrated that I won't let you use a book and that I don't know all the states. I am sorry that I don't know all the states and I need a book to help me. I am learning too, and I am embarrassed and sad that I don't know all the states off the top of my head." I explained to him that the lesson was teaching the class to follow along with what their teacher was saying.

Out of the blue he said, "Oh yeah! You are an aide, not a teacher."

That seemed to make sense to him. After we talked he was able to calm down. He even apologized to me. Children do listen better when they have been listened to.

—Jackie Freeman, special ed classroom aide for fourth and fifth graders

TOOL TIPS

1. Notice how often you interrupt with defensiveness, explanations, or advice.

2. Avoid giving advice. Have faith that your student might figure things out just because he or she has a listening ear.

3. It is okay to ask questions that invite your student to go deeper: "Can you give me an example?" "Anything else?" Repeat "Anything else?" until the student says, "No."

4. At an even deeper level, do you listen between the lines for the belief behind the behavior?

5. After listening, ask if this is an issue that could go on the class meeting agenda for more help. Respect the student's choice.(See the Curiosity Questions: Motivational [page 112], Curiosity Questions: Conversational [page 117], and Don't Back-Talk Back [page 255] tools.)

WHAT THE RESEARCH SAYS

Research shows that listening has a key influence on establishing respectful relationships with students. Ladson-Billings asked urban eighth-grade students to share their perspectives on their teachers.[46] Specifically, students were asked about what they liked about their teacher. The responses demonstrate the importance of teachers listening and the influence of listening on the quality of the teacher-student relationship which, therefore, influences student learning. One student said, "She listens to us! She respects us! She lets us express our opinions! She looks us in the eye when she talks to us! She smiles at us! She speaks to us when she sees us in the hall or in the cafeteria!" These student comments highlight the art of listening and demonstrate the importance of nonverbal communication when listening.[47]

CURIOSITY QUESTIONS: MOTIVATIONAL

Any authority that is not spontaneously recognized, but has to be forced upon us, is a sham; true authority and discipline come from within.

—Alfred Adler

The Curiosity Questions: Motivational tool is different from the Curiosity Questions: Conversational tool (page 117). The latter invites conversation, while the Curiosity Questions: Motivational tool is designed to motivate students with only a few words. This works because they have been respectfully asked a question that invites them to think and to decide what they feel motivated to do.

The quote above teaches us so much about the psychology of motivation. How do you feel and what do you want to do when someone demands something of you? Do you feel respected? Do you feel motivated to cooperate? Or do you feel like rebelling? On the other hand, how do you feel and what do you want to do when someone respectfully asks you a question? Are you motivated to think about it and maybe even cooperate?

Actually, physiology is involved as well as psychology. When someone makes a demand

"FOR YOUR INFORMATION, YOUR 'BECAUSE I SAID SO' TRICK DOESN'T WORK WORTH A DARN AT SCHOOL!"

of you, notice that your body stiffens, whether a little or a lot, and the message that goes to the brain is "Resist." When someone respectfully asks a question, your body relaxes and the message that goes to the brain is "Search for an answer." While searching for an answer you feel capable, connected, and more inclined toward cooperation. Just as you might feel more motivated to cooperate with someone who respectfully asks you a question, students might feel the same. As Adler's quote at the beginning of this section indicates, motivational questions help students develop discipline from within.

To increase your awareness, start noticing how often you tell instead of ask, and put a dollar in a jar every time you catch yourself telling. (How long would it take for you to have enough money in the jar for a nice vacation?) When you find yourself telling, think about how you could turn your words into a respectful question that would invite your student to feel respected enough to want to cooperate.

Caution: Note that the tool recommends "curiosity" questions, not "compliance" questions. Some teachers are disappointed when their curiosity questions don't work. Need we say again that there isn't any tool that works with every student every time? This is the reason we need so many tools. Still, let's take a look at why curiosity questions may not work.

1. There hasn't been sufficient training for the student to know what is expected and how to accomplish it.
2. You haven't taken time to create a connection before correction. One way to accomplish connection is through the Validate Feelings tool: "I know you are angry. What could you do to calm down before focusing on a solution?"
3. Your tone of voice implied an expectation of compliance instead of an invitation.

Simple motivational questions often invite students to use their personal power to search for answers instead of using energy to push back when told what to do. You will find several examples in the "Tool in Action" stories and the "Tool Tips" below.

TOOL IN ACTION FROM DECATUR, GEORGIA

I have a success story to share about asking questions instead of engaging in power struggles. We were outside at an exercise break, and I have a couple of students who are always late coming inside because they continue to throw the balls and play. I said, "I noticed everyone else is by the door, ready to come in, and you are still on the soccer field."

They said, "Eh, we'll be fine."

Normally I would want to get in a power struggle and tell them to move faster, but instead I said, "What needs to happen for us to be on time?"

As they got to the end of the field, they started running and got to the door on time for class. It was so nice to let them make the decision and to watch them make a good decision!

I have also noticed a change in my math group overall—they are often ready for class now without discussing it at all, and today one of them asked the others, "Are you ready to begin? Do you have your materials?" while they were chatting and getting ready for class.

—Elise Albrecht, middle school teacher, Cloverleaf School

TOOL IN ACTION FROM ATLANTA, GEORGIA

I have one student in my geometry class who I've had to keep telling, "Come on, let's get to work. We've got twenty minutes left of class," while he sits in front of a blank piece of paper.

By adjusting my language from telling statements to questioning statements, he has really turned things around. Now I'll ask him, "What's your plan to finish your classwork in the next twenty minutes?" or "What resources do you need from me to . . . ?"

At first he looked at me like my head was spinning around, but he quickly got to the point of realizing that he is in control of his actions.

This change has sparked a whole conversation on being present and mindful in class, and he is actually working with our school counselor now on practicing mindfulness techniques.

When he was prompted to examine why he wasn't getting his work done, he finally admitted that he wants to work but gets spaced out and can't stop thinking about all the stuff that he has to do later in the day. His real challenge has always been that he has trouble being present and mindful, but it always looked like he was just being lazy or defiant.

—Bryan Schomaker, M.A.T., lead high school math teacher, Howard School

TOOL TIPS

1. Simple motivation questions invite students to search for answers.

2. Avoid commands that invite resistance and rebellion, and ask questions that invite feelings of capability and cooperation. Examples:
   - "What is your plan for finishing your work by the end of class today?"
   - "What do you need to take so you won't be cold outside during recess?"
   - "How can you and your friend solve this problem together?"
   - "In our class meeting, what did we decide to do when this happens?"
   - "What is your plan for getting your desk in order before we leave for the day?"

3. See the Curiosity Questions: Conversational tool (page 117).

WHAT THE RESEARCH SAYS

Siegel and Bryson recommend using asking statements rather than telling statements during times of conflict to avoid power struggles.[48]

Asking invites constructive problem-solving, whereas neuroscientific research shows that "telling statements" increase a biochemical stress response and may produce a response that looks like rebellion or withdrawal. The researchers describe how asking works to invite the "upstairs" brain to engage in processing choices and planning, while telling triggers the reactive "downstairs" brain. Siegel and Bryson report that when we facilitate thinking by the "upstairs" brain, there is a decrease in stress levels and emotional reactivity.

CURIOSITY QUESTIONS: CONVERSATIONAL

To see with the eyes of another, to hear with the ears of another, to feel with the heart of another; for the time being, this seems to me an admissible definition of what we call social feeling.

—Alfred Adler

The root of the word "education" is the Latin *educare*, "to draw forth." Too often we try to stuff instruction in by telling, and then we wonder why our wonderful lectures go in one ear and out the other. When we engage in telling, the student may stiffen, and the message that goes to the brain is "Resist." On the other hand, asking with true curiosity invites the listener's body to relax, and the message that goes to the brain is "Search for an answer." Conversational curiosity questions help students develop the "social feeling" referred to by Alfred Adler in the quotation above, because they feel respectfully included.

Conversational curiosity questions take more time than motivational curiosity questions (page 112) because you are doing more than inviting a student to think of a solution to a simple task that requires attention, such as, "What do you need to do to get your work done on time?" Conversational curiosity questions require just what the name suggests: a conversation.

"Maybe little Jack Horner became argumentative because he was backed into a corner, leaving him no options."

A. BACALL

Before you engage in curiosity questions, it is important to wait until everyone has had time to calm down. Then find a quiet place where you can sit with the student and really listen to his or her responses to your questions.

The "Tool Tips" below include a script for curiosity questions. These are meant to give you an idea about what curiosity questions might sound like. However, it is important that you don't use a script in the moment, so that your questions are genuine and relate to the specifics of the situation.

TOOL IN ACTION FROM NOBLEBORO, MAINE

Stephen, age four and a half, has been having a really hard time with his classmates. He gets frustrated easily and then hits. During the morning work cycle, the teacher notices Stephen crying next to his mat. There are puzzle map pieces all over the floor. The assistant informs the teacher that Janet flipped his puzzle over after he hit her.

TEACHER: Stephen, I notice that you are very sad. What happened?

STEPHEN: Janet flipped my puzzle over, and I worked on it all morning.

TEACHER: I can understand why you are so sad. You put a lot of work into that. What caused Janet to flip your puzzle over?

STEPHEN: Well, I hit her. She was bossing me.

TEACHER: So you got mad and hit her?

STEPHEN: Yeah.

TEACHER: Then what happened?

STEPHEN: Then she flipped my puzzle map over.

TEACHER: So what did you learn from this?

STEPHEN: Maybe I shouldn't hit.

TEACHER: Janet looks sad too. What could you do to help her feel better?

STEPHEN: I could tell her I'm sorry.

TEACHER: Would you like some help?

STEPHEN: I can do it.

Notice the difference when a child decides to say "I'm sorry" instead of being told to say it. The apology comes with sincerity. Stephen came to this conclusion on his own (with a little help from curiosity questions) after feeling proud of himself for solving the problem and wanting to fix it.

—Chip DeLorenzo, M.Ed., head of school, Damariscotta Montessori School, Certified Positive Discipline Trainer

TOOL IN ACTION FROM POWAY, CALIFORNIA

My ninth-grade English class has followed a routine for the last three weeks: after reading, discussing, and developing a plot diagram of a short story, students have been assigned a three-paragraph literary analysis. Students have also been provided a rubric and a model essay. The model essay for each of the assignments was reviewed and discussed in class.

Tomas has handed in a one-paragraph essay for the last three weeks. I privately asked Tomas to meet with me after school on Thursday to discuss his essay. The conversation went like this:

TEACHER: So, Tomas, how are you doing?
STUDENT (STAMMERING UNCOMFORTABLY): Okay.
TEACHER: Do you know why I wanted to meet with you?
STUDENT: Maybe my grades?
TEACHER: Let's take a look at your essays.

He opened his binder and shuffled through a couple of pages until he came to his essays.

TEACHER: What is your understanding of what is needed in the essays?
STUDENT: I don't know.
TEACHER: Do you remember getting a piece of paper that listed the essay requirements and how you would be graded?
STUDENT: Yes.
TEACHER: Can you take out that piece of paper?

The student pulled out the piece of paper and together we looked at the requirements.

STUDENT: Oh, I didn't follow what was assigned.
TEACHER: What can you do about it now?
STUDENT: Do you think I can have until Wednesday to redo all of the
essays so far for full credit?

Previously in a class meeting, students had determined that they would like the opportunity to work toward mastery on all assignments, quizzes, and tests. Consequently, we decided that they could continually revise work for full credit (utilizing the Mistakes as Opportunities for Learning tool). We agreed to revisit this policy at the end of October. So far it has been amazing. Because of Positive Discipline strategies my students are empowered and are earning good grades. My class has gone from a typical bell curve to a J-curve: I have more students with A's than B's, more with B's than C's, and no one is failing.

—Diana Loiewski, teacher, Certified Positive Discipline Classroom Educator

TOOL TIPS

1. Students will listen to you *after* they feel listened to.

2. Stop "telling" and ask questions instead, such as (but using your own words):
   - "What happened?"
   - "How do you feel about it?"
   - "How do you think others feel?"
   - "What ideas do you have to solve this problem?"

3. See the Curiosity Questions: Motivational tool (page 112).

WHAT THE RESEARCH SAYS

Dr. Dan Siegel suggests that asking invites constructive problem-solving rather than telling statements, which will increase the student's biochemical stress response. Siegel and Bryson describe how asking works to activate the "upstairs" brain, which helps students process choices and engage in planning, while telling triggers the reactive "downstairs" brain. Siegel and Bryson report that when we facilitate thinking, there is a decrease in stress levels and emotional reactivity.[49]

Dr. Judy Willis, a neuroscientist, further explains how stress and emotion impact learning and includes specific implications for the classroom. After practicing as a neurologist for almost two decades, Dr. Willis became so interested in the neuroscience of learning that she decided to become a teacher and has since used her research to help educators better understand how to support student learning. Willis describes neuroimaging research that reveals the negative impact of stress and anxiety on learning. Neuroimaging studies provide support for the importance of student-centered learning focused on helping students feel a sense of belonging and significance in the classroom.[50]

Just as Siegel and Bryson report evidence showing that when students feel stimulated to learn rather than intimidated, memory and learning improve, Willis describes neuroimaging studies showing that stress-induced situations negatively impact the ability to learn and store new information.

CHAPTER FOUR

CLASSROOM MANAGEMENT

CLASS MEETINGS

Children learn more from each other than from what the
teacher says.

—Rudolf Dreikurs

Have you ever noticed that kids will often listen to each other even
though they haven't listened to you? During class meetings, we
have heard students say to each other the very words that, when we
used them, seemed to go in one ear and out the
other: "If you cheat, you won't really learn" or
"If you aren't a good sport, others won't want to
play with you." They sometimes hear these statements from teachers as lectures to be ignored
while hearing them from each other as good
advice.

Many teachers have found that class meetings make their job much easier because they
gain a whole classroom full of problem-solvers.
Students can practice the many social-emotional
skills they learn during class meetings throughout the day to create a cooperative classroom atmosphere.

These social-emotional skills are not learned
overnight any more than academic skills are

"We put our chairs in a circle,
and started talking, and the next thing
I knew we solved the problem."

learned overnight. Students learn and retain skills when they are practiced daily, and this is just as true for the skills learned in class meetings as for academic skills.

When Jane was an elementary school counselor and was first learning and teaching about class meetings, she would tell teachers to prepare for a "month of hell" because it takes time for students to learn the skills required for successful class meetings. However, we have found that the "month of hell" is no longer part of the process if you take time to train students in the Eight Essential Skills for Successful Class Meetings before engaging in class meetings to solve real problems. These essential skills (described in detail in *Positive Discipline in the Classroom*) are:[51]

1. Form a circle quickly, quietly, and safely.
2. Practice compliments and appreciations.
3. Respect differences.
4. Use respectful communication skills.
5. Focus on solutions.
6. Role-play and brainstorm.
7. Use the agenda and class meeting format.
8. Understand and use the Mistaken Goal Chart.

Some students learn all eight skills in just a few days. Others might need to spend a week or more practicing each skill. While learning the essential skills for class meetings, students are learning social-emotional skills, such as respect for self and others, listening to each other, brainstorming together as they focus on solutions, critical thinking, accountability, resilience (by practicing that mistakes are opportunities to learn), and all the other characteristics and life skills needed for successful living.

One special needs teacher didn't think the class meeting agenda would work because his kids needed "immediate" help when they were upset. Still, he decided to try it. He reported that it was almost funny to watch some of his students come into the room obviously upset after recess. They would march over to the agenda and write their name on it, then walk away visibly calmer. Putting their name on the agenda was their "immediate" solution because they knew they would soon get help during a class meeting (they have class meetings every day). That process helped them calm down.

The benefits of having daily class meetings (and weekly family meetings) are undeniable. We love when research validates our position, but we feel even more gratified to hear from teachers who experience the joy and benefits of the skills kids learn by participating in class meetings.

TOOL IN ACTION FROM DECATUR, GEORGIA

We had a class meeting where we brainstormed about interruptions (students making noises, comments, et cetera). One student said, "I know I'm doing it too, but it's so hard to stop!"

I have noticed that, although it is a constant struggle, they have become more patient with each other and say "Please stop" more often than saying unkind things like "Shut up" when someone is making noise.

One of the benefits I didn't foresee was their developing a little more empathy for one another's struggles with attention.

—Elise Albrecht, middle school teacher, Cloverleaf School

TOOL IN ACTION FROM MISSION VIEJO, CALIFORNIA

Today's class meeting accomplished everything in five minutes! I was actually concerned because there was nothing on the agenda to discuss. There hasn't been for two weeks! When I questioned them on it, they informed me that they are able to handle everything on their own now and usually do.

Sweet success! It's good to know they have truly embodied the principles they've been taught and apply them to their life now at this point.

—Joy Sacco, third-grade teacher, Carden Academy, Certified Positive Discipline Trainer

I have been working as an elementary public school teacher since 2003. I had serious trouble with my sixth-grade students. At that time, one of my colleagues introduced *Positive Discipline in the Classroom* to me. I read the book, and I could see why I had such trouble with my students. I was being too kind because I thought that would make me look like a good teacher and have a good reputation among my colleagues, students, and their parents. But I should have been kind *and* firm. I should have thought about how to teach in a way that improved a student's sense of responsibility, respectfulness, and independent resources.

After reading *Positive Discipline in the Classroom* and attending Positive Discipline workshops, I started to change what I taught and how I taught. My first change was truly connecting with students. When I took time for daily connection, my students responded to kind and firm correction when needed.

I started having class meetings every morning. The agenda included making a circle, compliments, a cooperative activity, and a hug. At 8:40 we made our circle, sitting on the floor together. When I sat on the floor with my students, I felt calm and connected with them. I had previously started my lessons standing in front of the classroom, with my students sitting in chairs. Making the circle was the beginning of a miraculous change in the class atmosphere and changed my attitude as a teacher.

At first students were shy about giving compliments, but they soon became eager to do so. I was surprised as I watched the cooperative atmosphere develop. There was no blaming or bullying, but lots of problem-solving and confidence building. At the graduation ceremony, one of my students told me, "I have learned to look forward to hearing words of appreciation from my teacher and friends. Whenever my friends speak my name, I feel extremely happy."

There is a lot of competition in Korean culture and our school, so I plan cooperative activities with students to develop social skills and connection before correction. We enjoy this active and fun time together.

We end our class meeting with hugs. I knew the power of hugs through teaching parents the hug activity in parenting classes. Now I hug my students every day. It makes a big difference because we feel connected.

As I reflect on this experience, our special class meeting time changed not only the students but also myself.

—Seonghwan Kim, Johyeon Elementary School, Certified Positive
Discipline Trainer

TOOL IN ACTION FROM SAN BERNARDINO, CALIFORNIA

Last Saturday I was at a former student's wedding reception and ran into many of my old students. After letting me know that she had so many good memories of my class and had stayed friends with many of her classmates, one girl said to me, "Over the years we have had our ups and downs, but we learned how to solve our problems from those class meetings. I'm so glad you taught us." I felt overwhelmed when she said that, and so grateful that I had learned about class meetings. She and another student I had taught were both getting their doctoral degrees.

I couldn't get that student out of my mind. So you see, all because of Positive Discipline and class meetings, I was successful with little five-year-olds.

—Colleen Petersen, retired schoolteacher

TOOL IN ACTION FROM GUAYAQUIL, ECUADOR

During our classroom meetings (which occur three times a week), we first acknowledge each other with compliments and appreciations. In this part of the meeting, students feel important and recognized for their talents, accomplishments, and more. We then revisit previous solutions to problems, checking in with students to determine if the solution worked. If the first agreed-upon solution did not work, students brainstorm more ideas. We then focus on our agenda with any problems that need to be discussed while focusing on possible solutions. The students involved in the problem identify one of the suggested solutions that they are willing to try. We wrap up our meeting by discussing future plans.

Positive Discipline has empowered my students, created a more positive and respectful environment, and helped to develop positive characteristics in students that help them today to be successful academically and socially and will continue to serve them well in the distant future.

—Jeremy Mathis, fourth-grade teacher

TOOL IN ACTION FROM SEATTLE, WASHINGTON

About two weeks ago, students in a fifth-grade class started bringing some Silly Putty to school and used it to occupy their hands instead of fidgeting. This week, the Silly Putty became a bit of a problem (being used inappropriately) and was put in "time-out" on a shelf. Then it disappeared. For one girl in particular, Liz, who had saved her money to buy the Silly Putty, this was pretty stressful.

On Tuesday they held a class meeting and talked about mistakes and how embarrassing it would be to acknowledge you did it. They came up with the solution of putting the Silly Putty back anonymously. Nothing happened.

Then the prime suspect, Clyde, "found" the Silly Putty in a cupboard but denied having taken it. The class was suspicious, but the teacher set very clear expectations that no one would be blamed without evidence.

Wednesday morning, shortly before their scheduled class meeting, students were working in small groups when Clyde blurted out, "All right, I did it!"

Not everyone heard this, but Liz did, and she asked to meet privately with Clyde. The two of them walked off to an empty room after requesting that adults not be present.

When I came in for an observation the teacher pulled me aside and expressed concern. He shared the history that Liz and Clyde were off talking and he didn't know exactly when they were coming back. Not only that, Clyde's name was on the class meeting agenda again, and the teacher didn't feel it was appropriate, given the events of the morning, that issues with Clyde be discussed again. (Good intuition!) I suggested that they hold the class meeting but just do compliments.

Liz and Clyde arrived just as the class meeting started and found places to sit in the circle. A student started the meeting and chose to do the compliments as "give or get," with no pass. Clyde sat kind of crumpled over himself as the first two students spoke. When he got the talking stick he sat up straight and complimented Liz for being a friend and listening to him.

Four students later, Liz complimented Clyde for being a good friend and listening to her. Two students after that, James (who had put Clyde on the agenda this time) complimented Clyde for being a good friend. Then another student and another complimented Clyde. One compliment was "I compliment you for being a friend, and I trust you." Clyde by now was no longer curled in himself and had a tear running down his cheek.

Several students asked for a compliment and could pick the student to give them a compliment (per our guidelines for compliments). Clyde began to slowly raise his hand. The next student asked Clyde if his hand was up and chose him to offer the compliment. Then more compliments for Clyde followed. The last one was from a boy who said, "I compliment you for being open with your emotions, the happy ones and the unhappy ones." After the meeting, one of the students remarked under his breath after the circle, "Clyde got nine compliments!" This is in a class of about twenty-five. No adult suggested this. No adult commented. It just happened.

The teacher reminded the students that they had had several struggles, and each time they had been up to the challenge. He told them that he felt they had once again met a significant challenge successfully. He explained to them that the problem-solving part of the class meeting would happen at the next meeting, and they ended with a brief fun rhythm activity.

When I met with the teacher afterward, we both sat stunned for a bit. He saw this as a watershed meeting for his class—partly because of how they welcomed Clyde back in, partly because James initiated the repeated compliments (James had been struggling with Clyde all year), and partly because of the courage modeled by Clyde and Liz.

Because this teacher had prepared the ground by teaching about mistakes, differences, compliments, and encouragement, these students had the skills they needed to rally like this.

—Jody McVittie, M.D., Certified Positive Discipline Lead Trainer

TOOL TIPS

1. Schedule daily class meetings.

2. Place an agenda in a visible place that is easily accessible for students. When students have a challenge, they can put it on the agenda. Or you can give a choice: "Would it help you to put this on our class meeting agenda, or to use the Wheel of Choice to solve this problem?"

3. Take dictation for younger students at specified times, such as just before recess.

4. Start every meeting with compliments.

5. Brainstorm for solutions to agenda items and write them all down.

6. Ask involved students to choose a solution that works for them.

7. Follow up during class meeting in a week to see how the solution worked.

WHAT THE RESEARCH SAYS

Class meetings are one of the best ways to provide experiences for students to feel belonging at school. Research shows that when students feel a sense of belonging at school, academic performance improves, as does social and emotional success.[52] Leachman and Victor report that class meetings help students develop a sense of responsibility, empathy, and self-motivation.[53] Edwards and Mullis explain the success and benefits of class meetings. Specifically, class meetings can enhance relationships, increase students' feelings of belonging, increase effective communication, and improve problem-solving skills as well as help facilitate a positive, caring, cooperative school climate for learning.[54] Urban schoolteachers in a qualitative examination of the efficacy of class meetings shared the comments below about how class meetings took care of problems proactively while validating students' concerns, thereby leading to fewer disruptions and conflicts.[55]

> "Students are meeting discipline expectations and learning to value who they are."
>
> "We've had a more positive, cohesive group and better school attendance."
>
> "Class meetings bring up simmering problems before they boil."
>
> "There has been a tolerance for others and social bonding."
>
> "I think less time is spent dealing with other situations in class. Usually kids will wait until the class meeting to discuss problems."

CLASS GUIDELINES

Permissiveness ignores the need for order.

—*Rudolf Dreikurs*

Involving students when creating rules and regulations for the class-room helps build a sense of community, connection, and ownership. This is instrumental in helping students feel capable and motivated to contribute, because they have been involved in the process.

In many cases, teachers may decide *what* and allow students to decide *when* and *how*. For example, let your students know that play-ground equipment needs to be treated respect-fully, and then allow brainstorming about the *how* and *when*.

"You can't just get up and leave without permission."

The whole class can be involved in creat-ing several routine charts: morning, recess, academic, end of the day, and so on. A morn-ing routine may include greeters at the door, a morning poem, and getting ready for the first academic subject. Some schools start the day with the routine of class meetings, starting with compliments to set a positive tone for the day.

In the following "Tool in Action," a teacher

shares how her learners developed general guidelines to create the classroom atmosphere they wanted, in order to ensure connection and optimal learning.

Drumroll, please . . .

It's been twelve days in the making, and I'm happy to announce that we've established our guidelines and expectations for our classroom. They are:

- Be safe
- Be kind
- Take care of our school and supplies
- Help each other learn
- Have fun

We started by sharing ways we could make this year a great one. After collecting forty or so ideas, we put the ideas into the categories listed above. In groups we brainstormed what we would say and do in order to be safe, be kind, take care of our school and supplies, help each other learn, and have fun. We then discussed and revised these as a group and created several drafts. We fancied them up and gave it our stamp of approval by signing our names.

The guidelines will be kept alive throughout the year and will give us a frame to pause and reflect and increase our awareness of the world around us. They will be reviewed and practiced over and over again.

We have been establishing our routines and having fun—well, at least I have!

—Ms. Leckie's Learners, Queen Anne Elementary

During my after-lunch classes, I noticed that many students ask to go to the bathroom. Believe it or not, it is an interruption to have students raise their hand not to participate but instead to ask to go to the restroom. I also noticed that sometimes it can be humiliating for students because they know that they are clearly interrupting the flow of the class when they are not responding with an answer to a question or an on-topic thought.

So I have changed my bathroom policy from "Ask" to "You're a young adult—make a good decision about when it is best to leave, pick up the bathroom pass, and wave it at me so that I know that you are leaving. Be responsible by going to the restroom and coming right back to class."

So far this year I have had no misuse of the bathroom pass and my lesson stays on topic! Students tell me that they love our bathroom policy, and they wish their other teachers would treat them the same way.

—Diana Loiewski, teacher, Certified Positive Discipline Educator

TOOL TIPS

1. Invite the students to help make a list of class guidelines. Examples:
   - Be kind
   - Be respectful
   - Take turns
   - Focus on solutions
   - Avoid interrupting

2. Divide into small groups and give each group one of these guidelines to role-play what it looks like when students do and don't follow the guideline.

3. When students aren't following a guideline, point to the list and ask, "Can you see which guideline needs to be followed now?"

4. Periodically discuss a guideline during class meetings for review and training.

5. Rotate students to take turns leading, such as taking care of the classroom jobs routine.

WHAT THE RESEARCH SAYS

Research shows that effective teachers have good organizational skills and work with students in advance to establish structure and routine. Studies indicate that behavior problems occur when students do not understand the classroom routines and procedures. Stronge reports in his review of qualities of effective teachers and best practices in education that teachers who involve students in the process of establishing and maintaining guidelines and routines are more effective in managing the classroom and providing quality instruction.[56]

COMPLIMENTS

We can build only on strength, not on weakness.
—*Rudolf Dreikurs*

Giving and receiving compliments is another art that needs to be taught and practiced—especially since compliments are not the same as praise. A compliment is something you appreciate about other people—not because they have lived up to your expectations but because of a contribution they have made to the well-being of others or the environment, or because of something they have accomplished to enhance their own well-being.

Sometimes you'll have students whose behavior is so challenging that it is easy to forget that their behavior is just the tip of the iceberg and exists because of discouragement. For these students it may not be easy to find a way to give a compliment. It is helpful to dig a little deeper to discover something that could be encouraging to a misbehaving student. Use some of the other tools, such as the Become a Mistaken Goal Detective tool (page 10) or

"Frequent and effective communication is the foundation of good classroom management. That is why I send a daily compliment to all of my students. The postage is expensive but the encouragement pays off tenfold.

any of the Understand the Mistaken Goal tools (pages 23–47) to discover the discouragement behind the behavior—and thus the need for encouragement. We love the truth of this inspirational quote (author unknown) that has been posted on Pinterest and other social media sites: "Thinking of your child as *behaving badly* disposes you to think of punishment. Thinking of your child as *struggling to handle something difficult* encourages you to help them through their distress."[57]

Compliments are an important part of class meetings because they set a positive tone for the rest of the meeting. They can also set the tone for the classroom atmosphere. Learning to give and receive compliments is a valuable life skill to help students look for the good and to verbalize their appreciation throughout the day.

The following activity, called Charlie, was created by Suzanne Smitha, a school psychologist, to help students experience how deeply hurtful it is to say mean things to another student and how encouraging it can be to find complimentary things to say.[58]

1. Hold up a chart-paper drawing of Charlie. (A simple outline or stick figure will suffice.) Introduce him as Charlie, who goes to another school and isn't very well liked.

2. Ask your students to think of comments they might hear that could hurt Charlie's feelings (such as "We don't like you," "You look funny," or "You can't play with us"). As they volunteer examples, crumple first one corner and then the next, all the way up the paper, each time a hurtful comment is made, until Charlie disappears in a wrinkled ball of paper.

3. Then suggest that Charlie is feeling pretty bad about all those comments, and your students are probably feeling bad too after seeing how much these words hurt Charlie. Ask the students to think of things they could say to Charlie to help him feel better. What does he need to hear to help him know he is an important part of the school? Are apologies in order? With each example of a positive comment the students suggest, smooth out a little piece of the chart paper until Charlie is whole again.

4. Ask how Charlie is different now. (He is, of course, still quite wrinkled.) Lead students toward the point they might learn from this activity: that no matter how hard we try to retract what we have said or how sincere our apologies, comments intended to hurt leave a little hurt within a person. It is, therefore, very important that we think before we speak and make every effort to be sure our comments to others are respectful at all times.

This very powerful activity has a lasting impact on students, as you will see in the following "Tools in Action."

TOOL IN ACTION FROM MORRISTOWN, NEW JERSEY

During the Charlie activity, students often squirm a bit or act as if it's silly (it's their job at this age, after all), but the activity always sticks with them. They love teaching it to younger students, and it really helps them at a time when verbal criticism is very frequent among their peers.

After presenting the Charlie activity a few years ago to a middle-school class, I was out in the hall later in the day while the students were at their lockers changing classes. I don't know what was said by one student to another, but the response was, "Ouch, that was a Charlie."

It's hard for them, with their peers, to say, "Hey, those words hurt me," but this student was comfortable enough to say the same thing using Charlie.

—Teresa LaSala, Certified Positive Discipline Lead Trainer

TOOL IN ACTION FROM HAMPTON, VIRGINIA

Last Friday I had the privilege of conducting the Charlie activity with a group of second graders. With my first crumple, they gasped. Then they became too enthralled by the freedom to say whatever came to mind and began laughing at the unkind things offered by one student after another. However, when the time came to make kind comments to comfort Charlie, they quickly redeemed themselves, and he was "unfolded."

One little girl, Sophie, who often says unkind things to her classmates, said, "He's still wrinkled." Her observation was a great segue, and the children closest to Charlie began trying to flatten out his wrinkled hands, legs, and feet. When I asked if anyone had ever felt like Charlie, most nodded, of course. And when asked if anyone had ever said unkind things like we'd just heard, most also nodded, and Sophie admitted, "Sometimes I say mean things because I want to hurt others because I'm hurting." I addressed this as best I could without getting too personal.

Then one little girl asked if she could hug Charlie. "Of course!" I said. And he was passed around to several to hug.

Little Kimberly noticed the result: "Now he's wrinkled because we hugged him."

—Brenda Garret, Certified Positive Discipline Trainer

TOOL IN ACTION FROM SHENZHEN, CHINA

Alvin, an eight-year-old, was viewed as a "headache student" in Ms. Happy Guan's class, where I was assisting. He was sitting next to me in the circle and could not stop moving and was constantly making funny faces and noises. However, when I asked him to talk, either he had nothing to say or his voice was too soft to be heard.

When we were practicing compliments, one student said to him, "Alvin, I thank you for making me happy by making silly faces." But this comment was made in a sarcastic tone. When it was Alvin's turn to talk, he said he had nobody to thank. I asked if he would like to thank Susan for lending him her pencil. He took a while to say the words, and when he did, he spoke very quickly with a robot-like voice.

I knew he was not used to this kind of interaction, which he felt was uncomfortable, and his feelings were hurt. I patted him on the shoulder and thanked him for his courage to practice saying "thank you."

During the first round of the Charlie activity, when everyone was hurting Charlie, Alvin said quite a few harsh words. However, he started lowering his head, then his back. At the end, he buried his head deeply into his knees. My heart was aching for him. I knew how much disrespect this boy had received from his school and his family.

Then when we were doing the second round, while everyone was encouraging Charlie, Alvin started sitting up slowly. There is no other image better than a "blooming flower" to describe him at that moment.

When it was the third round, "What would you say to your classmates if you were Charlie?" Alvin's eyes became bigger and brighter; his back was straight. He got the talking stick and said loudly: "If I were Charlie, I would say: 'Although I have shortcomings, I am a good person, so don't look down on me!' "

I saw the tears in Ms. Happy's eyes, and I felt the same—touched and proud of Alvin.

—Elly Zhen, Certified Positive Discipline Trainer

TOOL IN ACTION FROM PARIS, FRANCE

I welcomed my first-grade class, including John, whose personal history was filled with regular monitoring by a psychiatrist. This child came every day to school and behaved the same in class—head down, stomping, screaming, obviously unhappy. Along with his alarming lack of psychosocial skills, he showed a significant delay in academic learning. I even wondered if this child had ever been to school before first grade.

This behavior went on for several weeks until one extraordinary day when, during "practice compliments" circle time, a classmate thanked him for holding his hand during lineup. It was like a revelation to this heavily bruised child: he smiled out of such satisfaction that I was able to read the emotion, the intensity, and its immediate meaning: *I belong now, I am important; someone knows my name, and that makes me important.* John rebelled less and less after this, and embraced learning.

And yesterday, during the round of appreciations in the class meeting, the students thanked the classmates with whom they had played

141

during the previous break. The first one to speak often influences the kind of appreciations that follow. John, looking at his special needs assistant, said: "Nadia, thank you for helping me do my job. I am stronger now."

This shows that the time dedicated to John by the special needs assistant, the encouragement she gave John to show him how able he was, and the successive and progressive steps made to manage the work were all felt by the student, who expressed his gratitude using the round of appreciations during the class meeting. After receiving appreciations from his peers, he was able to give some words of appreciation in a very meaningful way.

—Florence Samarine, teacher at a public school

TOOL TIPS

1. Students will get over the embarrassment of giving and receiving compliments once they practice the skill.

2. Teach students to focus on what others accomplish and how they help others instead of things such as what they wear. Examples:
   - "I would like to compliment you for helping me with my math yesterday."
   - "I would like to compliment you for playing in the sandbox with me at recess."
   - "I would like to compliment you for working so hard on your project."

3. It is helpful to model compliments by giving several every day. Keep notes to make sure every student receives a compliment from you each week or so.

WHAT THE RESEARCH SAYS

Do you know you can improve student behavior by 80 percent just by pointing out what students do correctly?[59] Studies consistently show that teacher and peer compliments influence school connection and impact school culture. Both connection/belonging at school and the culture of a school are major variables identified as influencing overall student success—social, emotional, and academic.

Within the Positive Discipline context, class meetings provide a structure for students to give and receive compliments on a regular basis. Furthermore, teaching the essential skills of class meetings provides students an opportunity to learn how to give and receive genuine compliments. Often students will start out by complimenting a classmate's hairstyle or clothes, but through Positive Discipline activities students learn to give compliments that are more process-oriented and meaningful. Students learn to encourage each other, show appreciation for how someone helped them, or show appreciation for something like a fun game of soccer at recess.

These benefits are evident in the research. For example, Potter set out to determine if classroom meetings increased a student's ability to interact positively at school as well as at home.[60] This study found that students' ability to give and receive compliments improved, and overall the number of compliments increased as a result of regular class meetings using the Positive Discipline class meeting model. Students were generally more supportive of one another as well. In this study, class meetings were introduced in a fifth- grade classroom across a period of eight weeks. Teacher and student journals, as well as parent surveys, indicated an increase in students' positive interaction skills. Findings indicated that students increased their skills in three specific areas: listening, ability to compliment and appreciate others, and ability to show respect for others.

PARENT-TEACHER-STUDENT CONFERENCES

The educator must believe in the potential power of his pupil,
and he must employ all his art in seeking to bring his pupil to
experience this power.

—*Alfred Adler*

There was a time when inviting students to a parent-teacher conference was not even considered. And some parent-teacher conferences were discouraging, with parents of struggling students feeling blamed by teachers, and the teachers of such students feeling blamed by parents. The struggling student could only imagine what was being said about him or her, and none of it felt encouraging.

Having everyone talk together provides varied perspectives and opportunities for solution-focused conversations about both strengths and challenges. When everyone is working together to solve problems, the result is a supportive and encouraging experience for the student, parent, and teacher.

Conferences are more respectful when the student is included. After all, the student is well aware of his or her challenges and strengths and can add a lot to the process of finding solutions to minimize challenges and encourage strengths. Also, parent-teacher-student conferences provide an opportunity

PARENT-TEACHER CONFERENCES

"The bad news is your son failed every test this term. The good news is that mistakes are opportunities to learn."

to create a connection between home and school through collaboration and partnership. You can gain insight into the student's home environment, family values and expectations, and rules and routines. Parents have an opportunity to learn from your perspectives and professional insights. When the student is present, he or she has a unique chance to feel the support of both parents and teacher at the same time. When these important adults in the student's life all show their interest and concern, the effect is encouraging and motivating for the student and reassuring for the adults.

The book *Soar with Your Strengths* begins with a delightful parable about a duck, fish, eagle, owl, squirrel, and rabbit who attend a school with a curriculum that includes running, swimming, tree climbing, jumping, and flying.[61] Of course, each of the animals was born with strength in at least one of these areas, but each was doomed to failure in other areas. It hits close to home to read about the punishment and discouragement these animals encounter when parents and school personnel insist they must do well in every area if they are to graduate and become well-rounded animals. A major point of this book is that "excellence can be achieved only by *focusing* on strengths and *managing* weaknesses, not through the elimination of weaknesses."

Parent-teacher-student conferences can be an important part of the process to encourage students to manage their areas of weakness and soar with their strengths. When their teachers insist they try to earn all A's, students learn mediocrity. Sometimes teachers even penalize students by taking away the time they spend on their best subjects (where they feel encouraged) until they do better in their weak areas (where they feel discouraged). Instead, teachers could coach students to spend enough time on their weak areas to maintain progress and most of their time building on their strengths.

It is important to put yourself in the parents' and student's shoes as you prepare to talk about the student's strengths, struggles, or areas where growth is needed. Parents and students are more open to feedback when a relationship of trust and safety has already been established, as established by the Caring tools on page 55. Some teachers start the year off with a postcard greeting by mail. Open house is another opportunity to foster home and school communication. Warm, caring communication lays a foundation for respect and trust. Frequent communication using emails or newsletters continues this process of communicating plans and expectations to parents. Effective communication keeps parents informed and connected throughout the school year and creates a foundation for effective parent-teacher-student conferences.

TOOL IN ACTION FROM SAN JOSE, CALIFORNIA

Parent-teacher-student conferences are the norm at our school. As a parent, this process has been a huge benefit for me and for my two daughters throughout their elementary and middle school years.

Our twice-per-year conference sessions are student-led. Prior to the conferences, students reflect on their own learning and prepare work samples from each subject that they want to share with their families.

During the conference, the students lead, sharing what they know, how they feel about their learning, their successes, and their mistakes. They set learning goals for the rest of the year. They can also share what they need from the adults around them for support.

Both of my daughters really take ownership of their own learning and have a much greater understanding of what they know and what steps they can take to learn what they don't know. As a parent, I can see their independence, pride, and motivation through their sharing, which helps to relieve any of my parental anxiety about their education.

—Cathy Kawakami, Indigo Program School, Certified Positive Discipline Trainer

TOOL IN ACTION FROM ATLANTA, GEORGIA

Parent-teacher conference day had arrived. Moms and dads streamed in and out of my classroom as they learned about their children's progress, while also teaching me what I needed to know about each child's social, emotional, and educational development.

Sam's parents arrived with hope and some trepidation in their eyes. You see, the students I teach struggle in school, and Sam has really struggled—school has not been easy on any front. What comes so easily to others is enviable to the child with learning differences and challenges. A significant part of my job is to teach these students what they need to succeed through connection, respect, and encouragement. If I am able to accomplish that goal, I know that their hard work and perseverance will pay off in ways they cannot even imagine.

So as Sam's mom and dad sat before me, I knew I had to speak with both honesty and compassion. When Sam entered my classroom he did not come with confidence, academic prowess, or a sense of belonging. For the child who learns differently from others, teachers must build a learning environment where connection and hard work are valued and encouraged. Such an environment is vital for any academic progress.

Slowly, over the course of the school year, through class meetings, encouragement, and active problem-solving, Sam was beginning to blossom. I could see that he was going to be just fine—with a lot of hard work, appropriate instruction, and diligence, of course!

During the conference, Sam's parents almost visibly placed their hopes and dreams for Sam, their only child, on the small table between us. While I did my professional best to explain the nuances of Sam's learning, his progress, and his learning needs, I could see anticipation on their faces. It became apparent to me that I needed to connect with their hopes and dreams as well.

Because I had received the gift of not only teaching Sam to read but also connecting with him emotionally, while fostering a positive social environment in our classroom, I could genuinely see and appreciate the amazing person he is. I shared with his parents my honest belief in Sam's future as it related to all aspects of his growth and development. The tears of relief began to flow from both Sam's mom and dad. As I reached for the box of tissues, I knew that everything was going to be just fine.

The tenets of Positive Discipline not only reach and transform the child but also touch the teacher and all those who love the child.

—First- and second-grade reading teacher

TOOL TIPS

1. Has everyone (parents, teacher, and student) come prepared with answers to these questions?
   - What is going well?
   - What is needed to encourage and support what is going well?
   - In what areas would improvement be beneficial?
   - What is needed to support improvements?

2. During the conference, ask all participants to share what they have written. Let the student share first.

WHAT THE RESEARCH SAYS

The Harvard Family Research Project recommends having a two-way conversation in which teachers learn from parents as much as possible.[62] This approach builds respect and trust with the child's family and places the emphasis on building a relationship and learning from each other to support the student. When elementary students are included in parent-teacher conferences, their inclusion generates positive feelings and has been found to benefit learning. Furthermore, parents gain important insights regarding their child's relationship with the teacher. Research identifies a positive relationship between family involvement and student success. This relationship was found regardless of race/ethnicity, class, or parents' level of education.[63]

For example, Marcon examined 708 preschoolers and their parents' involvement over a three-year period. Participants in this study included mostly low-income African American preschoolers and their parents in full-day public kindergarten or Head Start programs. Parent involvement, which Marcon asked teachers to rate based on parent-teacher conferences as well as home visits and time spent volunteering at school, was compared with levels of student achievement. The study found that when parents were highly involved, their children, especially boys, performed better.[64]

CLASSROOM JOBS

Never do for a child what a child can do for himself.
—*Rudolf Dreikurs*

In the name of expediency, many teachers do things that students could do for themselves or for one another. One example is bulletin boards. Of course, bulletin boards done by teachers may look better than bulletin boards created by students, but this is a missed opportunity for students to feel capable, as well as experience the pride of ownership. We can guarantee that your students will be much more interested in the bulletin boards created by their classmates.

Classroom jobs give students an opportunity to contribute on a regular basis in a meaningful way. They promote responsibility and respect for others in the classroom, and students feel a sense of belonging and capability when they make needed contributions.

Involve the whole class in brainstorming a list of jobs that need to be done in the classroom and let the students decide how to rotate jobs so that no one is stuck with the worst or keeps getting the best. When teachers invite

"If you have a student who refuses to stay seated, put that behavior to work delivering messages for you, collecting completed work, handing out and collecting books, and taking around the wastebasket."

students to work together to make a class jobs list, students share ownership. This process alone has an immediate positive effect on students' sense of belonging and contribution.

This school year started with a bit of challenge. Some students always wanted to be first in line to hold the door for the rest of the class. When this challenge was brought up during our classroom meeting, the students enthusiastically began to think about solutions to such a challenge.

Everyone agreed to create a list of students who would like to be a "door holder," as they named this responsibility, and to rotate this job every day among the students who wanted it. The kids have placed the list next to the door, and every day they can check to see whose turn it is.

An amazing part of this problem-solving endeavor was that the kids themselves were the ones who followed through, without any guidance from a teacher. When someone shouts out that he or she would like to be the door holder, the answer is always "We will go with our agreement. It is not your turn. Check the list, please."

—Nataliya Fillers, Oak Farm Montessori School, Certified Positive Discipline Educator

It is very important to me to have all my students feel they are important to the group and to me. The Positive Discipline Classroom Jobs tool accomplished this goal far more effectively than I expected.

It is important to note that this tool was applied in a class of thirty-five third graders. Despite this rather large number, the goal was achieved with each individual assuming a specific responsibility in the classroom. This job assignment made each child feel part of an assembly where everyone could propose solutions to problems while being respectful of their peers, where all could feel heard, considered, and free to speak their minds.

As for me, I gave up having control over them in exchange for their

POSITIVE DISCIPLINE TOOLS FOR TEACHERS

participation and cooperation. Now the link I establish with my students is closer and more respectful. I observe them with affection and marvel every day at the success they are achieving. They know they can count on me for encouragement, but they also know they are capable of accomplishing many things on their own.

For example, when I am leading an activity, the timekeeper lets me know that I should get ready to finish by showing the sign indicating I have five minutes left. Another student in charge of compliments invited us to reflect, saying to the group, "Close your eyes for an instant and let us remember who has done something special for us, or who has tried to improve. Think it over so you can compliment them." I was amazed as they followed up on their reflection, naming each other and paying compliments: "Thanks for cheering me when I was sad," "Thank you for explaining the homework to me," "Thank you for inviting me to play," and "I recognize that you are making a big effort to wait for your turn to speak and not interrupt."

The feeling of belonging created by their individual job responsibilities coupled with the repeated experience of being heard and recognized resulted in increasingly fewer children with inappropriate behaviors since they no longer needed to misbehave in order to be noticed or to feel important.

This does not mean that we never had any more problems; the difference was that we learned to work out those problems together with mutual aid and cooperation. It takes patience, perseverance, and confidence in the process. Unlike employing punishments and rewards in order to change students' attitudes, which may yield instant but not lasting results, Positive Discipline yields results that are long-term.

—Sandra Colmenares, third-grade teacher, Certified Positive Discipline Classroom Educator

TOOL IN ACTION FROM CAIRO, EGYPT

I was faced with a very rebellious attitude from a student in my twelfth-grade class. He always questioned my authority in the classroom. It was a constant toss-up whether he would or would not do what he was asked, depending on his mood.

In confronting my confusion in managing this class of teenagers, I decided to ask my colleagues to help me search for solutions. Among the many different strategies the group brainstormed, I chose to empower this student by asking him to be responsible for taking attendance at the beginning of each class.

I was surprised by how much this request pleased him. He became even stricter than I was about noting classmates who arrived after the bell rang. He was never late himself, and he began his work promptly and without complaint. Our power struggle ended because I provided a way for him to feel a sense of belonging by asking for his help. The coded message for the mistaken goal of Misguided Power, "Let me help," really worked.

—Marjorie Vautrin, twelfth-grade teacher, Oasis International School

TOOL TIPS

1. Create a whole room full of assistants to make your job easier while helping your students feel needed and capable.

2. Brainstorm enough jobs for everyone. Examples: water plants, empty pencil sharpener, pass out papers, straighten bookshelves, monitor playground equipment, monitor cleanup time, be the meteorologist, manage recycling, manage attendance and office messages, be the morning greeter, et cetera.

3. Add the job of job monitor to oversee the completion of the jobs.

4. Post the job list in your classroom.

5. Rotate jobs so everyone becomes proficient in all jobs.

WHAT THE RESEARCH SAYS

A report by Durlak and colleagues in *Child Development* identifies the importance of students contributing in the classroom as well as the whole school community. Furthermore, a fundamental component of evidence-based programs (programs based on the best available and valid evidence identified in the field) is integrated learning of social and emotional skills. Providing students with daily opportunities to contribute through classroom jobs, peer tutoring, or as a Positive Time-Out buddy (see page 185) are just some of the examples of how Positive Discipline meets this evidence-based standard. This report cites specific benefits of contributing in the classroom, including students' feelings of satisfaction and belonging. Furthermore, contributing in the classroom has been shown to increase motivation and involvement. This research published in *Child Development* provides strong support for what Adler and Dreikurs recognized long ago about children's need for belonging and feeling significant, and the importance of their contributing in meaningful ways. Positive Discipline tools are designed to help teachers practically apply what the research identifies as important for long-term success.

CONTRIBUTIONS

We can teach responsibility only by giving the pupils opportunities to accept responsibilities themselves.
—*Rudolf Dreikurs*

We have heard many teachers complain about how difficult their job is because parents send their children to school with a sense of entitlement. This complaint may be true, but teachers can't change parents. They can, however, make sure their students learn the art of contributing, a skill that will serve them throughout their lives.

Adler believed that the primary need of all people is a sense of belonging and that *Gemeinschaftsgefühl* is a measure of mental health. As we mentioned in an earlier tool, *Gemeinschaftsgefühl* essentially means "social consciousness and a desire and willingness to contribute." Thus, belonging and contribution are equally important. Many parents have done a good job of helping their children feel a sense of belonging. However, the scales are out of balance when children are not also taught the importance of contribution. When contribution is missing, children develop a sense of entitlement.

"My class job this week is library helper. My teacher said I'd work with Dewey Decimal?"

Research shows that children seem to be born with a desire to contribute. Warneken and Tomasella found that children have a natural instinct to help others starting at a very early age. In one study, eighteen-month-olds and their mothers were brought into a room where they watched the experimenter drop clothespins. The toddler would watch for a few seconds before picking up the clothespin and handing it to the experimenter.[65] In another scenario the experimenter tries to put books in a cabinet with the doors closed. The toddler watches him bump into the cabinet several times before he walks over to the cabinet and opens it for the experimenter. If you want your heart to melt, go to this YouTube link and watch for yourself: https://www.youtube/kfGAen6QiUE.

Too often, even when children want to contribute, they are discouraged from doing so. A two-year-old may plead or demand, "Me do it, me do it." Instead of taking time to honor this desire to help, adults sometimes discourage the child's efforts by taking over. Perhaps the adult is in a hurry or doesn't think the child can do it "well enough." Parents don't realize that with such discouragements they are denying their children an important opportunity to fulfill their innate desire to contribute. It is important that this pattern not be repeated in the classroom.

As children grow older and become accustomed to having things done for them, they are at risk of losing their natural desire to contribute. They get used to having things done for them. Some seem to see it as a burden, or even an insult, if they are asked to do anything for anyone else, often at the same time they are making constant demands on others. In school they seem to want and expect the same special treatment they receive at home.

The more one wants to contribute (in his or her family, classroom, and community, and to the planet), the greater his or her overall mental health. Contributing promotes a sense of belonging and capability. We shouldn't rob children of these gifts by doing too much for them.

Classroom meetings provide the most comprehensive way to teach contribution, though there are many other ways. Anytime you involve students in problem-solving and focusing on solutions, they learn a little more about how to contribute in a meaningful way.

In a high school class of fifteen-year-old students I was doing Positive Discipline sessions. I was going to talk about the brain in the palm of the hand (page 173) and Positive Time-Out (page 185); however, the students' chatting was very annoying, and we could not concentrate or hear each other. At one point I decided to ask for the students' help and said, "I need your help. Tell me what we need to do to have a productive atmosphere and be respectful of what others say." They looked at me, surprised, and replied, "Three hours of detention."

They are in a very strict school where teachers give detention very often. I told them I was not willing to give them detention. Instead, I needed us to brainstorm and find another way.

They started thinking and making suggestions. The person responsible for deciding who would talk would pass the talking stick. I asked them more questions to help them think. At one point a big, heavy silence filled the room. I had, I think, asked too many questions and not given them enough space. I asked, "What is happening now?" and a girl said, "It's oppression." I laughed and asked, "Would there be something in between oppression and incessant chatter?"

Someone said, "What if we raise our hands when we need to talk?" Another said, "But that is what all teachers tell us to do." The girl who had used the word "oppression" said, "Guys, when we decide we want to raise our hand, we are free. When the teachers tell us to do so, then it is oppression. What do we want to choose?"

Now we had this deep, sustained silence once again. Then they all decided they could raise their hands and still be free! It took only ten minutes for them to reach this conclusion because they were invited to contribute their ideas, and in the time left the students were respectful and the class atmosphere was incredibly positive. And they learned a lot. They taught themselves what freedom was about!

—Nadine Gaudin, Certified Positive Discipline Trainer

As a parent and Positive Discipline trainer, I feel so fortunate that my children attend a school that practices Positive Discipline. The principal asked me to spend an hour in conversation with our new assistant principal to share the basic principles of Positive Discipline. When I made the appointment during summer hours, the only availability was while I had the children (Julian, eight, and Eva, seven) on a summer day, and so I suggested that they come with me.

My children know that I am a parent trainer, and they have assisted me in the preparation of my parenting class materials; they have often participated in some of the activities as I prepared laminated cards or other props for activities. So their presence at the meeting was much more than sitting at a smaller table while the adults talked. We invited them to share how different Positive Discipline tools are used in their classrooms, and the assistant principal and I were treated to a view of Positive Discipline from the child's perspective.

My son (entering grade three) explained how his teacher used the class meetings to solve problems. My daughter demonstrated the Charlie activity and showed the assistant principal a Wheel of Choice that she had drawn for our house. My kids also read the Asking vs. Telling activity. That was so fun to watch. In answer to the question "What can we do better as a school?" my son said that the substitute teachers can be taught some of the techniques, and my daughter wanted a cool-off space on the playground.

Witnessing the conversation between my children and the assistant principal, I was so excited for both of them in the coming year. The assistant principal emailed me later saying that she would never forget "crumpled Charlie"—I knew that she could see the depth of the work and witnessed the intention of her new team of teachers.

For my children, I was so excited that the Positive Discipline work really lived in their school days, and that they were so comfortable sharing with an adult completely new to them. As a Positive Discipline trainer, I was so inspired by the possibility of bringing children's voices into education for adults.

—Kristin Hovious, Certified Positive Discipline Trainer

TOOL TIPS

1. Think of all the things you do that could be done by your students (such as creating bulletin boards, morning greetings, and even teaching some lessons). Assign these tasks to your students.

2. Verbally appreciate how much they contribute to the positive classroom atmosphere.

3. Involve students whenever possible. For example, "Students, we are having a problem with disruptions right now. I need your help solving this challenge."

4. See the Classroom Jobs and Class Meetings topics (pages 150 and 124) for other ideas on providing opportunities for contributing in the classroom.

WHAT THE RESEARCH SAYS

Adlerian-based research shows a direct relationship between social interest (one's desire and willingness to contribute) and overall mental health. Social interest and belonging relate to adults' as well as children's perceived stress, coping resources, and resilience.[66]

Furthermore, the education director of the Center for Greater Good at the University of California, Berkeley, writes:

Schools don't need to reward kind behavior; the reward occurs naturally through the warm feeling that comes from helping another person. People who witness others doing unexpected kind acts often get a similar warm and uplifting feeling—what psychologist and researcher Jonathan Haidt . . . calls elevation. Haidt's research shows that across cultures, human beings are moved and inspired when they see others acting with courage or compassion, and this elevation makes them more likely to want to help others and become better people.[67]

This article identifies how rewarding students for acts of kindness is too common in our schools today and points out that programs that promote rewards go against what research shows about developing altruistic tendencies.

AVOID REWARDS

Reward and punishment do not produce inner stimulation, or
if they do, it is short-lived and requires continuous repetition.

—*Rudolf Dreikurs*

Students love rewards, and teachers see them as a quick and effective way to motivate students—especially since they work! But stop and think. What are students learning when they receive rewards for good behavior or good grades? Are they learning to get good grades and to behave respectfully for the inner rewards? Or are they learning that the external reward is the important goal, not the achievement or the contribution? Are they learning to think about how they can get bigger and better rewards? Are they deciding to stop a good behavior or stop getting good grades when they no longer want the reward?

Students love a lot of things that aren't good for them, like sugar. Small amounts of these things aren't harmful, but too much creates dependence (addiction). The third of the five Criteria for Positive Discipline discussed in the Introduction states that Positive Discipline "is effective in the long term." Sometimes we

"I tried everything to get my class to pay attention. I tried bribes, sarcasm, guilt, shame, and threats. Nothing works! Are you paying attention to what I'm saying?"

need to "beware of what works" when the long-term results are not good for students.

In the section "Contributions" (page 155), you learn the importance of helping students develop a sense of belonging and contribution. Experiencing a sense of belonging and feeling good about an achievement or about making a contribution are inner rewards that can be diminished by external rewards.

We all enjoy appreciation from others, but when does external appreciation become more important than inner satisfaction? Awareness can help us find balance, allowing us to enjoy external appreciation without it outweighing the joy of inner satisfaction.

TOOL IN ACTION FROM LIMA, PERU

It was difficult for me to believe that it was possible to apply discipline without rewards or punishments, since this is what I had used to previously nudge my students into good behavior. I had let them know what the consequences would be for those who did not meet the established agreements. That system rendered immediate results and gave me peace of mind.

But despite my doubts about the effectiveness of this new Positive Discipline methodology, I dared to test it. At the end of my experiment, I understood that I did not have to exert control over my students, but rather I could create a climate in which the children focus on solutions, propose improvement goals, and commit to effect the changes.

For instance, one of the problems in my classroom was that children took a long time to be ready when doing project work. This always happened after lunchtime, when they were supposed to clear all their eating implements and move their desks to form groups. This would take too long, and consequently they had insufficient time to complete the task at hand.

We touched on this subject in a class meeting, and they wrote their ideas for improvement as follows: "We want to reduce the time used to get ready at the time of project work, so let us first take care of our things and move the desks before lunch. We must set up the stopwatch online for ten minutes, to gauge our time."

To my surprise, the children arrived from recess and rearranged their desks without any indication from me. One of them assumed the responsibility of using the computer stopwatch and projecting the countdown on the screen to make it visible to all. Within ten minutes, most of them were already sitting, ready to begin, and the stopwatch was set up again to monitor the time it took the whole group to be ready. Those who lingered were encouraged by their peers to hurry, and all were glad as they improved and tried constantly to beat their own record.

I have confirmed undoubtedly that Positive Discipline works, and I have been amazed by the progress of my students. They no longer needed an adult to make sure they do the right thing because they want their classroom to have an atmosphere of mutual respect.

—Sandra Colmenares, third-grade teacher, Certified Positive Discipline Educator

TOOL IN ACTION FROM SAN DIEGO, CALIFORNIA

Dexter, my four-year-old son, started a new year of preschool. Dexter's pre-K teachers wanted to motivate their students to follow directions, participate in class, and engage in prosocial behaviors. So they decided to implement a sticker chart in the classroom. When a student received five stickers, he or she could take a prize from the prize box.

The first day of class was difficult for Dexter, but he got a sticker because it was the first day. The second day he did not get a sticker. The next two days he earned his stickers, but for the two days after that he continued to have difficulties.

Every morning on the drive to school I spoke to him about what he needed to do to have a successful day. I followed it up with "I believe you will make good choices today."

On the last day that he didn't receive a sticker, I asked him, "Is it important to you that you receive a sticker from your teachers?" He paused for a few seconds, then looked me in the eyes and said, "Well, it's important to the teachers."

This insight reinforced the idea that external motivators do not work for our children. The sticker chart became so distressing for the other students that some of them who loved school started to tell their parents they didn't want to go to school. Luckily the teachers realized the stress this chart was having on the children and discontinued it.

In the same class there was another four-year-old girl who received all five of her stickers in the first week, but the second week she was having difficulty following directions and was no longer motivated to earn her stickers. When her parents asked her about it she simply stated, "I don't need to earn any more stickers, I already got my prize." Once again, another failed attempt to externally motivate a four-year-old.

—Jeffrey Saylor, parent

TOOL IN ACTION FROM GUAYAQUIL, ECUADOR

Last year I started the year using a reward system. Many other teachers were using ClassDojo (a reward system). Without evaluating it or thinking about it, I thought I would follow suit. However, after becoming a Certified Positive Discipline Educator I learned about the negative effects of a reward system.

After establishing classroom meetings and setting up a classroom based on mutual respect, we discussed the system as a class. It was eye-opening to hear how this reward system made the students feel.

In the end, students wrote a very short note explaining how they felt. The classroom voted as a whole if they wanted to keep the reward system, or abandon it and focus on solving problems and recognizing mistakes as learning opportunities. The majority voted to abandon the reward system, and we haven't looked back. The overall classroom environment has been more respectful and less power driven.

—Jeremy Mathis, fourth-grade teacher, InterAmerican Academy, Certified
Positive Discipline Classroom Educator

1. Rewards teach *external* motivation. Positive Discipline tools teach *internal* motivation.

2. Help students enjoy the inner reward of feeling capable and making a contribution. Examples:
   - Instead of rewards, ask students to put challenges on the class meeting agenda so the whole class can be involved in finding solutions.
   - Ask for help: "I need your help right now. What are your ideas for respectful solutions?"
   - Ask, "What will help you feel good one year from now: an external reward, or accomplishing a goal for yourself and making a contribution that benefited others?"

WHAT THE RESEARCH SAYS

Kohn reports research showing that rewards (stickers, candy, praise) decrease students' internal motivation to repeat tasks that they are being rewarded for doing.[68] While teachers report that rewards quickly get students to work quietly, they fail to understand the long-term effect. Kohn argues there is a risk to rewards, because rewards don't help students develop internal motivation, self-reliance, or responsibility.[69] Fabes, Fultz, Eisenberg, May-Plumlee, and Christopher set out to study the effects of rewards. Their findings revealed how rewards undermined children's prosocial motivation. When children in their study were rewarded for helping, during subsequent trials in which children were given free choice, children's internal prosocial motivation to help diminished.[70]

Educational research as far back as the 1970s has shown the negative effect of rewards on internal motivation and the learning process. Lepper, Greene, and Nisbett found that children interested in drawing who received no reward for their artwork spent significantly more time on an art project compared to children in the group assigned to receive rewards for their work. This research showed especially that when rewards are contracted ahead of time, they seem to have a negative impact on interest and motivation. It should be noted that this occurred even when there was a baseline showing the children had a high interest in drawing.[71] The negative impact of rewards on internal motivation has been observed and recorded in older student samples as well. Deci reported that rewarding college students with money has a negative impact on motivation. Even college students identified by researchers as intrinsically motivated became less motivated when paid as a reward.

Garbarino closely examined interpersonal interactions (language and emotional tone) when rewards were used. In tutoring groups in which fifth- and sixth-grade students tutored younger students, Garbarino found differences in communication in the reward group compared to the no-reward group. In the group receiving the reward the tutors made more negative comments than the tutors in the no-reward group. Also, tutors' emotional tone was more positive in the no-reward group.[72]

Mueller and Dweck's research showed that even verbal rewards or praise undermine students' motivation and performance.[73] Dweck's in-depth research on praise illustrates how verbal rewards impact individuals' mindset.[74] Students who receive feedback based on effort and process develop a growth mindset, whereas students who receive praise develop a fixed mindset. Students with a fixed mindset seek easier tasks and avoid doing work that doesn't come easily. On the other hand, students with a growth mindset seek more difficult tasks and seem validated by the internal feelings that come from putting effort into something and striving forward even when it is difficult.

CHAPTER FIVE

CONFLICT RESOLUTION

AGREEMENTS AND FOLLOW-THROUGH

The success of a teacher depends to a large extent on his ability to unite the class for a common purpose.

—*Rudolf Dreikurs*

Oftentimes teachers will decide what students should or should not do, make an announcement about their decision, and then refer to it as an agreement—even though the students had no involvement in making the agreement. For instance, the cartoon on the right shows a student unwilling to sign a contract that has been created only by the teacher.

In both cartoons, one of the parties makes an executive decision,

"What was our agreement?"

"I can't sign that behavior contract unless my attorney reviews it."

rather than involving the other in the agreement—and invites rebellion. Indeed, an agreement without full involvement is an edict, and edicts are not very well received by students. Involvement increases acceptance and commitment.

There was a time when kids sat in neat rows and obediently did whatever the teacher required. Many teachers may long for those "good old days." But should they? Would these teachers want for themselves the same submission to authority they wish for their students? Or do they want the freedom and respect to ask questions and challenge the status quo? How can students learn accountability and problem-solving when their individuality is stifled by teachers who model submissiveness?

Such a model of education is destructive to self-esteem, personal growth, and the fulfillment of human potential. Instead, let's focus on how far we have come in creating an atmosphere of equality, dignity, and respect for all people. Yes, we still have a long way to go, but we have made progress. Use the following steps for agreements and follow-through as one way to maintain dignity and respect for everyone involved:

1. Have a friendly discussion where students and the teacher can each voice their feelings and thoughts. This discussion can be done in class meetings or one-on-one.

2. Brainstorm together for solutions and find one that everyone agrees to try.

3. Agree on an exact time by which the agreement is to be met. (You'll see the importance of this later.)

4. If the agreement is not kept, ask, "What was our agreement?" When this question is asked in a friendly manner, students usually feel motivated to follow through. If the agreement does not work, go through the steps again, starting with a discussion about why it didn't work.

Meet with students individually when there are specific concerns. Taking time to meet one-on-one shows you care. Use curiosity questions to explore the students' perceptions as you explore a plan for agreement. You can start by asking, "Would you be willing to hear my ideas?" or "Would you like to hear what has worked for other students who have had this problem?"

The Agreements and Follow-Through tool serves as a reminder of how important it is to take time to involve students if you want cooperation, mutual respect, accountability, and responsibility.

TOOL IN ACTION FROM SAN DIEGO, CALIFORNIA

My success story involves two Positive Discipline tools: Agreements and Follow-Through by using Curiosity Questions. At our school, the classes determine for themselves agreements about daily procedures and activities, including how to use the outdoor play equipment. One of the agreements made by the kindergartners and first graders was how to take turns on the swings. It was decided by the students that if the swings are full, the waiting person stands a safe distance from the swinger and counts, each time the swinger's feet come forward, to thirty. Then it's time for the swinger to give up the swing to the waiting student.

One day I was supervising lunch duty and a kindergarten student came up to me and let me know that a swinger was not following the agreement. I walked over to the swings and asked the student if he knew what the agreement was about taking turns on the swings, and he said he did.

I asked, "Did the person waiting count to thirty?"

He said, "Yes."

I asked, "What is supposed to happen after a student counts to thirty?"

He said, "Get off the swing."

The student stopped swinging, hopped off, and found another activity.

Success! Thank you to our wonderful teachers who take the time to create these agreements with the students. This is proof that rules do not need to be determined by adults and that children are more likely to cooperate when they have a voice in the decision-making process.

—Donna Napier, office manager, Innovations School, Certified Positive
Discipline Educator

TOOL TIPS

1. If you say it, mean it, and if you mean it, follow through. (Curiosity questions can be a great way to follow through.)

2. The key is to be kind and firm at the same time.

3. "I know it is hard to experience the consequences of your choices. I respect you too much to rescue you."

4. "We'll keep our agreement until we have time to come up with a new one that works better."

WHAT THE RESEARCH SAYS

In reviewing more than a hundred studies, Marzano identified the quality of the teacher-student relationship as the foundation for effective classroom management.[75] Teachers who were categorized as having high-quality relationships with their students had 31 percent fewer discipline-related problems. One of the most important characteristics identified in developing a positive relationship with students is cooperation. It is recommended, based on this research, that teachers establish agreements about class rules and procedures through group discussions. This team approach helps develop group cohesiveness and encourages cooperation. Furthermore, talking one-on-one with students to discover mutually agreed-upon solutions increases cooperation and develops problem-solving skills.

UNDERSTANDING THE BRAIN

Mind and body are inseparable; they are only parts of the whole individual, who can use all his functions for whatever goal he has set for himself.

—*Rudolf Dreikurs*

Have you ever "lost it" and reacted in a way you later regretted? Maybe you even told yourself, "I knew better. Why didn't I wait until I calmed down so I could control my behavior and act more rationally?"

Maya Angelou has said, "When we know better, we do better." But this is not necessarily true. Sometimes we don't do better even when we know better, and there is a good reason why. When people become upset, they react from the part of the brain responsible for the fight, flight, or freeze reaction. Brain science and research show that when we are in the fight, flight, or freeze state, rational thinking goes out the window. So unless you are a saint or superhuman, no matter how much you beat up on yourself for reacting irrationally, it is likely that you will do it again, as will your students.

It can be helpful for teachers and students to understand what is happening in their brains when they react instead of acting thoughtfully

"I know that some of your students are very disruptive, but don't let your temper explode. Count down before blasting off."

and rationally. They will still react, but understanding how the brain functions can help bring a speedier recovery from the fight, flight, or freeze impulse and support self-regulation and focusing on solutions.

Dr. Daniel Siegel demonstrates how the brain works by using the palm of his hand as a concrete model to show how different parts of the brain function in response to stimuli. He advises that we must "name it to tame it." When you and your students understand what is happening in your brain in response to feeling challenged or stressed, you can also learn self-regulation tools to "tame it." You can watch Dr. Siegel's demonstration on YouTube at https://youtu.be/gm9CIJ74Oxw. Once you watch this video you can teach what you have learned to your students using the following guide:

1. Ask your students to hold up their hands in an open position and to follow along with what you do.
2. Point to the area of your palm down to your wrist, and explain that this area represents the brain stem, which is responsible for the fight, flight, or freeze response to stress or danger.
3. Fold your thumb into your palm. The thumb now represents the midbrain (limbic system), where you have stored early memories that created fear and feelings of not being good enough. The midbrain works in conjunction with the brain stem to evoke the fight, flight, or freeze reaction.
4. Then fold your fingers over your thumb to make a fist. Your folded fingers represent the brain's cortex. The prefrontal cortex (point to the front of your fist where your fingertips touch the palm of your hand) is where rational thinking and emotional control take place.
5. What happens when our buttons get pushed and we "lose it"? We flip our lids (keeping the thumb in place, let the rest of the fingers open up and out).
6. Now our prefrontal cortex is not functioning. In this state we cannot think or behave rationally.

Kids (and adults) love understanding what is happening in their brains when the fight, flight, or freeze impulse takes control. This helps them appreciate why it is important to learn strategies for "taming" the impulse, that the best time to solve a problem or conflict in the classroom is after calming down, and thus the need for Positive Time-Out (see page 185).

Positive Time-Out is very different from punitive time-out. Positive Time-Out helps students calm down and cool off before trying to solve a problem, and they understand why it's so important. It's a great life skill for students to learn: "When I take time to calm down, I can think more clearly and come up with a solution that is helpful to everyone." When students (and teachers) take time to calm down, they can respond with empathy, insight, and good judgment rather than merely reacting in response to stress.

TOOL IN ACTION FROM LONDON, ENGLAND

After teaching my grade ten students (fifteen and sixteen years old) about the brain in the palm of the hand and Positive Time-Out during the second week of school, I actually had a need to use this knowledge in my classroom the following day.

I had a few students who continued to be disruptive and disrespectful in the class after numerous warnings. I could feel myself about to flip out. I calmly told the class I was feeling reactive and needed everyone to take a five-minute break outside the classroom because I needed a time-out. I demonstrated with my hand where I was at and how I was about to flip my lid.

They looked a bit shocked because they weren't expecting me to ask them to leave the room in the middle of class. I took a few minutes, did some deep breathing, got a cup of tea (as we do in England), and calmed myself down.

When the students returned to the classroom five minutes later, I calmly shared what I was feeling and why: the nonverbal communication among students was a distraction to me, and the inappropriate comments felt disrespectful.

Some of the students shared that they felt the same as I did, and we had a great discussion about nonverbal behavior and about taking time to think about behavior and whether it is respectful to the entire group.

The students' behavior improved, and I felt the students respected me for practicing what I taught and modeling the fact that even adults need a time-out when they are about to flip their lids.

Coincidentally, that evening was back-to-school night and I was going to be meeting all of their parents. I decided that I would share an experiential activity with the parents and give them a taste of what their children were learning in the class. So I demonstrated the brain in the palm of the hand and shared how I had used this concept with the class just that day.

As much as the parents were surprised that some of their children may have misbehaved in class, they felt relieved that even teachers may have some of their same struggles with children, and they appreciated that they now had a tool they could use at home with their children when situations escalated. I stressed to them the importance of modeling at home, and I am hopeful they absorbed this point.

These tools are so useful to me even after many years as an experienced teacher. When I have a challenging group of students, it's a good time for me to take out my Positive Discipline tools and start using them once again.

—Joy Marchese, tenth-grade teacher, American School of London, Certified Positive Discipline Trainer

TOOL TIPS

1. It is never effective to try to solve a problem from the fight, flight, or freeze state of your brain.

2. Teach your students about using the palm of the hand as a model for the brain by viewing Dr. Daniel Siegel's demonstration.

3. Wait until after a cooling-off period, when you and your students can access the rational, thinking part of your brains, to solve problems.

4. Teach methods for calming down. Examples: Positive Time-Out (page 185), counting to ten, taking deep breaths, going to the Wheel of Choice or the Anger Wheel of Choice (page 178), and putting the problem on the class meeting agenda (page 124).

WHAT THE RESEARCH SAYS

Dr. Daniel Siegel provides the neuroscientific explanation for why it is so important for teachers to understand the brain, especially as it relates to students' stress response.[76] Studies show a direct relationship between students' perceived stress and academic success. This relationship between stress and performance has been demonstrated even in older students. For example, female college students who were purposely told that male students do better in math subsequently performed less well on the math test given as part of the research study.[77] Siegel suggests that when working with students, it is important to continually assess whether or not we are engaging the upstairs brain (the part responsible for thinking, imagining, and planning) or triggering the downstairs brain (which regulates basic functions such as strong emotions, breathing, and the instinctual fight, flight, or freeze reaction needed when there is danger).

Also, Siegel and Bryson point out the importance of understanding the brain research showing that in some ways the brain is not fully developed until late adolescence. For example, Choudhury, Blakemore, and Charman used neuroimaging to study aspects of brain development during adolescence.[78] In their study, 112 participants ages eight to thirty-six performed computerized tasks that involved taking an emotional perspective, either from the participant's own point of view or from that of another person. The findings showed how executive functioning, empathy, and emotional perspective taking are still developing throughout adolescence. These research findings have important implications for classroom management. Positive Discipline helps teachers apply management tools that research shows match the developmental, social, and emotional needs of their students.

WHEEL OF CHOICE AND ANGER WHEEL OF CHOICE

Kids are our greatest untapped resource. They have a wealth of wisdom and talent for solving problems when we invite them to do so.

—*Rudolf Dreikurs*

Focusing on solutions is another primary theme of Positive Discipline, and students are great at focusing on solutions when they are taught the skills and encouraged to practice them. Teachers don't have to play the simultaneous roles of police, judge, jury, and punisher, and students feel capable and motivated to cooperate when they are respectfully involved in problem-solving.

The Wheel of Choice provides a fun and exciting way to involve students in learning and practicing problem-solving skills. Use the following directions for getting your students involved in creating a Wheel of Choice.

1. Show your students the sample of the Wheel of Choice on the next page created by first- and second-grade students.
2. Draw (or ask a student to draw) a circle on a large sheet of paper (some teachers use paper plates to provide individual wheels) and divide the circle into pie slices.
3. Brainstorm possible solutions to typical problems such as fighting, not taking turns, name-calling, and cutting in line. Once you have all agreed on several solutions that would be respectful and

helpful, write these solutions in the pie spaces. Leave enough room at the outer edge for symbols or pictures.

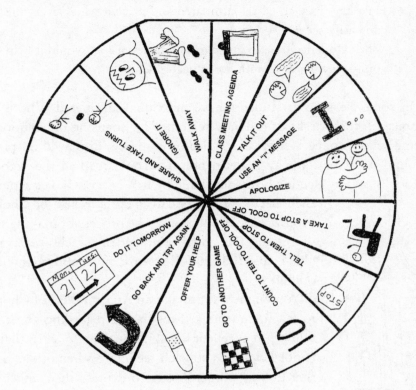

4. Ask your students to draw symbols or pictures to represent each solution. You may want to assign a team of students to work on a symbol for each solution.

5. When the wheel is finished, ask for student volunteers who would like to role-play the person or persons who is/are having a problem (for example, a fight over sports equipment). In the middle of the role-play, ask another student to hand the role-players the completed Wheel of Choice and

"I couldn't think of a science fair project so I just re-invented the wheel."

179

invite them to choose one of the solutions they think will be most helpful.

6. Have the finished wheel laminated and place it where everyone can easily see it.

7. When students are experiencing a conflict, ask, "Would it help you to find a solution on the Wheel of Choice?"

In some classrooms students have individual laminated Wheels of Choice on their desks as a handy reference for focusing on solutions. Some schools have Wheels of Choice prominently displayed on playground walls or hallway bulletin boards. You'll read in the second "Tool in Action" section how some hang their Wheel of Choice around their necks. Students can make a Wheel of Choice for a variety of solutions. The process of making the wheel and the visual reminder of the choices available helps students feel a sense of capability and cooperation.

"I finally discovered how to stop playground fighting. I forbid students from discussing politics during recess."

You might want to add an Anger Wheel of Choice to teach students self-regulation regarding anger. It will be an excellent life skill for them to learn that it is not helpful to squelch feelings and emotions and that it works much better to express their anger in socially acceptable ways. Use the following activity to help your students create their own Anger Wheel of Choice and to practice the skills through role-playing.

1. Involve your students in a discussion about what invites them to feel angry. Write their thoughts down on a flip chart.

2. Ask them to share some disrespectful or hurtful ways people express their anger and write them down on a flip chart.

3. Brainstorm together appropriate ways to express anger. Write them all down.

4. Ask for volunteers to create an illustrated Anger Wheel of Choice that includes their favorite choices.

5. During class meetings, role-play to practice their ideas.
6. Display the Anger Wheel of Choice in a prominent place in the classroom.
7. When a student is angry, you might ask, "Would it help you to use the Anger Wheel of Choice to find a way to express your anger?"

Students can use a Wheel of Choice for a variety of challenges. We have seen students use the Wheel of Choice to brainstorm ways to prepare for exams, to find options for cooling off, or to solve other specific problems. Students feel empowered and capable when they come up with solutions, and using a Wheel of Choice provides a visual reminder that there are many choices.

TOOL IN ACTION FROM BLOOMINGTON, ILLINOIS

The Wheel of Choice was very popular with students in preschool through middle school. Each class worked on their wheels early in the school year by first brainstorming a list of possible problems they might have at school. Next they brainstormed ideas about how to solve each of the problem situations. Often they role-played possible solutions to be sure the solutions were respectful and had the power to solve the problem without hurting anyone.

When all of their ideas were shared, the class came up with a Wheel of Choice with between four and eight different solution choices that they could try when problems arose. The number of choices reflected the age of the children. We noticed that younger children could handle only two to four choices with ease, but older children enjoyed having many choices.

Actually, the students that created that first Wheel of Choice were five and six years old—kindergartners! They took it and ran with it, listing so many choices for solving problems that I was blown away. It was also their idea to leave some blank spaces for new creative ideas that came up.

The places where most problems occurred at our school were

common areas: the hallway, the library, the lunchroom, and the play-ground. We had different classes share wheels for each of the common areas. For outside areas, we laminated the wheels and replaced them as needed. I also have photos somewhere of the middle school students who painted the big Wheel of Choice on the playground as a class project.

I can remember many times when I was on the playground and prob-lems came up. One such day I was supervising in kindergarten and two students came to me with their complaints against each other. I listened for a short period and then said to them both: "I trust you two to solve this. Why don't you go over to the Wheel of Choice, try a couple of solutions, and come back and let me know what worked?" Note that I asked them to come back and let me know what worked; in Positive Discipline we call this the Same Boat tool (page 237).

The two children looked at me and then at each other, somewhat surprised. They didn't say a word, but turned together and went to the place where the wheel was hanging on a cord. Very soon they were back, hand in hand this time, with their report of which solution had helped them solve their problem.

This tool is so liberating, not only for children but especially for adults who suffer from the delusion that children need our help to solve their problems.

—Dina Emser, former director of Blooming Grove Academy, Certified Positive Discipline Lead Trainer

TOOL IN ACTION FROM BRADENTON, FLORIDA

Each year we create a Wheel of Choice in my primary classroom. At a certain point in the school year, I noticed that the Wheel of Choice was not being used as much as I had hoped. I offered the class an extension in order to ignite an interest in this tool. I was thinking particularly of a four-year-old boy who always refused my invitations to use the Wheel of Choice when I knew he really needed it and could benefit from its use.

The children made their own portable mini wheels out of small paper plates, selecting, writing, and drawing four of their preferred things to do to problem-solve. Then we punched holes and used a piece of yarn so they could wear their wheel around their necks.

All the students had so much fun making their own wheel and were very happy with them. The fact of creating and wearing their own personal wheel made it more relatable, and it surprisingly worked very well for the boy.

When this boy took his portable wheel home, his mom told me that he was very excited about it and shared with her and his grandmother how to use the wheel. She said that she couldn't believe her eyes that evening when she saw him get in a conflict over something with his father: the boy was about to flip his lid, but instead of his usual reaction, which was to throw a tantrum, he ran straight to his Wheel of Choice and said, "I choose to walk away," and he did walk away!

—Saleha Hafiz, Center Montessori School

TOOL TIPS

1. Hang the Wheel of Choice and the Anger Wheel of Choice in a prominent location in the classroom.

2. When there is a conflict, ask students if they would like to use the appropriate Wheel of Choice to find a respectful solution or socially appropriate way to express anger.

3. It can be helpful to give students a choice: "What would help you the most right now—to use the Wheel of Choice or to put this problem on the class meeting agenda?"

4. You might want to use the Wheel of Choice program on the Positive Discipline website, www.positivediscipline.com/teachers. It includes fourteen lessons to teach students the skills for using a Wheel of Choice.

WHAT THE RESEARCH SAYS

Research indicates that students who are capable of generating appropriate solutions to a problem demonstrate a higher level of overall mental health. In addition, studies show that students who demonstrate aggressive behaviors struggle to identify solutions in social conflict situations.[79] Using the Wheel of Choice provides a tool for students to develop these independent problem-solving skills. Students acquire a sense of resourcefulness when they learn there are many positive solutions for problems they encounter.

An action research study using the Wheel of Choice showed increases in students' ability to problem-solve and a decrease in both verbal and physical aggression over an eight-week period. Surveys done before and after the wheel was introduced indicated that students developed positive strategies for conflict resolution. Student journals showed that students were able to write down positive forms of conflict resolution after thinking about the problem. Verbal aggression decreased from the first week (twenty-two incidents) to the eighth week (four incidents). Teacher observational notes documented that students used the Wheel of Choice for successful problem-solving. The Wheel of Choice lessons introduced to students during class meetings included (1) make an apology, (2) tell the other person to stop, (3) walk away, and (4) use an "I" message.[80]

POSITIVE TIME-OUT: COOLING OFF

Where did we ever get the crazy idea that in order to make children do better, first we have to make them feel worse?

—Jane Nelsen

Positive Time-Out is not the same as punitive time-out. Positive Time-Out is a special place designed by students to serve their need to calm down. Another huge difference is that once students design their Positive Time-Out space (and create their own special name for it), they are not sent to it—they choose it. They are learning self-regulation and self-control.

It is okay for a teacher to ask, "Would it help you to go to our calming-down space?" That is very different from sending them there. It is especially helpful to give a student a choice: "What would help you the most right now—our special cool-out space or the Wheel of Choice?" After the students have completed time-out-buddy training and mastered guidelines for quiet listening, the teacher can also ask if the student would like to have a time-out buddy to accompany him or her.

Research shows that punitive time-out is ineffective because enforced separation from the group denies the child's basic need for inclusion and social

"May I be excused? The pressure is getting to me."

belonging. This deprivation creates the potential for power struggles or revenge. Punitive time-outs provoke the opposite effect from what is needed: instead of calming down, the student can become even angrier and more distressed.

Cooling off helps students learn to handle their emotions more successfully. Teachers find that even after just a few minutes of cooling off, students can focus on brainstorming for solutions or re-engage in assignments that previously seemed overwhelming.

It is important to take time to train students so that they understand how Positive Time-Out can help. Allow students to work together to create a Positive Time-Out space. Brainstorm with the entire class to define what the Positive Time-Out space might look like. If your students need help, provide examples. For younger students the Positive Time-Out area might have cushions, books, stuffed animals, and an iPod for listening to soft music (no interactive screens), or a notebook with models of relaxation exercises for calming down. Older students may create something as elaborate as a Hawaii-themed corner with beach chairs and umbrella, a mural, and other decorative details, or something as simple as a beanbag beside a shelf with magazines and paperback books. *Jared's Cool-Out Space,* written by Jane Nelsen and illustrated by Bill Schorr, is a great resource to read to the class to teach the process and benefits of Positive Time-Out and to inspire creative ideas.

TOOL IN ACTION FROM CHICAGO, ILLINOIS

Last year I had the chance to attend an incredible workshop on Positive Discipline for Lycée Français teachers with Béatrice Sabaté. The workshop provided me with the inspired recognition that there are reliable methods I can use to deal with the challenges I was encountering in the classroom.

One of the tools that caught my attention was *le temps de pause* (Positive Time-Out). I thought right away about two of my students who had difficulties staying focused for a long time. Would these two students take advantage of this *temps de pause*? How much time would they need? Would they return to class with a refreshed ability to focus and complete their work? Would all the students use the *temps de pause*? I really wanted to try.

One day I explained to all the students in my group that sometimes it is difficult to be attentive for a long time and that we could create a little space to rest for a few minutes. I explained that this option was not meant for only one student for a long period of time but was meant to give all students who needed it enough time to rest. The students really liked this idea! Then each of the students chose two pictures of items they wanted to put on a poster to hang in the relaxing area. On the poster there was a basketball player in action, birds forming a heart, tropical fishes, a snake, a shark, and more. We decided together on a convenient place to put the poster, and our Positive Time-Out space was created!

At the next class, I explained again the purpose of the *temps de pause*, and during the class (and throughout the rest of the year) I was amazed to see that only the two students who struggled to be attentive asked me for permission to have *un temps de pause*. Only one of the two sat by the poster and rested at a time. Looking at the pictures on the poster, these students could explore a world of the imagination that allowed them to momentarily escape the demands of their classwork. They would stay only a few minutes and then come back with the group to participate happily in the activities. The other students were not bothered at all by their brief departures.

This *temps de pause* was so easy and quick to put in place and so useful for all of us. Everyone benefited, everything was positive, it was magic!

—Nathalie Meyfren-Rado, Lycée Français de Chicago

TOOL IN ACTION FROM SOLANO BEACH, CALIFORNIA

As part of becoming a Certified Positive Discipline Trainer, I spent a year helping children develop social-emotional skills and holding well-functioning class meetings using the tenets of Positive Discipline at a Montessori school in Solana Beach, California.

We were learning about self-regulation and using Positive Time-Out in a classroom of nine- to twelve-year-olds, a group made up of an equal number of girls and boys. When we discussed during the class meeting what name they wanted to give the Positive Time-Out space, half chose "Dragon's Lair" and the other half picked "Tranquil Ocean." Each time we voted, the outcome was stubbornly exactly the same.

Obviously, we had to table the task of naming our Positive Time-Out space until the students became more skilled at compromise. After three class meetings, they decided together on "Dragon's Ocean"— the place where dragons go to cool down! They were all pleased with this name, and both boys and girls used the space happily when they needed to calm down.

—Julie Iraninejad, Certified Positive Discipline Trainer

TOOL IN ACTION FROM FORT WAYNE, INDIANA

At the beginning of the year, our students in the primary classroom (ages three to six) helped us set up the Positive Time-Out space. During our daily classroom meetings, we often talked about the importance of this space, where children can go to take a break when they feel they need time to cool off and feel better before trying to solve a conflict. This special area was providing individual, personal space for any child who felt the need to be alone.

We asked students if they could think of some rules for using the Positive Time-Out space, since with twenty students in the class it was very much in demand. We also asked them to think of some objects they could put in the area to make it more restful. We asked them to work on naming the space as well. The children decided to add some books (which they periodically change), a mirror, "feeling" cards with pictures, and a small basket with marbles. We had a wooden child-size barn in the classroom, and the children decided to put the barn in the area. Just recently we also had a suggestion from a boy who said it might be a good idea to add a small CD player and earphones to listen to music.

They decided to name it "Our Personal, Special Space."

—Nataliya Fillers, Oak Farm Montessori School, Certified Positive Discipline Educator

TOOL IN ACTION FROM NEW YORK, NEW YORK

A kindergarten class was transitioning from French to English with agitation and noise. The teacher usually nagged and raised her voice to get them quiet.

I happened to be there to observe a child who was dealing with impulsivity. I asked the group, "Is this the way English class is supposed to start?" Most of the kids regrouped and settled down in silence—except for the impulsive child. I moved closer to this child and asked discreetly, "Do you need more time to get ready? Do you want to use the reading corner to calm down?"

He happily went to the library corner.

The class had started by the time he finished his first book. He complained, "But I can't see what's happening from here!"

I answered him, "You bet! You needed your soothing time for a while. But if you are ready to join the group and remain seated and calm, you can join your class now."

With enthusiasm and happy compliance, he did just that.

—Floriane Prugnat, school counselor, Certified Positive Discipline Trainer

TOOL IN ACTION FROM MÁLAGA, SPAIN

When we are very upset, we access our midbrain (the amygdala), where the main objective is fight, flight, or freeze. The purpose of Positive Time-Out is to help students calm down until they can access their prefrontal cortex, where rational thinking takes place.

The attitude of teachers in those moments of midbrain distress—their empathy, firmness, and kindness—is essential in helping students learn self-regulation until they are able to reclaim the rational brain and see the distressing situation with a problem-solving attitude.

Positive Time-Out is *not* a period for thinking in the child's regular classroom seat. It is a separate space, a special place and time, created to help the child escape the usual demands of classroom tasks, relax, and focus on the natural flow of his own mind and feelings. Calming down contributes to the child's ability to develop causal thinking and engage in reflection. Only through calm thinking can the child reach the stage of recognizing responsibility and discovering solutions.

The other day I was substituting in a class where a student began pounding on the table and insulting a girl in his group. I turned to him calmly and asked him to come out into the hallway with me. Since he was already in his "reptilian brain," he seemed ready to fight or run away.

I told him I was not punishing or scolding, I just wanted him to tell me what had happened that upset him so much.

He said he did not want to read the book.

I asked if it would help him to go to the corner of the room where we had created a Positive Time-Out table. He could draw or do a puzzle instead of feeling forced to do something he did not want to do.

He willingly went to the table and began to work on a puzzle. When he finished, he was totally calm and joined the rhythm of the class without further problems. I noticed that the other children had also calmed down and seemed willing to welcome him back to the group.

—Macarena Soto Rueda, school consultant, Residencia Escolar Virgen de la
Fuensanta de Coín

TOOL TIPS

1. Some teachers have found it helpful to teach calming strategies such as counting slowly, taking deep breaths, or even meditation techniques.

2. Students find it helpful to know about flipping their lids and why it is helpful to calm down. (See the Understanding the Brain tool on page 172.)

3. Do not send students to the Positive Time-Out area. Instead, ask, "Would it help you to go to our cool-down area?" Even better, provide choices: "Which would help you the most—our cooling-off space, using the Wheel of Choice, or writing your problem on the class meeting agenda so everyone can help?"

4. Let the student decide when he or she is ready to return to class from Positive Time-Out.

WHAT THE RESEARCH SAYS

Research using brain scans at the Mindful Awareness Research Center shows the negative effects caused by isolation during a traditional time-out punishment.[81] The effects within the brain can look the same as the effects of physical pain, such as what would be present with physical punishment or even abuse.

Eisenberger, Lieberman, and Williams used neuroimaging to examine how social exclusion and physical pain are similar in terms of the brain's chemical response. Participants were scanned while playing a virtual ball-tossing game in which they were ultimately excluded, and their neural images were compared to those of individuals experiencing physical pain. The study's findings show that social isolation and physical pain share a common neuroanatomy.[82] This finding raises serious questions about why many parents and educators still believe that putting a child alone in the corner is beneficial. Research shows that while traditional punitive time-out is one of the most popular discipline tools used by parents and educators, it is not effective in helping children or adolescents self-regulate, problem-solve, or make positive behavior changes.

All human beings have a profound need for connection. The research support for the importance of students feeling connection and belonging at school is abundant.[83] Positive Time-Out provides an important tool for helping students calm down so they can problem-solve and respond more appropriately to classroom guidelines. While traditional time-out intensifies the emotions and demands of a stressful situation by isolating and excluding the student, Positive Time-Out helps students learn to manage their emotions through a procedure based on their own choice. Since the Positive Time-Out space is a student-designed part of the classroom, students who choose to go there can still feel they belong to the group while they take a short period to rest from the stress created by the demands of others. Once students feel better, they can re-engage actively with the group and connect with others successfully. Usually students who have had a positive opportunity to calm down work much more cooperatively to identify solutions that will be helpful to themselves and others in the long term.

"I" MESSAGES

It is part of our general prejudice against children that we assume that we know what they mean without really listening to them. We keep our own mouths so busy that we fail to hear what comes out of theirs.

—*Rudolf Dreikurs*

Adler emphasized the concept of "private logic," meaning that everyone perceives the world in unique ways through the "lenses" they create from beliefs based on their life experiences. We can all agree about this logic but seem to forget it when we want to blame or judge someone else for how they see things.

Too often students (and adults) blame others for their feelings by saying, "You make me feel _____." This is not true. No one can make anyone else feel something. They might invite you to feel something, but you always have a choice. One way to help your students take responsibility for their feelings is by teaching the skill of using "I" messages. The following scenarios provide examples:

SCENARIO ONE: Henry cut in front of Serena. Serena got mad and shoved Henry. Henry got mad and shoved back, and soon they were scuffling. A teacher intervened and scolded both of them. Then Henry and Serena got into a shouting match about who was right and who was wrong.

"IF I HAVE TO WEAR THIS TO SCHOOL I'LL GIVE MYSELF A WEDGIE AND SAVE THE OTHER KIDS THE TROUBLE."

SCENARIO TWO: Henry cut in front of Serena. Serena said, "I feel mad when you cut in front of me, and I wish you would go to the back of the line." Henry said, "Sorry," and went to the back of the line.

You may be thinking, "Well, that is unrealistic. Why would Henry apologize and go to the back of the line just because Serena told him how she felt and what she wanted?" Because sharing "I" messages invites cooperation instead of rebellion.

Another secret is that they had learned and practiced the art of "I" messages, which includes the following formula: "I feel _____ about _____, and I wish _____."

When people have a feeling, such as being mad, and go straight to an action without thinking about what they are feeling, their action is usually a thoughtless *reaction*. This invites another thoughtless reaction from the instigator, until the interaction has devolved into a chain reaction of unhelpful, hurtful behaviors. Reactions almost always involve a judgment and a retaliation.

When people express a feeling, they have to stop and think about what their feeling is. Then they take responsibility for the feeling by naming it and expressing it. Using an "I" message is not judgmental. It is a simple statement. It is nonreactive and usually invites responsibility and positive actions from others.

After sharing the above examples, ask your students to make a list of things other people do that invite them to feel annoyed or angry (that is, what bugs them). The list might include things such as cutting in line, gossip, and not being invited to join a game. Let them know it is okay to exaggerate when they are brainstorming to make it more fun.

Then share an example of how to use the "I feel _____ about _____, and I wish _____" formula: "I feel hurt when you don't let me join the game, and I wish you would let me take a turn in the game." It can be helpful to role-play certain situations, such as bullying, pushing at the water fountain, or not helping to return the play equipment, to give students the opportunity to practice using "I" messages. Let them practice until they feel comfortable sharing their feelings and wishes. You will find several examples in the "Tool in Action" stories below.

Self-regulation (taking responsibility for one's feelings) is an important social and life skill. "I" messages require self-regulation, and students seem to enjoy learning this language and practicing it.

TOOL IN ACTION FROM LONDON, ENGLAND

About a week after teaching my tenth-grade students how to use "I" messages (I always joke with them that I don't mean messages on the iPhone), I had a student ask if he could come and speak to me about his essay grade. He came to me and said, "Ms. Marchese, I feel confused about my essay grade because I worked really hard on the assignment and I don't understand why I received such a low grade."

This was brilliant! If he had approached me with his usual tone, he might have said, "Ms. Marchese, I don't think the grade you gave me is fair!"

With this approach, I would have felt inclined to defend the grade I gave him. However, because he used an "I" message and shared that he was feeling confused, I wanted to help him understand and to feel better.

We sat down for about thirty minutes and went over every part of the essay and rubric. In the end, I didn't change his grade, but he felt better knowing what he could have done to improve, and I felt like a better teacher. A win-win situation! I did compliment him on his use of "I" messages and expressed my gratitude to him for approaching me in a respectful manner.

When I teach "I" messages, I always share the example of how they may use it with their parents to discuss their curfew, such as "I feel left out because I am the only one of my friends that has to be home at eleven, and I wish that we could negotiate a later time that we can both feel okay with."

The students love this example, and many of them will go home and use it. Most of the time the students are successful at negotiating a later curfew because their parents don't get defensive, and they appreciate the positive way that their teenagers are communicating with them.

When we give our students the opportunity, they show us how truly intelligent they are.

—Joy Marchese, tenth-grade teacher, American School of London, Certified Positive Discipline Trainer

TOOL IN ACTION FROM PORTLAND, OREGON

In our classes we teach the children to express "bugs and wishes"— "bugs" to express what is bugging them, and "wishes" to express what they want. This just happened with a five-year-old I get to work with:

HE: I want to give Kevin a wish.

I: You mean a bug and a wish?

HE: Nope. Just a wish.

I: Okay.

HE (TO KEVIN): I wish you would play with me!

—Steven Foster, special ed teacher, Certified Positive Discipline Lead Trainer, and coauthor of *Positive Discipline for Children with Special Needs*

TOOL IN ACTION FROM PORTLAND, OREGON

I was in a Head Start classroom and sitting at a table where the kids were making bracelets from very, very tiny beads. The only part of the process that they needed help with was tying the bracelet off at the end.

One boy asked me to tie the knot for him (a very reasonable request). My adult fingers struggled with the elastic string and I kept *not* tying a knot. At one point I growled and said, "This string is bugging me!"

My little friend didn't miss a beat. He said, "And what do you wish?"

—Steven Foster, special ed teacher, Certified Positive Discipline Lead Trainer, and coauthor of *Positive Discipline for Children with Special Needs*

TOOL IN ACTION FROM LIMA, PERU

Reciprocal treatment among students improved thanks to the "I" Messages tool, which we modeled in a class meeting. I explained that we would be learning to express, in a respectful manner, the things that bothered us. We would develop two lists, the first indicating what bothered us and the second spelling out how we would like the other person to behave. Then, using the two lists, each student had the opportunity to practice how to express concerns by saying phrases like "It bothers me when _____ and I would like _____." Another time we practiced possible answers: "I'm sorry. I did not know you minded."

When the group was ready, we fixed up a cozy place in the classroom (with a rug and pillows) where students could talk calmly and resolve conflicts. Sometimes I sat at a little distance to watch without intervening, while being able to hear what they were saying and record their dialogues. They said things like: "I feel upset when you pick my colors without permission, and I would like you to ask first." The other replied, "I'm sorry. I will not do it again." Another exchange: "I feel sad because you asked me to play and then you went with the other girls and left me alone. I would like you to carry out what you say." The other replied, "Sorry, I didn't realize it. Will you play with me during the next break?"

Problems are easily solved before they turn into major conflicts. One day a boy approached me to tell me he was upset with his friend, and before he had time to tell me anything, another kid inquired, "Have you sat down to talk with him?" The boy left and I saw him talking to his friend. Later I asked him how he felt and he answered, "Everything is fine, don't worry."

—Sandra Colmenares, third-grade teacher, Certified Positive Discipline Educator

TOOL TIPS

1. It can be fun to use a toy ladybug and a toy wand as symbols for expressing "bugs and wishes." Invite students to use these symbols for practicing the art of using "I" messages.

2. To help your students retain the "I feel _____ about _____, and I wish _____," formula, allow time for them to practice periodically.

3. During a class meeting you might ask, "Who has an example of using this formula recently?" It is a valuable social and emotional life skill to understand that others may not feel the same and may not give them what they wish for. Still, it is important to learn skills to respectfully express feelings and wishes.

WHAT THE RESEARCH SAYS

"I" messages are an integral part of effective communication, especially when working to respectfully resolve conflicts with others.[84] Teacher and peer use of "I" messages provides students with validation and helps them feel understood. "I" messages facilitate effective communication, especially during times of conflict.[85] Kubany and Richard investigated communication of negative feelings in a sample of twenty high school students reported to be in close relationships. Findings showed that accusatory "you" statements evoked strong and more negative emotional responses compared to "I" statements.[86] In a sample of children living in Hong Kong, researchers found that children are more receptive to "I" messages than to comments that used "you" and were critical or negative.[87] A diverse sample of kindergarten and first-grade students and their teachers participated in a social-emotional problem-solving program that specifically included effective communication strategies such as "I" messages. The researchers documented a decrease in students' physical and verbal aggression.[88]

PROBLEM-SOLVING: FOUR STEPS

> The crucial factor is the shared responsibility, a process of thinking through the problems which come up for discussion, and an exploration about alternatives. Shared responsibility is best accomplished with the question "What can we do about it?"
>
> —*Rudolf Dreikurs*

Many of the Positive Discipline tools teach the importance of problem-solving: Class Meetings, the Wheel of Choice, Agreements and Follow-Through, Parent-Teacher-Student Conferences, Curiosity Questions (both types), Control Your Own Behavior, "I" Messages, Focus on Solutions, and many others. They are all designed to create what Adler and Dreikurs referred to as "a sense of social interest and community feeling." The Problem-Solving: Four Steps tool provides a process for students to practice this valuable skill.

The steps are:

1. Ignore it.
2. Talk it over respectfully.
3. Agree together on a solution.
4. Ask for help if you can't work it out together.

"Do I get part-credit for trying?"

Many wonder why "Ignore it" is a problem-solving step. How do you solve a problem if you just ignore it?

Well, how often do we make a big deal out of something so minor that it would fade away if ignored? You can have students role-play the following two scenarios to learn that ignoring can be one of many solutions.

SCENARIO ONE: Two students, who have been coached to play their roles by exaggerating while making sure no one gets hurt, are walking down the hall in opposite directions. The first student accidentally bumps into the second student, who shoves back. The first student, in turn, shoves the second student. Stop the role-play when the point has been made—usually after ten to fifteen seconds.

Process the role-play by asking what each student is thinking, feeling, and deciding to do. Then invite all the other students to share what they learned from watching this role-play.

SCENARIO TWO: The same two students are walking down the hall in opposite directions. The first student accidentally bumps into the second student. The second student keeps walking.

Process the role-play by asking what each student is thinking, feeling, and deciding to do. Then invite all the other students to share what they learned from watching this role-play.

Follow this role-play by inviting the students to create other scenarios for what the two students could do instead of fighting or ignoring. They might come up with some creative variations, such as apologizing, laughing, or turning to give each other a high-five. Whatever they come up with, invite students to role-play the new scenarios.

Introduce the other three problem-solving steps to your students. Facilitate a discussion of each of the steps to help students gain a better understanding of what they mean. For example, the step "Ignore it" might involve taking some Positive Time-Out to calm down before coming back to follow the other steps.

The second step, "Talk it over respectfully," might involve sharing "I" messages and listening to the other person's point of view. It might mean each person taking responsibility for how he or she contributed to the problem and sharing what each is willing to do differently.

The third step, "Agree together on a solution," might require a brainstorming session to first create a list of possibilities.

The fourth step, "Ask for help," could mean putting the problem on the class meeting agenda to get the whole class involved in brainstorming for solutions, or asking an adult for help.

Divide students into three groups and ask them to first discuss each step and then to create a role-play to demonstrate each one. They can decide who will play each role, being sure to include the important roles of observing students who are all affected by what goes on.

It won't be long before you will catch your students practicing the art of finding solutions without any interference from you.

TOOL IN ACTION FROM BRADENTON, FLORIDA

A second-grade boy came in from recess upset and crying. "I'm not mad that my pants got pulled down, I just want to know who did it," the child sobbed. Upon my inquiry, he told me that about eight classmates were playing tag when his pants were somehow pulled down, exposing his underwear. He felt several friends saw his underpants as a result. Vance named those eight children, both boys and girls, who had been playing with him, and I called them into a smaller, private office to problem-solve out of sight of the other children.

When all the children and I were in the office, I asked, "Who has a problem?"

Vance answered, "I do."

"What is your problem, Vance?" I questioned.

He said that someone pulled his pants down while they were playing tag, and he wanted to know who did it so he could solve it.

No one confessed. I reminded the children that we were looking not for blame but for solutions. As if I hadn't said that, one child raised his hand and said that he'd seen Sammy do it. Sammy turned his head swiftly toward that child and said, "Uh-uh, I didn't do it." Then first another and then another child chimed in that they too had seen Sammy do it. As the eyewitnesses united around one story, Sammy claimed innocence with tears.

At this point, I reminded them again that we were just looking for solutions, not blame. Vance wasn't mad; he just wanted to know who had done this. No one was going to be in trouble. I began to feel that the others were telling what they had seen and Sammy was lying in his own defense.

I felt sick. I wanted to say to Sammy, "Just admit what you did; you won't be in trouble, and then we can simply solve the problem and move on." But as his huge tears flooded his face, Sammy stuck to his story of innocence while the others stood by theirs.

As I was about to try to make some all-encompassing statement that would move us onward without final closure, a small girl piped up. "I did it by mistake," she revealed. "I was chasing Vance and I fell. As I fell, I landed on him and accidentally pulled his pants down as I was falling." We were shocked. The eyewitnesses couldn't believe they were wrong about what they thought they'd seen. I was hit with a bolt of awareness that maybe eyewitnesses couldn't be trusted to accurately report what they saw, and because of this, they should not be brought into the problem-solving arena.

Today when something like this happens, I don't ask who has something to contribute or who saw something related to the issue. I simply let the children involved talk to each other and solve the problem peacefully.

—Mattina, second-grade teacher, Center Montessori

TOOL IN ACTION FROM SAN DIEGO, CALIFORNIA

As part of our problem-solving process, we use what we call "check-in." It combines Positive Discipline tools such as Curiosity Questions, "I" Messages, and Asking for Help. Not only is there a check-in procedure for adults to help students, but there is a check-in process that happens between students if someone is hurt, either physically or emotionally, or if there is a misunderstanding or a disagreement.

For example, if a student bumps into another one, the first student would stop and check with the other student by asking "Are you okay?" and "Do you need anything?" The injured student could say,

"My elbow is scraped and I need a Band-Aid and an ice pack." The two students would come to the office for assistance.

If a student is feeling hurt by something another student said or did, they ask for a check-in with the other person. This could be with an adult present or just between the kids. The student is allowed the opportunity to share with the other person how he or she is feeling: "It makes me sad when you don't include me in your games." Then the other person would have the opportunity to respond: "Well, sometimes you don't want to play the game we are already playing." The dialogue goes back and forth until they have reached an understanding or settled on a plan to do something different.

In our society, most children (and many adults) do not have these kinds of problem-solving skills. It is testimony to the dedication and commitment of our teachers that they take the time to connect with their students respectfully and teach these skills using the platforms of the morning meeting and class meetings.

—Donna Napier, Innovations School, Certified Positive Discipline Educator

TOOL IN ACTION FROM DECATUR, GEORGIA

My class had been having a lot of trouble with not watching where they throw and kick basketballs and soccer balls, and students consequently getting hit in the head. The class came up with a bunch of solutions and decided on the rule of moving to another location for soccer.

They've since been asking me to supervise them when they want to play soccer. I hear them reminding each other not to kick the soccer balls into the basketball games. It is really helpful and has made break time so much easier to supervise.

—Elise Albrecht, middle-school teacher, Cloverleaf School

TOOL IN ACTION FROM ATLANTA, GEORGIA

We like to think of our classroom as a community of learners where we all learn together. To help develop this collegial atmosphere, I stress with my students, from the beginning of school, that we are all teachers and learners. We each have information to share and information to receive from one another.

To help in forming this spirit of cooperation, I need to first "know my learner." For most of my students, this is only their second year of formal full-time school. Developmentally, they may not all be at the same place. To further their sense of empowerment and to promote a sense of responsibility for their own learning, we initiate the "Ask three before me" rule.

The children are encouraged to become problem-solvers. If there is something they don't understand or are not sure of, they are to ask three classmates what to do before coming to a teacher. This practice is something I encourage from the first week of school. The advantages may include:

- A sense of ownership and responsibility toward their learning
- A feeling of control over a situation
- Problem-solving
- Defusing attention-seeking behavior
- Eventual elimination of undue attention-seeking behavior

As our school year unfolds and the teacher and the assistant are working in small groups, this plan allows the teachers and the students to continue with their lesson virtually uninterrupted. It may take a bit longer for those who like to hear an answer only from the teacher to get on board. Proper modeling and rehearsing of what "Ask three before me" looks like is a must. So is recognition of those who followed the plan, whether the one who asked a question or those who answered the question. Positive feedback to all parties builds the spirit of cooperation and encourages the others to do the same.

—Patty Spall, first-grade teacher, St. Jude the Apostle Catholic School

TOOL TIPS

1. Invite some students to create a poster of the Four Problem-Solving Steps to hang in the room.

2. Create a special place in your classroom or just outside your room where students can go to follow the Four Problem-Solving Steps.

3. When you see the need to intervene in a problem, offer a choice: "What would help you the most right now: using the Wheel of Choice, using the Four Problem-Solving Steps, or putting this problem on the class meeting agenda?"

WHAT THE RESEARCH SAYS

Longitudinal research, in which data is gathered for the same students over time, has shown that students who learn problem-solving skills early in school are less likely to develop behavioral difficulties. Shure and Spivack report that teaching interpersonal cognitive problem-solving skills improves students' impulsive behavior.[89] For example, one study showed that students who learned problem-solving skills in kindergarten and first grade showed improvements compared to the control group. Group comparisons were made through fourth grade, showing consistent results in favor of the students who learned problem-solving skills.[90]

Research also confirms the importance of using a systematic process for promoting students' social and emotional growth.[91] One of the standards identified through evidence-based studies is integrated daily practice of social and emotional skills. Positive Discipline's Problem-Solving: Four Steps tool, as well as other tools such as Class Meetings, provides a format for daily practice as part of the structure and routine of every school day. Research on the efficacy of classroom meetings identifies class meetings as beneficial to students, as daily practice improves students' ability to use problem-solving skills.[92]

CHAPTER SIX

TEACHER SKILLS

ACT WITHOUT WORDS

Talking is one of the most ineffective things to do. Silent action by a teacher is always more effective than words.

—*Rudolf Dreikurs*

Do you sometimes have the feeling that your students don't hear a word you say? You are probably right—especially when a mistaken goal is involved. For example, if a student's mistaken goal is Undue Attention and you try to motivate behavior change through verbal lectures or reprimands, you are actually reinforcing the student's goal of seeking attention as his or her mistaken way to find belonging and significance.

If your student's mistaken goal is Misguided Power, your words may invite a power struggle as he or she lets you know "You can't make me." If your student's goal is Revenge, your words are likely to deepen his or her hurt feelings and invite more hurtful behavior in retaliation. If your student's mistaken goal is Assumed Inadequacy, your words are likely to deepen his or her mistaken belief of not being good enough.

Too often the words you use are based on reacting to the behavior. Acting without words requires that you stop and think about how to respond proactively.

"I don't need to go to a gym. One of my classroom management strategies is to circulate frequently around the room. I figure I walk three miles a day."

A. BACALL

It requires you to get into the student's world and understand the belief behind the behavior so that you can encourage new beliefs that motivate new behavior.

Using nonverbal signals is one way to act without words, and may help to get your students involved. During class meetings, have students brainstorm a list of silent nonverbal signals that are respectful and helpful. Some examples: smile and point to what needs to be done; hold up an index finger as a reminder to use quiet voices; clap three times and have the student echo these claps as a reminder for silence. Nonverbal signals are always more effective if students are involved in creating those signals and agreeing to them in advance.

Sometimes acting without words isn't appropriate or helpful in the situation. Another Positive Discipline teacher tool related to Act Without Words is the One Word tool. In that case, the signal is replaced by one word. The last "Tool in Action" story shared in this section includes a teacher success story using this tool. The "Tool Tips" section provides specific examples to show how using one word may be most effective.

Finally, there are times when the most effective thing to do is to get close to a student who is off-task. Your proximity alone may be all the student needs to get back on task—especially if your intent and energy convey connection before correction (see page 86) rather than intimidation.

It is often said that actions speak louder than words, but the *energy* behind those actions has the loudest "voice" of all. You will feel the energy of these teachers who share this in the following "Tool in Action" story.

TOOL IN ACTION FROM RALEIGH, NORTH CAROLINA

In large urban high schools of more than two thousand students, the process of changing classes creates repeated, disruptive events throughout the school day. Although changing classes has the positive benefits of giving students regular breaks and needed interaction with their peers, these short periods of heightened social and physical activity can make it difficult for teenagers to transition to the calm of class discussions and instruction.

When thirty or more vivacious teens enter a high school classroom, they inevitably collect in small social groups and continue their hallway discussions. The teacher has the challenge of gaining their attention quickly so that the work of the day can begin. When the ringing of the automated school bell is not enough, I try to model polite interruption, since the social exchange among peers is of utmost importance to these adolescents.

Instead of attempting to make myself heard above the noise of thirty teenage voices, I walk over to the light switch and turn the lights on and off several times to signal to students that I'm ready for class to begin. They have learned what this signal means, they can all see it happening, and they know they need to bring their conversations to an end, take their seats, and listen for instructions. Without speaking a word, I have their attention. Equally effective is the device of raising my hand in the air as I place a finger over my lips. I find a small group of students who are watching me and perform this action with them first. These students know it is time to end conversation, and they raise their hands as well. Gradually I move from group to group, not saying a word but simply keeping my hand raised. If necessary, I do the "zip your lips" motion. Without one word spoken about the need for quiet, the teacher can begin.

—Sally Humble, Ph.D., retired English teacher, College Board Workshop
facilitator/consultant

TOOL IN ACTION FROM TOOELE, UTAH

Once, when teaching sixth grade, I lost my voice but still had to teach a full day and keep twenty-eight students engaged in learning activities. It makes me smile that it was this day that taught me the power of this Positive Discipline tool—that actions do speak louder than words. Amazingly, it was one of my best days teaching! All I could do was whisper, so utilizing proximity, writing messages, and using smiles and gestures made a big difference in communicating. The benefits of using this tool were so clear that once my voice was restored, I started incorporating those behaviors more in my everyday teaching, with great success.

I have had many people comment that they have been amazed at how eye contact, smiles, and energetic whispers or softer tones have engaged a large group of kids when it seemed as if only yelling could get their attention and work effectively. I have adapted the motto of a former president: "To speak softly and carry a big smile."

—Jessica Duersch, sixth-grade teacher, Certified Positive Discipline Educator

TOOL IN ACTION FROM ATLANTA, GEORGIA

I have found a fun way to reach students who have a hard time tuning out the "busyness" of our classroom during centers time. At any one time, there are four different centers going on around us, but I have found that using a charades-type approach for instruction keeps the students' focus on me and makes a simple project more challenging.

I begin by posting a few sign-language words on the whiteboard. The basic words are "hello," "please," "thank you," and "you're welcome," to name a few. I begin each lesson with the following nonverbal signals:

1. Snap fingers to get the students' attention. I sign for them to look at my eyes, and I look at theirs.
2. I sign what supplies they will need, such as scissors, pencil, and glue stick.
3. I proceed to act out, charades-style, the steps necessary to complete the art project, using some sound effects (like popping the cap off the glue stick). The students seem to enjoy the sound effects almost as much as creating their art projects.
4. I encourage them to sign back to me with any questions they have.

The other children, even though they are busy with their centers, all turn and notice the quietness of our center. We all have fun (me included) challenging our other senses to complete a task.

—Tricia Loesel, first-grade teacher, St. Jude the Apostle Catholic School

TOOL TIPS: ACT WITHOUT WORDS

1. You may have noticed that students tend to tune out adult lectures.

2. Kind and firm actions usually speak louder than words. For example, let students know you will begin the lesson when they are ready. Then sit quietly until they are ready (assuming you have taken time for training with the tool; see page 69).

3. Put on your gym shoes and circulate. Proximity is an action that often speaks louder than words.

4. Perfect the look that kindly and firmly communicates "Nice try."

5. Kindly place your hand on a student's desk as a silent signal.

6. For younger students, start the year with a class procedures poster with symbols/pictures. An example would be hand to ear for listening.

7. Use your sense of humor to create some of your own silent signals. For example, you could hold up a small inflatable palm tree to signal you need a Positive Time-Out.

TOOL TIPS: ONE WORD

1. One word is often all that is needed for a friendly reminder.

2. One word to avoid is "Don't." Instead try:
   - "Pencils" as a reminder for students to get out a pencil for note-taking
   - "Eyes" when students need to visually attend for learning
   - "Books" to signal students to be ready with their book out
   - "Clean-up" before leaving the classroom
   - "Solutions" when kids are arguing or fighting

3. Combine nonverbal signals with the One Word tool for multisensory instructions.

TOOL IN ACTION FROM EUREKA, ILLINOIS

Often we teachers use lots of words and then wonder why kids tune us out. A typical example in my first-grade classroom was at recess. I noticed my tendency to talk on and on about the weather, what kids would need to wear, and what they needed to do to show me they were ready. It was another time to lecture kids when all they wanted was to go outside and play.

I decided to try out the Positive Discipline tool One Word. As the time approached for recess, I looked at our schedule, looked at the clock, and said, "Recess." It was funny and gratifying to see the kids look at one another and at me, and then begin to get ready. I got my coat and headed for the doorway of our classroom. Calmly the kids lined up behind me. With one look over my shoulder I could see they were ready, and even quieter than usual—they were probably in shock—and off we went.

It was another energy saver for me, and I noticed that the students were very cooperative and seemed to appreciate fewer words. I believe my actions showed respect for their capability to know how to get ready for recess.

When talking so much, I didn't show faith in them (another Positive Discipline tool). When I talk less, they have the space to access their inner capability and figure things out for themselves.

—Dina Emser, former director of Blooming Grove Academy, Certified Positive Discipline Lead Trainer

WHAT THE RESEARCH SAYS

A meta-analysis of classroom management interventions designed to decrease disruptive behavior showed that using a wide variety of non-verbal cues, such as moving closer to students or a silent signal (example: finger to lips for quiet), is extremely effective for redirecting students who are not on task. Furthermore, having prearranged non-verbal signals, such as the teacher raising a hand to signal students to take their seats, is recommended in the literature.[93] McLeod reports that effective teachers use classroom management skills that include the use of proximity (specifically, moving toward trouble spots) to encourage attention. School culture has an effect on student behaviors. Students who report satisfaction with their school received fewer verbal reprimands compared with students who are dissatisfied with school. Also, effective teachers are located near problems when they occur and, therefore, can respond quickly and quietly.[94]

DO THE UNEXPECTED

For as long as the teacher gives in to her impulsive reaction, unaware of its meaning, she will fortify the child's mistaken goal instead of correcting it.

—*Rudolf Dreikurs*

Research studies show that effective teachers are more spontaneous and flexible in how they respond to problem situations. Using the element of surprise or humor can help redirect students in a positive way.

Many teachers find that when they want to yell, it is actually more effective to whisper and stay calm. One teacher would pick up a bullhorn and whisper into it. Another teacher used exaggerated sign language to gain the attention of his students. Spontaneously doing the unexpected can get students' attention, keep their interest, and help them stay focused.

Understanding that there is an underlying purpose for students' misbehavior (see the four "Understand the Mistaken Goal" tools, beginning on page 23) can help teachers avoid falling into the trap of reacting impulsively, which may actually reinforce the misbehavior. For example, if a student's mistaken goal is Undue Attention, a reactive impulse might be to give negative attention by nagging or coaxing. Using humor might involve getting this student to create a joke contest and get other students to sign up for the joke of the day.

If the goal is Misguided Power and you find yourself engaging in a power struggle, you might get out a set of toy boxing gloves and say in a joking manner, "Meet me after class." Of course, this is effective only if your sense of humor is obvious. After lightening the situation with humor, you could follow by saying, "I realized we are in a power struggle, and I care about you too much to fight. Let's calm down, and then meet for a problem-solving session."

When you understand the purpose behind the misbehavior, you can see how it may be helpful to do the unexpected.

TOOL IN ACTION FROM EUREKA, ILLINOIS

As I became more aware of Positive Discipline, I got better at remembering what it felt like to be a child. The Do the Unexpected tool helped me be entertaining and funny to gain cooperation and break the stress or pressure of the moment for all of us. When kids were distracted during a lesson, I would go over and begin talking to the wall or the window, describing whatever process I was trying to teach.

If they were talking, I would go to my desk and read my book, begin to sing a silly song, or go to a child's desk and invite her to get up and do some exercises with me. As soon as the kids noticed, I would motion for them to join us.

Doing the unexpected allows all of us a break from the pressure of the moment to do something physical, musical, or funny and then to get back to business with better energy. It helps me stay out of my bossiness and crabbiness as a teacher and remember that these are kids—they like to be entertained and surprised.

—Dina Emser, former director of Blooming Grove Academy, Certified Positive Discipline Lead Trainer

One day it seemed all my special education students were out of control as they lined up after recess to go back to class. Instead of yelling, I just sat on the ground and waited for them to notice. Soon everyone quieted down. They looked at me curiously. One even offered to help me up.

—Jackie Freedman, special ed instructional assistant, fourth- and fifth-grade classroom, Certified Positive Discipline Educator

TOOL TIPS

1. Turn on some lively music and declare that it's dance time. After a few minutes, turn off the music and declare that it's now work time.

2. To get the attention of students, stand on your desk and don't say a word, or lie on the floor. (This may not be your style, but we know teachers who have done both.)

3. Change seating arrangements. Say, "Everyone pick up your books and move to another desk." This movement can change classroom dynamics quickly among students who may be chatty or distracted by those immediately around them.

WHAT THE RESEARCH SAYS

Emmer and Stough summarize research on the critical role of classroom management, identifying the need for teachers to be capable of making split-second decisions.[95] Effective teachers are comfortable reacting to difficult situations spontaneously. Research on teacher decision making identifies the need for teachers to quickly modify management strategies based on the needs of the situation. Research also shows that new teachers are often less comfortable changing a task when students become restless. This inability to assess and respond to the changing demands of the classroom can decrease teacher effectiveness.

LIMITED CHOICES

We cannot protect our children from life. Therefore, it is essential to prepare them for it.

—*Rudolf Dreikurs*

Wouldn't it be nice if students would just do what they are told? After all, teachers know what they need, so why give choices?

To answer this question, let's go back to the beginning of this book, where we created the list of characteristics and life skills we want for children, such as self-reliance, self-regulation, respect for self and others, responsibility, problem-solving skills, and so on. These skills are not learned through blind obedience. They are developed when teachers use the Positive Discipline tools that provide repeated practice for students to learn them.

Also, not having a choice invites a sense of powerlessness and rebellion. Having a choice, even when limited, creates a sense of useful power and encouragement that invites students to think and choose. When they feel encouraged, they are more likely to choose cooperation.

Limited choices are most appropriate when students don't have a choice about "what" but do have a limited choice about "how," "where," or "when." Students

"In general, do the right thing."

may not have a choice about doing assignments, but they could have a choice about when and how they do them.

What if your student doesn't want to pick one of the limited choices and wants to do something else? If the something else is acceptable to you, fine. If it is not, say, "That isn't one of the choices." And then repeat the choices, followed by, "You decide."

If the limited choice still doesn't work, become a behavior detective. Maybe you haven't created a connection before correction. Maybe you haven't validated the student's feelings or point of view. Maybe another tool would be more effective, such as curiosity questions, joint problem-solving, or putting the problem on the class meeting agenda.

The next "Tool in Action" story provides an example of a teacher who used many Positive Discipline tools for connection and understanding before offering a limited choice.

TOOL IN ACTION FROM ATLANTA, GEORGIA

In my kindergarten class, Owen, a new student to the school, consistently avoided doing his work, especially during the morning language arts block. As a new student, Owen had struggled with the transition. He often had difficulty managing his emotions and demonstrated low frustration tolerance. In daily class meetings Owen avoided giving his classmates compliments. And when problem-solving he often sought solutions that solely benefited him.

Conversations with Owen's parents helped me better understand Owen. Owen's parents shared that Owen was an only child and that they both worked very long hours and traveled. Owen's parents openly admitted that when they were with him, they avoided conflict because they had so little time together as a family. Owen's avoidance of doing hard tasks in the classroom made sense in the context of his family and home life.

I often use limited choices to help guide students' behavior. Once I understood that Owen was perfectly capable of doing his work but just avoided things he didn't particularly like, I decided to use limited choices to motivate Owen and guide him to develop a more responsible work ethic.

The first time I used limited choices with Owen, he had some trouble managing his feelings, but it worked like a charm. I gave the class directions to write about their favorite "Super Kids" character so far this school year. Owen did not start working, but instead fiddled with the supplies in his pencil box. I then went to Owen, bent down, and said, "Owen, you can write about your favorite character now or with me at ten o'clock. It's up to you."

Owen knew the daily schedule and that recess was at ten o'clock. At first Owen protested, "I don't want to miss recess. I don't know what to write."

He started to cry, but then wiped his tears and started to work. When the students were out to recess, I opened Owen's journal and read what he had written: "It is hard for me to pick my favorite Super Kid. All the kids are so nice. I like them all. It is like my new school. Everyone is nice and my friend."

As I read the entry in Owen's journal, I knew we were making progress. He had decided to do his work and earn the privilege of going to recess. More importantly, he had chosen to share how he felt about his new school and new friends.

—Meg Frederick, kindergarten teacher

TOOL TIPS

1. Having no choice is discouraging. A limited choice is empowering.

2. Offer appropriate and acceptable choices.

3. Provide at least two possibilities that are okay with you. Examples:
   - "Do you want to read this book or do homework during free time today?"
   - "What would help you now—going to our cool-off space or the Wheel of Choice?"
   - "Would you like to hand in your report neatly handwritten or typed?"
   - "Would you like to sit here or over there?"
   - "Would you like to put this problem on the class meeting agenda or use the four problem-solving steps [page 199] together to find a solution?"

4. Remember that even limited choices work better after you have made a connection before correction.

WHAT THE RESEARCH SAYS

Research shows that providing students with limited choices can increase academic motivation while decreasing problem behavior.[96] There are several rationales offered as to why this strategy is helpful for student learning. Most important, studies on the brain demonstrate how the mental task of processing choices keeps students engaged, self-directed, and feeling empowered, thereby increasing the internal locus of control. Kern and Parks summarize recommendations based on their research findings. Most important are that (1) teachers should not view offering choices as a loss of power or authority, nor should they remove choices in an effort to regain control over students, and (2) limited choices should be viewed as a management strategy to help students feel empowered.

LOGICAL CONSEQUENCES

If we allow a child to experience the consequences of his acts, we provide an honest and real learning situation.

—*Rudolf Dreikurs*

Notice the wording in the Dreikurs quotation above: "If we *allow* a child to *experience* the consequences of his acts . . ." Allowing a child to experience consequences is very different from *imposing* consequences, which are usually just poorly disguised punishments. Allowing students to experience consequences the Positive Discipline way means having faith in students to learn from their experiences in a supportive environment. A supportive environment means omitting all "I told you so" lectures. It means omitting all punishment. It means not rescuing. It means not trying to prevent all mistakes—except those that are life-threatening or hurtful to self or others. Once you have followed all the "omits," there are several "dos" for creating a supportive environment:

PLAYING THE
SANTA CARD

"My teacher said if I continue to be disruptive in class, she will tell Santa that I'm naughty. Then he will bring me only educational toys."

1. Simply validate your students' feelings, and then have faith in them to work out the consequences of their choices and learn from their mistakes.

2. It is okay to ask if they would like some help. If the answer is yes:

a. Ask if they would like to put the challenge on the class meeting agenda so their classmates can brainstorm for solutions that might be helpful.

b. Help students explore the consequences of their choices/behaviors through the Curiosity Questions: Conversational tool (page 117). In this way, students are gently led through a process of answering questions that invite them to "think it through" for themselves.

Imposed logical consequences (punishments) are designed to make sure students *pay* for what they have done. On the other hand, helping students explore the cause and effect of their behavior helps them learn from what they have done.

Positive Discipline does not advocate external controls (i.e., rewards and punishment). Positive Discipline's focus is on long-term results. Each Positive Discipline Tool teaches internal self-control and helps students engage in a process of identifying the problem and searching for solutions.

The idea of "No more logical consequences—at least hardly ever" can be a huge paradigm shift for educators who have relied on a management system based on rewards and punishment. Teachers trying to make this shift often ask, "Why isn't it okay to use stickers as rewards for good behavior—especially since students like them?" or "Shouldn't the student go to the principal's office for misbehavior or face some negative consequence?"

Removing enforced consequences requires a shift from relying heavily on external reinforcement through the use of rewards and punishment (identified by research as ineffective in the long term) to developing a classroom management system based on mutual respect and internal locus of control.

Under some circumstances logical consequences are appropriate. Remember that privilege = responsibility. When students don't want to take responsibility, it may be appropriate for them to lose the related privilege.

The three R's and an H are a good tool to help you decide when a consequence is a natural, logical effect of a behavior rather than a disguised punishment. If the three R's and an H are met, the consequence is a solution with the student assuming responsibility.

THE THREE R'S AND AN H CRITERIA
1. Related
2. Respectful
3. Reasonable
4. Helpful

Allowing students to experience the effects of their behavior is important for their development. However, too often teachers (and parents) rescue students, preventing them from learning from the natural flow of events. If a student forgets something and the teacher rescues him, there is no opportunity for the student to experience the reality of being forgetful. When students are rescued, they cannot develop confidence in their ability to handle problems independently.

Try the following activity to help you gain a better understanding of the long-term results of punishment, rewards, logical consequences, and focusing on solutions.

FOUR ALTERNATIVES TO DEALING WITH CHALLENGES

1. Get a blank piece of paper and divide it into four quadrants, saving a little room at the top. Think of a challenge you are having with a student. Write it down at the top of the paper.
2. At the top of each quadrant write each of the following discipline methods: Punishments, Rewards, Logical Consequences, and Focusing on Solutions.
3. Next, fill each quadrant with descriptions of what each discipline method might look like in the context of your challenge. Create several descriptions for each quadrant.

4. Now pretend you are the student who is presenting the problem. As you read the descriptions of the discipline method in each quadrant, notice what you are thinking, feeling, and deciding.

5. Go to "Creating a Results Road Map" on page 6 and look at the "Challenges" list and the "Characteristics and Life Skills" list. Which of the discipline methods inspired you to learn any of the things written on the "Characteristics and Life Skills" list? Did any of the discipline methods motivate you to engage in any of the items on the "Challenges" list?

Many teachers who complete this activity experience how rewards and punishments may work temporarily, but they do not teach the characteristics and life skills we hope our students are learning. The Logical Consequences tool can be effective when applied properly. However, in most cases, focusing on solutions creates the best long-term results.

TOOL IN ACTION FROM GUAYAQUIL, ECUADOR

Positive Discipline has caused a dramatic and positive change in my classroom environment. I have always taken pride in my management skills and my ability to create a positive classroom community. My students in the past have experienced a climate in which we have addressed problems when they came up, handled them in a respectful and appropriate manner, and delivered consequences as needed. However, we didn't realize how often those "consequences" were actually disguised punishments.

After the Positive Discipline workshop, I came to the realization that we were not truly solving problems. Of course, we would address the problems, find a way to manage them (often with a consequence), hope that the student had learned his lesson, and then move on. However, we did not focus on the root of the problem, and students did not have much participation in the process. Now, all my students know that in my classroom, we focus on real solutions.

Now, solutions come almost entirely from the students. They have become deeply invested in not only solving their own problems but also helping others find respectful solutions to their problems.

Before this change in my approach, students would come to me with a problem and the expectation that I would impose a consequence as a remedy. Now, students still come to me with problems, but their request for help is different. They say, "Mr. Mathis, I had a meeting with John about a problem we are having, but we weren't able to come up with a solution. Can I add this problem to our next class meeting agenda?" This new approach has completely eliminated the "tattle tale" mentality and changed the way students think about solving problems.

—Jeremy Mathis, fourth-grade teacher

TOOL TIPS

1. Help students explore the consequences of their choices.

2. When it seems appropriate to use a logical consequence, be sure it meets the privilege = responsibility formula. Here are two examples:
   - "You can sit with your friend when you come to me with a plan for how you will handle the privilege respectfully."
   - "You can make up for your missed assignment by teaching a special unit to the class."

3. Whenever possible, focus on solutions.

WHAT THE RESEARCH SAYS

The Center on the Social and Emotional Foundations for Early Learning is a national resource for disseminating research and evidence-based practices to early childhood programs across the country. The center's research identifies the effectiveness of logical consequences, especially when used with other positive strategies.[97] Studies have included samples of young children who demonstrate noncompliant, aggressive, and oppositional behaviors with a focus on families with multiple risk factors from diverse ethnic and socioeconomic backgrounds. There are clear, far-reaching benefits to helping students understand the cause and effect of their choice and experiencing the logical consequences of those choices. On the other hand, research shows punishment (which unfortunately is more commonly used compared to logical consequences) does not have long-term positive outcomes.[98] In fact, punishment may lead to fear, which has a negative impact on learning. Punishment negatively influences motivation and concentration. Furthermore, students may learn to please the teacher to avoid punishment rather than acquiring skills and knowledge for their own development. In the case of physical punishment, the student may become fearful of and avoid the punisher as well as develop negative feelings and perceptions about school.

HAVE FAITH

The educator must believe in the potential power of his pupil, and he must employ all his art in seeking to bring his pupil to experience this power.

—Alfred Adler

What does it mean to have faith in students? It doesn't mean abandoning students to figure out everything for themselves. It means having more faith in how much they can handle, even if it means they have to struggle. Having faith means knowing that they can benefit from some struggle. Struggle builds resilience and a sense of capability as students learn how much they can do. And, most important, having faith in your students means empowering them to use their deep wisdom and caring to deal with some challenges that might seem impossible to adults.

You can offer support that invites them to think by validating feelings. You can also offer some guidance through curiosity questions (see the Curiosity Questions: Motivational [page 112] and Curiosity Questions: Conversational [page 117] tools). You show faith by not rescuing, fixing, or controlling, and instead get students involved in helping and problem-solving.

"I am going to close my eyes and cover my ears. I expect the students who took my chair, my desk, and my chalkboard to bring them back."

Patience is probably the most difficult part of

showing faith in your students. It almost always seems more expedient to solve problems for students. This is particularly true if you believe teaching means students should be passive receptors of your knowledge, or if you attempt to settle conflicts through punishments or rewards.

Dreikurs pointed out that students will know if you genuinely have faith in them and their ability to strive and move forward. Allow them to feel a little disappointment. Allow them to work through their feelings. Allow them to problem-solve on their own. They will need these skills in the future.

Encouraging yourself and your students requires a lot of faith—faith in yourself, faith in your students, and faith in the Positive Discipline tools to produce the results you hope for. As you read the following "Tool in Action" story, notice the teacher's kindness, her firmness, and the faith she has in herself, her student, and the tools being used.

TOOL IN ACTION FROM POWAY, CALIFORNIA

Every Friday we have a vocabulary quiz in my tenth-grade English class. Last week was unusually busy, and we didn't have a lot of class time to study the words that appeared on Friday's quiz. Typically, when I give a quiz or test, I proctor the exam from the front of the classroom.

This past Friday, Jordan was obviously looking at his neighbor's quiz. I whispered in his ear, "How else do you think you might accomplish a good grade?" He immediately apologized.

After class, all the students had exited, but Jordan stayed behind. He was horrified at what he had done. He said, "Ms. Loiewski, I am terribly sorry. I only looked at one answer, and I promise I didn't look at any others."

"Okay, what is your plan for next week?"

"I promise I will study more, and I will even help other students study."

For the next vocabulary quiz, Jordan was highly motivated to perform better. In our homework basket, he placed a paper with all of the words written out with definitions and sentences. When I asked him about all this extra work, he responded that he had fun studying and really wanted to earn 100 percent.

—Diana Loiewski, high school teacher, Certified Positive Discipline Educator

TOOL IN ACTION FROM PARIS, FRANCE

When I see what happens with my students in my class as well as at home, I'm impressed by the power of Positive Discipline! My last experience in my class was really amazing.

Three-year-old Marc pushed his friend Arthur during recess. He pushed so hard that Arthur fell on a branch and peed in his pants. The recess teacher brought the two crying little boys to me, saying, "I wonder how you are going to use your Positive Discipline to deal with this."

I asked what had happened. The boys were both crying, and I couldn't understand a word they said. Then I said to Marc, "Go back to play, and we'll talk about it when you feel better."

Marc went back out to recess, and I started changing Arthur, who was wet. Five minutes later Marc came back to tell me he wanted to say sorry to Arthur. I asked Arthur if that was okay. It was, and so Marc said, "Sorry." I told him he could go and play. He came back five minutes later, saying, "I wonder, how is Arthur? I would like to help him get changed and stay with him." I asked Arthur if Marc's idea was okay with him. And soon they were sitting on a bench together. How cute! Finally they went back to play outside, holding hands.

—Nadine Gaudin, teacher, Certified Positive Discipline Trainer

This story beautifully illustrates that adults often make things so much more complicated than they are because they don't have faith in children—both in their innocence when accidents happen and in their ability to have compassion and to solve problems. Nadine knew that her children needed some time to calm down before they could access their rational brains and solve their problem without adult interference. Of course, Nadine takes time for training (during calm periods), teaching them concern for others and respectful problem-solving.

TOOL IN ACTION FROM VISTA, CALIFORNIA

During a class meeting a student submitted a concern that she hoped her peers could solve. My heart sank as she explained, "It bugs me that the woman that helps me at Starbucks has cancer and I wish I could help her." (See the "bugs and wishes" activity on page 196.) I sat quietly and held back tears.

Thank goodness that I was at the end of the circle and last to speak! As the talking stick was passed around, the class excitedly offered ideas to cheer her and raise money for her. Instead of choosing which idea to follow, we did every single one and spent the entire school year focused on extending our love to the barista. We raised enough money to help her with medical bills, pay her rent on occasion, and shower her with cards and pictures! She did successfully complete her treatment and now has a clean bill of health! Teachers empower students to develop phenomenal and inspiring social interest when they teach problem-solving skills and have faith in what their students can accomplish.

—Joy Sacco, Carden Academy, Parent/Teacher/Certified Positive Discipline Trainer

TOOL IN ACTION FROM PETALUMA, CALIFORNIA

I have read Jane Nelsen's book *Positive Discipline* every year for thirty years or more. I have used her "related, respectful, and reasonable" tools in my Montessori classroom as well as hosted a yearly book study for parents whose children are enrolled at the school.

One piece of advice I always remember is how things get worse before they get better. When the adults in a child's life set a fair limit and follow through with kindness, firmness, and detachment, a child who is not used to this may test the adult to the limit to see if the adult will cave in. Riding this wave of discomfort instead of throwing in the towel and saying "This Positive Discipline stuff does not work" can be one of the biggest challenges, but the long-term positive effect is far greater than "swatting at flies" for an eternity. You just have to have faith in them.

Recently our group of three- to six-year-olds tested this faith. We had just finished eating snacks together, as we do every day first thing in the morning. My assistant was at the rug with all of the children and said, "As soon as I see everyone seated and ready, I will call you to go to work." We didn't know how it started, but one person started flopping on the rug, and before we knew it the entire group was out of control, copying and adding their own disruptive and disrespectful behavior. My assistant said, "I am leaving the circle and will return when you are all seated."

Both adults in the room proceeded to go about our business while listening, watching, taking notes, and making sure that everyone was safe. At times I would walk in without a word and remove an object that was in someone's hands. The children continued to have access to water and the bathroom but were not allowed to leave the area until they were all seated. One boy and girl were invited out after remaining seated despite their peers' behavior. They went to work. Another child had not gone to the rug in the morning as he is sensory-sensitive and starts his day with headphones and music. During the two hours—yes, two hours—that this went on, he worked away from the chaotic area with noise-canceling headphones on. I put earplugs in my own ears and the ears of the two children who were working.

For the two hours there was running, sock throwing, chasing, crawling, yelling, dancing, pulling of shirts, pushing, picking up people, taking out materials, rolling, tripping, and general loud disruption. There were a few cries from several of the children of "Everyone sit down!" but to no avail, because the children asking were not modeling it themselves. At one point a child said, "Everyone, we are all teachers." Another child said, "It's hard to concentrate."

During this time the teachers remained friendly and detached, firm and loving. There was a little farm dog in the room with us, and she remained in the arms of one or the other of the teachers. The children who were working continued to do so and the teachers continued to work with them. My assistant even sat down and read to one of the students while they worked. You could hear the noise ebb and flow. Then the noise stopped and all of the children sat down.

My assistant and I returned to the rug and I handed my assistant a pad and pencil. She went around the circle and asked, "What did you do that contributed to what just happened here?" At first there were a few attempts to point fingers, with "He did this" and "She did that," but when we said that everyone had had a part in the disruption and we were not blaming others but looking at ourselves, it stopped. Then, unanimously and honestly, each child reported what his or her part in the event had been: "I threw socks, ran, and chased," "I was running in circles, trying to get friends to go to their names on the rug, rolling people, yelling," and so on. Then we asked, "What made it stop?" They all said, "I sat down." My assistant said, "That was all I asked."

One child, having observed his classmates being quiet when the adults read stories to the group, asked if he could be a leader and read a book. That prompted another child to ask to read as well. They sat down in chairs at the circle and took turns reading. Every child was attentive.

The biggest surprise of all followed when I said to all of the children who leave before lunch, "It is time to go, so I will call your name to get your things and line up by the door." Many said, "You mean it is time to go home?" "Yes," I said. "If you are staying for lunch I will call you to go wash your hands." A child asked if she could call the children's names, and she took over that role with grace and confidence.

Since this exercise in the classroom the children have not re-created the chaos. They have been reminding each other of the solution. The days that have followed have been more ordered, a result of their own desire to create that order.

In a recent family class that my assistant and I took through the Blue Mountain Meditation Center in Tomales, California, I read these words of Eknath Easwaran in an article entitled "Wisdom in Action": "If as a child I have not been told no by my parents, then when I become an adult, I will not be able to take no from anyone at all. In relationships with children, love often expresses itself in the capacity to say no when necessary. . . . If we cannot say no to our children when necessary, we will actually be teaching them to have more self-will. . . .

Only when we are detached in good measure from our own ego can we encourage our children to grow to their full stature in their own way, by saying, 'We will support you as long as you turn your back on what is selfish and self-willed.' "

As Jane said, not shame, blame, and punishment but a limit with love.

—Andrée Young, Red Barn Montessori

TOOL TIPS

1. Express faith: "I have faith that you two can figure out a solution that works for both of you."

2. Avoid rescuing: "Do the best you can, and then I'll help." When you know students are capable, rescuing communicates that you think they are not.

3. Offer a choice: "Do you want help from the whole class during a class meeting, or to use the Wheel of Choice?"

4. Use encouragement to show faith in a student's ability: "I notice you are sticking with that problem, even though it is hard for you."

5. Have faith in students to use their power for heartwarming social interest when given the opportunity.

WHAT THE RESEARCH SAYS

Rosenthal and Jacobson's 1960 study identified the prevalence of the "Pygmalion effect" in schools.[99] Specifically, the researchers examined the hypothesis that there is a relationship between teachers' beliefs and expectations about student potential and student achievement. In their study, a nonverbal intelligence test was administered to all students in an elementary school at the start of the school year. The test was disguised as a test that would predict intellectual "blooming" and was labeled "The Harvard Test of Inflected Acquisition." Rosenthal and Jacobson then randomly selected 20 percent of the students (so the selections had no relation to actual test scores), but teachers were told that the 20 percent were "above average" students who showed "unusual potential for intellectual growth" and could be expected to "bloom" academically by the end of the school year. At the end of the school year, researchers retested all students. Those children who had been randomly labeled as "intelligent" showed a significantly greater increase in test scores compared with the other students, who had not been labeled as likely to excel. The data supported Rosenthal and Jacobson's hypothesis that teacher expectations and beliefs affect student achievement. They concluded that the teachers' expectations regarding the intellectual ability of certain students led to an actual change in the intellectual performance of those same students, even though they were a randomly selected group simply labeled by the researchers as more capable of growth.

Yatvin, a former school psychologist and professor at Portland State, points out how Rosenthal and Jacobson's research as well as replication studies in other schools reveal the power teachers have when they show faith in their students.[100] Yatvin reports that the positive effect of teachers having faith in their students has been observed in very specific ways. A teacher's smile, nods of approval, or willingness to provide more opportunities for a student to ask and answer questions, and a kinder tone of voice, even if these responses occur unconsciously, influence student performance in a positive way.

SAME BOAT

We can overcome the existing intense competition and its damaging effects if we treat all the children as a group—by putting them all in the same boat.

—*Rudolf Dreikurs*

Conflict usually diminishes when you put students in the same boat—that is, treat them the same—instead of trying to figure out who is to blame. Jane learned this quickly as an elementary school counselor. In the beginning, when two students were sent to her office because they had been fighting, she would make suggestions for solutions, none of which satisfied either party. They just wanted to play the "it's unfair" and blame games.

Her great lesson came when two boys were sent to her for fighting and she said, "I have faith in you two to solve this problem. I'll step outside my office, and you can come tell me when you have a solution." Less than two minutes later they came back with a solution. One of the boys said, "I tore his T-shirt, so I will bring him another one tomorrow, but it doesn't have to be new because the one I tore wasn't new."

It also works well to ask who would like to put a problem (or fight) on the class meeting agenda. Class meetings provide students with the skills

"**Did I throw <u>which</u> spitball?**"

and practice to work out problems together. They love learning and repeating the sentence "Are you looking for blame or are you looking for solutions?"

Dreikurs explained the strategy of putting children all in the "same boat" by noting that too often children in a family will team up against adults for attention or power (two of the goals of misbehavior). Peers at school will do the same thing, teaming up against the teacher. Putting students in the same boat facilitates students working together to collaboratively come up with solutions.

TOOL IN ACTION FROM VISTA, CALIFORNIA

Two second-grade boys were visiting my classroom for after-school care. They were playing nicely on the floor when all of a sudden they jumped up and ran toward me, each shouting that the other had kicked him. They reached my desk and desperately pleaded their cases, each trying to outshout and blame the other.

I informed them that there was no reason to look for blame because children don't get into trouble in my classroom; instead, we talk things over and find solutions. I then asked if they would each like to be heard by the other so they could find a solution together. They said yes.

I then gave them a paper with the "I" message format to use as a guide: "I feel _____ about _____, and I wish _____."

I invited one boy to go first. He got right in the other boy's face and said very loudly, "I feel really silly, because I lied about you kicking me, and I wish I knew how to get out of this!"

The other boy burst out laughing and said, "I feel like laughing. I can't think of anything else to say."

They continued their game and forgot the argument.

—Joy Sacco, Carden Academy, Certified Positive Discipline Trainer

TOOL TIPS

1. Instead of taking sides when students fight or have a problem with one another, treat them the same. Instead of using individual names, say: "You two."

2. Give a choice: "Would you two like to go to the peace table, use the Wheel of Choice, or take some Positive Time-Out?"

3. Show faith: "Let me know when you two have brainstormed ideas and have a solution you both feel good about trying."

4. Class meeting agenda: "Would you two like to add this problem to the class meeting agenda?"

5. Practicing problem-solving during class meetings gives students the skills to work out problems together.

WHAT THE RESEARCH SAYS

Putting students in the same boat is one tool that helps teachers remember the importance of placing the problem back in the hands of their students. Teachers' management style impacts group dynamics. Lewin, Lippit, and White's classic study on group leadership showed how democratic leadership (based on mutual respect and cooperation) helps students engage in collaborative problem-solving, rather than working at odds.[101] In many of Dreikurs's writings he points out how classrooms reveal group dynamics that match Lewin's model. Dreikurs used Lewin's leadership model and Adlerian psychology to develop a democratic classroom management model to help teachers provide freedom and order. Lewin's research on group dynamics demonstrated that this approach was optimal compared to either authoritarian or laissez-faire styles. Specifically, this research showed how democratic leadership helps individuals feel a sense of cohesiveness and facilitates students working together to solve problems.

TONE OF VOICE

> We ourselves so many times instigate misbehavior on the
> part of the child because of the tone we use.
>
> —*Rudolf Dreikurs*

Have you sometimes caught yourself using a loud or disrespectful tone of voice without realizing what you were doing? Rudolf Dreikurs pointed out decades ago that when we speak to our students they hear more in our tone of voice than in the words we use. You may have experienced this before: when a class is noisy, teachers may raise their voices in an attempt to gain control. We suggest using a softer tone, or even whispering, to gain students' attention. This models quiet and respectful behavior.

Try listening to yourself and other teachers. Pay close attention to the tone of voice you're using. When your stress level goes up, students can hear it in your voice. This is why self-care (page 271) is so important.

Tone of voice is of major importance in how we communicate kindness and firmness to individual students and the class. Too often a tone of firmness without kindness initiates a power struggle. On the other hand, kindness without firmness can invite students to take advantage.

**"Let me have the water gun, Jerome! I'm trying
to maintain a sunny disposition and you are
raining on my parade."**

Your tone can communicate your confidence and belief in your students. With your tone of voice, you can quickly validate or discourage. A trusting, encouraging tone helps students feel a greater sense of connection—this can be a powerful tool in helping students experience belonging and significance at school.

The difference between a consequence and punishment is often evident in your tone of voice. You can kindly and firmly tell a student that not getting his homework in on time will lower his grade. However, if your tone depicts a threat, a valid logical consequence immediately becomes punishment. Remember that your tone of voice greatly impacts students' feelings and perceptions about school and learning.

TOOL IN ACTION FROM RALEIGH, NORTH CAROLINA

As a high school English teacher and now a principal, I regularly use the Positive Discipline tool Tone of Voice. When I talk to students who have made a mistake, using a soft voice and calm tone allows students their own emotional space to reflect on what they have done. When students are agitated or upset, using a calm tone and low volume defuses the situation. Trying to understand why the student made the choice he or she made also helps. I want the student to see that we are all working toward solutions, and I want them to participate as well.

For example, when a student has cheated or has an honor violation because he has taken a shortcut, my calm response lets the student know it is a safe place to develop his own way to work this out. I use questions such as "Can you imagine how that would make someone else feel?" and "Does that make sense?" and give the student time to sort out a response that is meaningful to him.

Students may cheat because their parents are putting pressure on them that they can't live up to, because they have difficulties managing time, or because they may be rescuing a friend who asks, inappropriately, for help. Students often do not see the impact that their cheating has on their classmates, their teacher, or themselves. I usually ask students to write an essay on those impacts of their cheating, as well as to brainstorm solutions for future choices.

Finally, every discipline situation ends with a positive statement about the consequences. I make sure I tell students that from this point on I only think positively of them and am proud that they turned their mistake into a learning experience.

—Dr. Tom Humble, high school principal and AP English teacher

TOOL IN ACTION FROM GUAYAQUIL, ECUADOR

I asked permission from one of our fifth graders to share a portion of her persuasive essay here. Paula is a lovely girl. She decided to work on this topic because her dance teacher at ballet academy screams at the students. Paula is very shy, and she usually feels anxious to express her opinions out loud because she doesn't like to make mistakes and is concerned about what others might think about her. She is a perfectionist. I think that writing down her experiences was very helpful to her. I was surprised that she was able to express her feelings, allowing us to know her a little bit better. I hope you enjoy her essay.

—Karina Bustamante, school psychologist, InterAmerican Academy,
Certified Positive Discipline Trainer

Teachers Shouldn't Scream

Why do dance teachers scream? No one knows but them. Is it because they don't like how you dance and they think yelling will make you dance better? I don't know. The thing I do know is that they shouldn't because it doesn't make anything better.

I have been thinking a lot about this screaming because I don't like how it feels. I am one of those students who gets screamed at. It doesn't feel nice. So I decided to research the topic for my persuasive essay. I wanted to prove that screaming wouldn't make anything better.

Many times kids don't really listen when a teacher yells. Or they might only listen at the moment the teacher yells. After the teacher looks away, they will keep doing what they were doing. That is because behaving only happens when a student wants to. The nicer the teacher is with the student the more the student will want to behave because they will prefer the teacher.

Dance teachers usually don't yell for misbehaving. (Sometimes they do.) Dance teachers usually yell to make you dance better. They scream while you're dancing to tell you your mistakes. I believe if they just told you in a nice way after you dance what you could do to improve, the student would want to listen.

Yelling can have a negative effect on a student's behavior. Students could get used to being given instructions with a raised voice. That makes students only listen to their teacher when she or he is yelling. Eventually teachers would be giving instructions yelling.

Sometimes screaming might make the teacher become a disliked teacher. The more the teacher screams the less the student likes him or her. That causes the student to misbehave or not listen to corrections because of their disliking for the teacher. It will be even harder to get the student's attention then.

Do you think yelling teachers have ever seen themselves on tape? Probably not. They should. The teachers will see how awful they look. They will see how graceless it is. Even though that is the minimum of the problems about screaming, it causes students to really dislike their teachers.

Yelling is not only disgraceful, but it is also considered an abuse. Shouting at a kid can harm their brain very badly. It is almost a bigger abuse than physical harm. Some experts say it is a threat to a child's sense of security, safety, and confidence.

A way screaming can affect a child's brain is with concentration problems. Children who are often exposed to yelling for a period of time have a hard time concentrating. Not being able to concentrate can affect the child's academic learning at school or at dance classes. That is because since the child can't pay attention he or she can't learn or memorize dances quickly. That is not good.

—Paula Moyano, fifth-grade student

After graduating from college in 1971, I was thrilled to get my first teaching job. I was further blessed to have a wonderful principal who said, "Whisper when you want to yell." I followed this wisdom during my thirty-seven years in the classroom. I used this "whisper technique" my entire career with great success. It helped me keep and model calm even in the most hectic kindergarten classroom moments. If I absolutely could not get the group's attention, rather than yell or use a harsh tone, I simply dropped a large book on the floor! The room got quiet in a flash.

—Jody Davenport, retired kindergarten teacher

TOOL TIPS

1. Think about your long-term goal to encourage, and be mindful of your tone of voice.

2. Your tone of voice will change if you take time to sit or stand so you are eye to eye with your student.

3. Be aware of your facial expressions and body language, as each impacts tone of voice.

4. It is okay to apologize if you have used a disrespectful tone of voice. Students are very forgiving.

5. Be kind to yourself and take time to breathe (or take a longer break, if needed) before you speak.

WHAT THE RESEARCH SAYS

Brain scans show that children respond more to the tone of an adult's voice than they do to the words that are being spoken. Researchers found that even sleeping infants react to different tones of voice. Graham, Fisher, and Pfeifer studied what sleeping babies hear and reported distinct neural processing of the emotion in a tone of voice.[102] Using a tone that communicates one message and language that communicates another has been shown to have a great impact on a child's sense of self and feelings of safety.[103] On a more positive note, research shows that using a positive, supportive tone promotes cooperative classroom behavior and results in higher academic achievement.

HUMOR

Learning takes place in play, without any concern for success and failure.

—*Rudolf Dreikurs*

Have you noticed how appropriate humor in the classroom can quickly lighten problem situations? Humor can help shift students out of fight, flight, or freeze thinking.

We have known teachers to stand on desks, wear funny hats, pop on a clown nose, and lie down on the floor to bring humor to a frustrating situation. This kind of physical humor doesn't fit everyone, but it can be fun. Some teachers start every class with a joke or a funny cartoon.

We would like to emphasize *appropriate* humor. Be mindful that the humor doesn't cause anyone to feel uncomfortable. Appropriate humor can help students gain new perspective and often can replace anger with laughter.

Humor can enhance learning by reaching a part of the brain that opens new pathways to learning. That is why we decided to find a cartoon for every Positive Discipline tool. Our motto: "Laugh and learn."

Of course, humor is not just for problem

"How to Do Well in School Without Studying is over there in the fiction section."

situations. As you'll read in the research section below, teachers who use humor effectively are respected and well liked by students.

Teaching literature in high school affords me many opportunities to find the humor. Whether you have a well-honed sense of humor or not, when the classroom teacher is having fun teaching, students realize they can have fun too. This realization brings joy to the learning process and draws students into the learning experience.

Once I remember trying to have my students see that a common motivation for some characters was their insecurities. One perceptive student—perhaps in an attempt to call my bluff on simplifying complex characterizations—asked: "So are you saying that everyone is insecure?"

Bingo! "Yes. Yes, I am. And I'm insecure, too."

I try to use that insecure persona to create humor, to create a paradox in the classroom, where the teacher is often surrendering a mantle of being right. We make jokes in class about the growth mindset, something that teachers at my school are all working on. Sometimes when I make a mistake, I can react badly, but I try to model comfort and humor when making mistakes.

Now my students have picked up on the growth mindset idea in the news and joke about it. But with the joking comes a sense of being liberated. If the focus is on growth, then students find a freedom to maneuver, to take risks, and to appreciate others' mistakes (without censoring them).

I find a classroom with laughter brings joy to learning. I search for "aha" moments as well as "ha ha" moments.

—Dr. Tom Humble, high school principal and AP English teacher

TOOL TIPS

1. Nonverbal signals, such as a wink and a smile to communicate "Nice try, but not here," can be effective when delivered with a sense of humor.

2. Encourage your students to bring jokes and cartoons to share in class.

3. Be sensitive to when humor may not be appropriate (sarcasm or humiliation).

4. Teach kids to use humor (sometimes in the form of exaggerations) while role-playing.

WHAT THE RESEARCH SAYS

Research shows that when teachers use humor effectively, students benefit in a variety of ways. Specifically, students feel more connected to their teacher and learning improves. Furthermore, studies show that appropriate humor in the classroom results in students being more motivated, and they perform better academically.[104] In fact, students report that they value the personal and social qualities of a teacher more than the teacher's intellectual ability. Students clearly value a sense of humor in teachers, and research supports the benefits when teachers create a positive learning environment using humor and are willing to share jokes in the classroom.[105]

DECIDE WHAT
YOU WILL DO

Be consistent. If you have set limits, stick to them. If you say
"No," mean it, and don't change your mind.

—*Rudolf Dreikurs*

There is so much focus in Positive Discipline on getting students involved in solutions, validating their feelings, asking them questions, understanding their behavior, connecting with them, and so on. Do you ever wonder, "What about me?"

Actually, all of this is about you. Involving students in decision making will minimize misbehavior and will increase your joy as a teacher. When students feel encouraged, you will feel encouraged as well.

And there are times when you don't need to get students involved. You can simply decide what you are going to do. Kindly and firmly let your students know, and kindly and firmly follow through. Notice the "and" in "kindly and firmly." It is best if you get students involved more often than you decide for them, but trust your judgment that you will know which to use when.

One day Jane was observing a fourth-grade classroom, and the students were being a little disruptive. The teacher got very quiet and seemed

"Obedience school was okay, but the teacher
responded to my unwanted behavior with
penalties. I never learned any long-term
behavior modification, so I'm still barking
and ignoring orders."

to be staring at the back wall, where there was a clock. The kids started whispering, "She is counting. Be quiet." Soon all the students were sitting quietly at their desks and the teacher started her lesson.

Later Jane asked, "How high do you count and what do you do after you get there?"

The teacher said, "Oh, I'm not counting. I have just decided I won't teach until they are ready. They think I'm counting, and they get quiet. It works for me."

The tool Decide What You Will Do helps teachers successfully implement kind *and* firm classroom management, which research identifies as improving teacher effectiveness.

TOOL IN ACTION FROM EUREKA, ILLINOIS

All of us have classes that we will always remember. Mine is a group of first graders who were super-smart, creative, and powerful! The majority of these kids were either firstborn or only children, and they were used to running the show. I remember sometimes feeling that they could do a better job of organizing the day than I could!

By the end of the day, I would feel bone-weary, with my throat scratchy and my voice tired from trying to compete for airtime with these kids. I decided to try something different, to decide what I would do rather than trying to change what the kids were doing.

I brought my library book from home, and I told my class that I was no longer willing to raise my voice to be heard. Anytime they weren't listening, I would go to my desk, take out my book, and read until they were ready.

They looked a little surprised, and the day started off pretty well. It seemed that even the heads-up about what I planned to do was helpful to them, and to me. But sure enough, later in the day, several of them interrupted with side conversations, talking over one another, voices louder and louder, and I almost forgot my plan. However, I caught myself before raising my voice and entering the fray. I moved over to my desk, took out my book, and began to read. Ah, heaven!

It didn't take long for the kids to notice and for a chorus of *shhh* to follow. Whispered terse directions came from the kid leaders, and they all quieted down. I waited a minute, then quietly put my book down and returned to the group with no comment about their behavior.

I was amazed at how quickly my actions impacted the behavior of the children. I kept my self-respect, respected others in the group, and experienced increased energy. It set a great precedent for handling classroom noise and distractions. One of the best parts for me was feeling good at the end of the day about the way I had conducted myself.

—Dina Emser, former director of Blooming Grove Academy, Certified Positive
Discipline Lead Trainer

TOOL IN ACTION FROM PORTLAND, OREGON

In a Head Start classroom during free play, a four-year-old boy named Adnan kept knocking over the block structures that several other children were working on, and then he laughed. The other children, as well as the teachers, had tried to get him to stop. Adnan kept promising to be more cooperative.

Finally a teacher who had had Positive Discipline training said to him, "Adnan, your friends are really getting mad at you. I can't stop you from knocking over the buildings; only you can do that. Let me tell you what I will do, though. If you knock another building over, I will ask you to play in a different part of the classroom."

The teacher reviewed Adnan's understanding of what would happen. He clearly stated that he would need to play elsewhere if he knocked over another building.

A few minutes later Adnan did it again. The teacher very calmly followed through and said, "Adnan, I need you to pick a different place to play." Adnan looked shocked and screamed that he wouldn't knock any more buildings over. The teacher calmly repeated that he would still need to move. Adnan tried to run past her to the block area, but she simply headed him off and pointed to a different area.

Crying loudly, Adnan went to the dramatic play area. After a few minutes he came and asked if he could go back to the block area. The teacher told him that he could try it again after lunch. She also asked him what would be different. He said, "I won't knock stuff over." The teacher wisely asked him what he would do. He replied, "I'll ask Josie if I can help her build."

After lunch Adnan and Josie built together.

—Steven Foster, special ed teacher, Certified Positive Discipline Lead Trainer, and coauthor of *Positive Discipline for Children with Special Needs*

TOOL IN ACTION FROM SAN DIEGO, CALIFORNIA

The boys in my special education classroom were constantly rushing, running down the hall to the lunch area. One day I said, "If you boys run, I will ask you to return to class and walk." That day at lunch I followed the boys to the lunch area and saw they had run again. I stood in front of them and kindly and firmly reminded them of what I had said. When they started to complain I shook my head, pointed back to the classroom, and said, "Try again." After a few moments of eye rolling and complaining, they walked back to class and walked to the lunch area.

—Jackie Freedman, special ed instructional assistant, fourth- and fifth-grade classroom, Certified Positive Discipline Educator

TOOL TIPS

1. It is usually most effective to get students involved in decision making. However, sometimes it is appropriate to decide what you will do. Examples:

   "I will post homework for the week on Mondays and give full credit for work turned in on time."

   "I will teach when you show me you are ready to learn."

   "I will be in the classroom for thirty minutes after school to answer any additional questions."

2. Be sure to follow through with what you say you will do. (See "Agreements and Follow-Through," page 168.)

WHAT THE RESEARCH SAYS

Classroom-based research has used careful observation, description, and measurement to help identify effective action plans for teachers.[106] Walker reports that the authoritative classroom management style (characterized by a kind *and* firm approach because of the focus on the teacher-student relationship as well as clear order and structure) positively influences students' academic and social development. Students in an authoritative classroom demonstrated higher achievement. Walker also reports that authoritative teachers can reduce the percentage of dropouts.[107] On the other hand, research shows that indulgent and permissive management styles (too kind, lacking firmness or an action plan on the part of the teacher) have a negative effect on academic performance as well as students' social and emotional development.[108]

DON'T BACK-TALK BACK

> In a moment of conflict, words are meaningless; only actions count.
>
> —*Rudolf Dreikurs*

After reading the words in the cartoon, you might ask, "Are you kidding? You want me to learn what isn't being said when my student just told me to 'f—— off'? I have to let this student know, loud and clear, that she can't talk to me that way."

We know. This is a hard one. Even when a student says something less inflammatory, such as "This is a stupid assignment," it may take a saint to resist talking right back to show who is boss: "Well, you can just go talk to the principal about that!"

Since we are not saints, how do we avoid reacting to back talk?

It helps to be ready with some practiced skills. And the first skill is to try hearing what is *not* being said and listen for the belief behind the behavior. Is this student really saying, "I'm sick and tired of being bossed around, so I refuse to take it from someone who can't physically hurt me"? Or maybe even "I refuse to treat you respectfully when you don't treat

"If you want to communicate with a disruptive student, learn to hear what isn't being said."

me respectfully"? Maybe the way the student is feeling has nothing to do with you. Your student may talk back to you because of the hurt she is experiencing in the outside world, and your classroom is the only place where she feels safe to express her frustration.

We could make a hundred other guesses about the belief behind the words, but you get the point. There is a hidden belief behind every behavior. Teachers are more encouraging when they address the belief, and the hidden need to belong, behind the behavior. Yes, the hidden message of back talk is a need—a need for belonging, a need for recognition, a need for connection, a need for hope, a need for skills. The caption for the cartoon could say, ". . . hear what the student needs."

When you respond to a student's back talk with your own back talk, you are modeling the exact behavior that is so upsetting to you. Instead, take some deep breaths and be prepared to be curious about the student's need. Model respect and caring instead of disrespect.

The following activity can increase your awareness of reactive back talk and provide active responses that you can practice. First we will present typical teacher responses to back talk and then some responses that could be life-changing for you and your students.

Pretend you are a student. Notice what you are thinking, feeling, and deciding in response to the following teacher back talk.

1. "Don't talk to me that way, young lady!"
2. "How far do you think that smart mouth is going to take you?"
3. "You are in detention. Don't come back to class until you can be respectful!"
4. "No recess for you. You can sit in the thinking chair until you are ready to apologize."
5. "You might as well have a red card with your name embossed on it."
6. "You can now write 'I will be respectful' five hundred times before tomorrow morning."

If you were the student, what would you feel motivated to do in response to these teacher commands? Would you want to cooperate, rebel, withdraw, or get even? Our guess would be any of the last three choices.

Now, imagine again that you are the student. How would a student respond to these nonreactive statements by a teacher?

1. "Hmmm. I wonder what I did to upset you so much."
2. "Wow! You are really angry. Do you want to tell me more about it?"
3. "I need to sit quietly and take some deep breaths until I can be with you respectfully."
4. "What would help us right now—some Positive Time-Out or putting this issue on the class meeting agenda?"
5. "I know how it feels to be so angry. I'm glad we have the skills to work things through once we have calmed down."
6. "Do you know that I really care about you?"

If you were the student hearing these teacher statements, what would you think, feel, and decide in response? Hopefully, you would feel a sense of connection and maybe feel inspired to change your behavior.

TOOL IN ACTION FROM JANE

After a workshop where we did an experiential activity on understanding the belief behind the behavior, we took a break. An eighth-grade teacher walked back to his classroom to see how the substitute teacher was doing. On his way, he saw two students fighting. When he tried to break up the fight, one of the students said, "F—— you."

Instead of reacting, the teacher gently touched the student's arm and said, "I can see how angry you are. Come walk with me."

The student jerked his arm away but started walking half a step behind. The teacher said, "I'm guessing you are feeling hurt by something. Do you want to talk about it?"

The student might have felt overwhelmed by this sudden kindness instead of the usual expected punishment. Whatever the reason, he got tears in his eyes and told the teacher how angry (a cover-up for hurt) he felt because of an argument with his brother.

The teacher just listened until the student got it all out and calmed down. Then he said, "Do you know why I knew you were feeling hurt about something? It hurt my feelings when you said, 'F—— you.' I knew you wouldn't say that unless you were feeling hurt and needed to strike back at anyone in your path. I'm glad you felt safe talking to me. I'm glad you know I care. Would you be willing to meet with me after school, and we can talk about some ideas that might be helpful to you?"

The teacher told us about this incident when he came back to the workshop. He asked others to brainstorm some ideas for what to say when he met with the student again. The participants came up with several ideas, such as creating an Anger Wheel of Choice, but the idea the teacher liked best was to just spend some time talking with the student about his favorite things to do. He would not even mention the upsetting incident unless the student brought it up first. Focusing on what was positive in the student's life would help him see that he had the power to separate himself from his brother's taunting. This teacher had a deep understanding of the power of encouragement (through spending special time with this student) to motivate behavior change.

TOOL TIPS

1. Many teachers model the opposite of what they want to teach when they react and talk back to a student who has back-talked.

2. Avoid taking the back talk personally—as hard as that can be.

3. Imagine this student wearing a T-shirt with the words "I'm hurting. Validate my feelings (not my words)."

4. It's okay to say, "Ouch. That felt hurtful and disrespectful. I need some time to calm down before we discuss this further."

5. Be sure to get back to the student when you feel calmer and can address the belief behind the behavior.

WHAT THE RESEARCH SAYS

Students perceive effective teachers as adults who avoid ridiculing a student or creating situations in which students may feel embarrassed in front of peers (as may occur if a teacher chooses to back-talk back). Studies show the importance of the teacher's ability to use active and reflective listening skills. Students identify their best teachers as paying attention to and caring about what they have to say. A teacher's ability to communicate with and respond to students with a respectful, caring attitude is directly related to student success as measured by academic achievement.[109]

CONTROL YOUR OWN BEHAVIOR

We can change our whole life and the attitude of people around us simply by changing ourselves.

—*Rudolf Dreikurs*

"My fortune says, 'You will be successful in getting students to control their behavior, if you first control your own behavior.'"

D o you sometimes expect your students to control their behavior when you have not controlled your own? We don't mean to instill guilt; rather, we want to create awareness. We often catch ourselves behaving in ways we aren't proud of once we have taken time to calm down and assess our actions.

Teachers are not perfect, and neither are students. It is quite normal to react when challenged. We need all the tools we can learn to help us have more control over our behavior and skills for apologizing to repair the mistakes when we don't. As we have said many times, students are wonderfully forgiving when we take time to genuinely apologize.

It has been said that if you know better, you do better. This is not necessarily true. Sometimes we know better and still get caught up in reaction and forget everything we know in the moment. When we do calm down, we are often far too critical of ourselves. Review the Mistakes as Opportunities for Learning tool (page 80) and the four R's of Recovery from Mistakes (page 81). Use them, and teach your students to use them. The goal is improvement, not perfection. Thus it is okay to teach something you haven't mastered yourself (such as perfect control), so you can also model using mistakes as opportunities for learning.

It is okay to let your students know you are taking a time-out for yourself when you need to calm down. Remove yourself from the situation and get centered before attempting to solve a problem. If you can't leave the scene, count to ten or take deep breaths.

When you calm down, apologize. By apologizing, you create a connection and a feeling of closeness and trust in your classroom. In this atmosphere you can work together for solutions. When you model this openness to learning, your students will follow your model and be focused on solutions.

TOOL IN ACTION FROM SAN JOSE, CALIFORNIA

At our parent cooperative preschool, one of the ways we help parents control their behavior while working in our busy preschool classroom is by letting them know that it is okay to "tag out" with another parent when their own child is involved in a classroom conflict.

With as many as twenty-four active preschoolers in the class at once, there are many opportunities to help children resolve conflicts. Many parents shared that they tend to feel even more challenged and more inclined to "lose it" when their own child is involved in a conflict. Many times their "mama bear" instincts kick in, and they create problems with the classroom dynamic.

In our parent class meeting, we all came to an agreement that it is okay for the parent to step away if her own child is involved in a conflict. That parent asks another parent or the teacher to intervene to help the children resolve their conflict. The parent moves to another part of the classroom and gets an update later. The security of knowing that they can step away without the other parents thinking badly of them has created a culture of mutual adult support and has helped everyone keep their cool and control their behavior.

—Cathy Kawakami, Almaden Parents Preschool, Positive Discipline Trainer

TOOL TIPS

1. Remember that modeling is the best way of teaching, so take time to think about what behavior you are modeling.

2. Just like students, most of us tend to react instead of acting thoughtfully. Prepare a record sheet and for a week use a check mark to record the date and time of every occasion when you react rather than act thoughtfully.

3. When you notice you are reacting, use a specific plan to help you control your actions. Choose a plan you can easily teach your students to use as well. For example: take deep breaths, count to ten, or put your hand over your heart.

4. When you do react, it is good to apologize. See the four R's of Recovery (page 81) and the Understanding the Brain tool (page 172).

WHAT THE RESEARCH SAYS

According to social learning theorist Albert Bandura, most behavior is learned observationally through modeling.[110] Bandura's classic research confirms the importance of the Positive Discipline tool Control Your Own Behavior. Bandura's research shows how students observe adult behavior around them and imitate what they see. Probably the most famous of Bandura's studies included thirty-six boys and thirty-six girls between about three and six years of age as well as one male and one female role model. After viewing a film in which the adult role model was aggressive, children who were left alone in a room with the same props that were in the film copied the behavior they had observed.[111]

Awareness of Bandura's learning theory has influenced classroom instruction. Research on effective instruction in the classroom supports modeling as an effective instructional tool for academic as well as social-emotional learning. Furthermore, research has shown that modeling can be used across disciplines and in all grades and ability-level classrooms.[112] Harbour, Evanovich, Sweigart, and Hughes reviewed findings in support of evidence-based practices for maximizing student success. These practices include modeling desired academic as well as social behaviors.[113]

TEACHERS HELPING TEACHERS

Paradise could be attained if man knew how to apply his knowledge for the benefit of all.

—Rudolf Dreikurs

Too often teachers feel isolated from adult support as they teach alone in their classrooms. They may not seek the help of their colleagues out of fear that they will lose credibility if they admit that they sometimes get stuck about how to deal with a behavioral challenge. The Teachers Helping Teachers tool is a fourteen-step process (developed by Lynn Lott and Jane Nelsen) where teachers can learn to be supportive of each other in an encouraging atmosphere. During this process, they gain many insights into the belief behind the discouraging behaviors of their students as well as many specific ways to be encouraging.

Since this is such a powerful process, many teachers appreciate the extra help they gain by practicing these problem-solving steps in a live Positive Discipline in the Classroom workshop (dates and locations can be found at www .positivediscipline.org). If you'd like to practice this with your local group of teachers, you can use the steps below to facilitate your own Teachers Helping Teachers process.

TEACHERS HELPING TEACHERS PROBLEM-SOLVING STEPS

1. Invite another teacher to sit next to you. Explain what the Teachers Helping Teachers Problem-Solving Steps are and how he or she is now a co-facilitator with you to help others.

2. Ask a scribe to write on a flip chart the teacher's name, the grade he or she teaches, and a fictitious name for a student he or she would like help with.

3. Ask the teacher to give a newspaper-type headline of the concern (just a few words). Ask the group for a show of hands of those who have had a similar concern or feeling. (This is encouraging to the teacher who has volunteered to get help, as you can point out how many people he or she will be helping.)

4. Ask the teacher to describe the last time the challenge happened, providing enough detail for a short (maybe sixty seconds) role-play. To help the teacher focus on specifics, ask, "What did you do and say? What did the students do and say? And then what happened?"

5. Ask the teacher, "How did you feel?" If he or she has trouble finding a feeling (or says, "I felt frustrated"), show the Feelings column on the Mistaken Goal Chart (page 12, Column 2) and ask him or her to choose the feeling that comes closest. Ask the group, "How many of you have felt the same?"

6. The teacher and the rest of the group can now find the mistaken goal in Column 1 and the belief behind the behavior in Column 5. Point out that this is just a working hypothesis and move quickly to the next step.

7. Ask the teacher, "Are you willing to try something new?"

8. Set up a role-play. Invite the teacher to role-play the student. Ask for volunteers to play the other parts (student and 2 or 3 bystanders), starting with the lines they heard during the description of the problem. Remind them that it is okay to have fun and to exaggerate.

9. Stop the role-play as soon as you think the group has had time to experience feelings and decisions (usually less than a minute). Process by asking the role-players, starting with the person who played the student, what they were thinking, feeling, and deciding as the people they were role-playing.

10. Ask the group to brainstorm suggestions the teacher could try. Be sure suggestions are addressed to the scribe at the flip chart, so the volunteer teacher doesn't feel bombarded by advice. For ideas, invite the group to refer to the last column of the Mistaken Goal Chart, make suggestions from their personal wisdom, and/or take a look at the Positive Discipline Teacher tool cards (available at https://www.positivediscipline.com/products/teacher-tool-cards).

11. Ask the teacher to choose one suggestion to try (even if he or she claims to have tried all of them).

12. Bring back the volunteers to role-play the suggestion the teacher chose, with the teacher playing himself or herself (so he or she can practice). (If a punitive suggestion is chosen, have the teacher play the student so that he or she can experience the student's reaction.) At the end of the role-play, process the thoughts, feelings, and decisions of each role-player, starting with the person playing the student.

13. Ask for a verbal commitment from the teacher to try the suggestion for one week and report back to the group.

14. Ask the group for appreciations for the volunteer: What help did they learn for themselves by watching this? What ideas did they see that they could use?

You may want to try these steps in a small group of two or three to get the hang of it. Most people have a difficult time sticking to the steps. They want to provide too much information and analyze everything. There is an Adlerian principle called "holism," which means every small part relates to the whole, and this helps to explain why it is important to avoid overanalyzing. Essentially, if you can deal with a small part that can be role-played and find a solution that might work for this small part, the whole will change and your answer to the greater problem will become clear. By sticking to the steps, everyone gains insights and learns ways to encourage, even when the solution doesn't seem to work.

These steps have been very carefully designed (and used for more than thirty years) to follow the Adlerian model. The model does not work if we introduce more information or give more advice other than what is asked for in the steps. Keep practicing. You will learn how to use the model and become more comfortable within its structure.

A lot of information comes out when the role-players are spontaneous (as opposed to sticking to the script reported by the teacher). One time during the Teachers Helping Teachers problem-solving process, Jane was role-playing a teacher who had presented a problem with a defiant child who didn't respond to any of her pleas for cooperation. The frustration she felt as the teacher was so overwhelming that her only response was, "You little stinker."

The real teacher burst out laughing and said, "That is exactly how I felt." She may not have allowed herself to realize that this was what she was feeling and thinking while describing the scene, but she felt so relieved when it came out in the role-play—she felt understood. She was now even more open to finding ways to encourage her student (and herself in the process).

Brainstorming for solutions produced some good ideas that the real teacher tried in the second role-play. Everyone else felt encouraged and supported because even the observers could identify and gained some ideas for some tools they could use with their students.

TOOL IN ACTION FROM BLOOMINGTON, ILLINOIS

Our staff practiced the Teachers Helping Teachers Problem-Solving Steps every other week in our staff meetings. Over the course of several years, we got quite good at the steps and found the process took less and less time. We were often surprised (at least in the beginning) by how much good energy we generated as a team during the process, even though meetings took place at the end of long school days.

We started each new session with a follow-up from the teacher about the problem from the previous meeting. Often this sharing was quite positive, and we noticed that the teachers seemed much more encouraged to report on what they had tried than when they originally reported the problem.

We were surprised to notice that many times teachers came back to the next meeting with the feedback that the problem behavior had not shown up in the two weeks since our last session. At first we chalked this up to coincidence—it was just a strange set of circumstances that a problem that had so confounded a teacher before would suddenly disappear from his or her classroom for two straight weeks. When this pattern continued to happen with a fair amount of consistency, though, we came to the conclusion that our teachers were leaving these meetings so encouraged that they did not invite the same behavior from discouraged students. They were somehow changed by this process— they were no longer alone with the challenge. They had shared openly with colleagues who listened and gave their best input with possible new solutions to try. There was no judgment, only a meeting of the minds and ideas of a group of dedicated teachers working together to improve their relationships with children.

The Teachers Helping Teachers Problem-Solving Steps had a unifying effect at our school, empowering teachers to support one another and students to do their best.

—Dina Emser, former director of Blooming Grove Academy,
Certified Positive Discipline Lead Trainer

TOOL IN ACTION FROM CHINA

The Teachers Helping Teachers tool is really a fruitful process. I found five other teachers to do it with me. Everybody enjoyed it and learned a lot. We conducted the process in order to help a child named Daisy, who is reluctant to answer questions. By going through the problem-solving steps, we concluded that Daisy had the mistaken goal of Assumed Inadequacy, and that her belief might be "I can't belong. I give up. Leave me alone." The participants brainstormed many tools for the teacher to choose from. She chose the Have Faith tool and the Take Time for Training tool.

We all learned the importance of trusting the process. For example, in the second role-play, our teacher played herself and another participant played the role of Daisy. When Daisy refused to answer a question and crawled under her desk, the teacher made the question easier. When that didn't work, she became anxious and wanted to give up, instead of doing what she said she would do, to have faith and take time for training. When I asked about Daisy's feelings, thoughts, and decisions, the teacher role-playing her told us that she knew her teacher would give up on her and not call on her again if she refused to talk. When her teacher heard her words, it suddenly dawned on her why it seemed that she had tried everything but nothing helped: Daisy could feel that her teacher did not have faith in her and would give up on her.

Both the volunteer and other participants learned that they needed to stick to what they say they are going to do, instead of repeating their old behaviors.

—Zhai Xia, Certified Positive Discipline Educator

TOOL TIPS

1. Practice using the Teachers Helping Teachers Problem-Solving Steps (presented in more detail in *Positive Discipline in the Classroom*) with a few other teachers.

2. At least once a month, invite a teacher to present a challenge where the whole staff can be involved in the problem-solving steps.

3. Keep a special folder in the faculty room where teachers wanting help can sign up to present a concern.

4. Remember to keep it confidential. Even though Teachers Helping Teachers is an encouraging process, others may not understand when they hear details out of context.

WHAT THE RESEARCH SAYS

Teacher peer consultation practices influence teacher effectiveness and hold important implications for teacher education, educational leadership, and instruction.[114] Peer consultation builds a community culture of collaboration and results in improved teacher development and teacher confidence. Positive Discipline's Teachers Helping Teachers tool provides a specific structure for collaboration and support. A sense of community among teachers is an important variable that influences the sense of community among students.[115] Not surprisingly, modeling appropriate interpersonal skills influences students' social and emotional growth. Teachers' sense of community directly relates to job satisfaction and overall teacher effectiveness.[116]

SELF-CARE

Good teachers...work at preventing illness and take good care of their bodies in order to teach at optimum levels. Your pupils need you well and enthusiastic in the classroom.

—*Rudolf Dreikurs*

Taking care of yourself is the best gift you can give your students. This can be difficult, as teachers are usually up very early and have long workdays. Today, teachers are often required to supervise after-school activities as part of their work responsibilities. Coaching athletics, supervising academic clubs, and attending school events in the afternoons and evenings make for a very demanding workload. Not to mention that a teacher's workday involves much more than direct instruction—lunch duty, carpool, and hall monitoring, as well as being available to help individual students before and after the school day, are all assumed responsibilities of most classroom teachers.

Honestly, most teachers can't even go to the bathroom when they need to because students can't be left in a classroom unsupervised. All this being said, it is important to remember that taking time for yourself, getting plenty of sleep at night, and planning ahead so you eat well and

"That's my survival kit. It has a meditation tape, aspirin, and rose-colored glasses."

stay hydrated can make a huge difference in the long run. Teachers who have self-care plans are less likely to get sick or experience work burnout, and are more likely to remain patient with their students.

ACTIVITY

In a faculty meeting or with a group of teachers, take time to set personal goals and encourage each other. For this activity, get into small groups of two or three.

1. First, spend a few minutes on your own identifying three to five personal goals for self-care. Write each down. This can serve as a guide for your self-care plan moving forward.
2. Share your individual self-care goals within your small group. When sharing, be as specific as possible. Think about ways you can track your progress. For example: if you plan to walk three times a week, mark the days in your calendar and then check off each time you walk, to track your success.
3. Brainstorm ways to help keep self-care a priority. Are there specific things you could do to encourage yourself and each other?
4. Make an agreement in your small group to check in regularly regarding one another's progress and provide encouragement and support for the group members to follow through.

Research shows that taking time on a regular basis to plan and attend to self-care can greatly decrease stress and increase self-efficacy. Teachers have many time constraints and busy schedules. Often taking just a few minutes for sharing and offering mutual support can make all the difference. When teachers come together and connect, it builds a sense of group cohesiveness. In fact, research shows that a sense of belonging serves as a protective factor in decreasing overall stress.

When I realized self-care was important, I started to watch myself and realize that when I was tired I would yell more in my class and give out more punishments. I would get annoyed really easily and get off track with my kind and firm behavior. So I decided to invest in more self-care.

As a teacher, I find it difficult, because I always think about my students first. I always think about my class and how I can do better activities, organize things that are both educational and fun for the kids. Preparing is important; however, if I'm tired, I get off track no matter how much preparation I've done.

I now know that I have to go to bed early, that I have to take a tea break, relax after a day of teaching, see my friends quite often, and try to do sports three times a week. Doing that influences my way of teaching, and I become more of the teacher I want to be.

The way I act with my students depends on how I take care of myself. It is an obligation as a teacher to take care of myself.

—Nadine Gaudin, teacher, Certified Positive Discipline Trainer

TOOL IN ACTION FROM LIMA, PERU

Positive Discipline urges us to believe in the ability of children to make decisions about how to respond to situations presented to them and to have faith in their capacity to adapt to the world. This philosophy gave me tools to interact with my students in a closer, respectful, firm, and loving way. These tools are invaluable to me professionally and personally. Not only have they transformed my teaching, but they have also changed me as a person and keep on changing me every day. I believe that to the extent that I am friendly and loving toward myself, I will also be so with kids. I believe that if I am able to perceive my mistakes as opportunities to grow and learn, I will also be patient when my students make mistakes. Therefore, Positive Discipline not only applies in the classroom but colors your very existence. This has been the best self-care I can imagine.

—Sandra Colmenares, third-grade teacher, Certified Positive Discipline Educator

TOOL TIPS

1. Make a list of the things you like to do that feed your heart, your body, your mind, and your soul.

2. Get out your calendar and make time for yourself *every* day.

3. Give up all guilt about taking time for yourself, or for taking time to be with people who boost your energy and your joy.

4. Keep a gratitude journal.

5. Ask for help when you need it. After all, you aren't asking for anything you would not be happy to give. Allow others the blessing of giving to you.

6. Laugh and learn from your mistakes—another great gift to yourself and others.

WHAT THE RESEARCH SAYS

Student teachers report more successful student teaching experiences when they attend to a self-care plan. Self-care improved their abilities to self-monitor and recognize "signs of stressors."[117] Eldar and colleagues followed three teachers in their first year of teaching and interviewed each teacher to evaluate teachers' difficulties in relation to teacher support.[118] Important factors related to teacher stress and burnout included how comfortable they felt at the school, involvement of the principal and other peer teachers for support, teachers' relationships with their students, and attitude toward the work. In addition, Emmer and Stough summarized how teacher emotion impacts classroom management and burnout.[119] They concluded that the teacher education curriculum should include how teacher emotion affects classroom decision making.

A longitudinal study in the Netherlands taking place over a five-month period showed how lower perceived self-efficacy in classroom management and emotional stress precede teacher burnout.[120] Researchers report relationships between teacher self-efficacy, job stress, and burnout. It is our hope that using the Positive Discipline Tools for Teachers will serve to increase teachers' sense of self-efficacy and awareness about the importance of self-care.

WANT TO LEARN MORE?

We want to thank the teachers from all over the world who took time to share their success stories for this book. If you are a teacher or educator reading this book and it is your first exposure to Positive Discipline or you simply want to learn more, there are many resources to help you as you learn and practice Positive Discipline tools.

For professional development in Positive Discipline, there is a non-profit, the Positive Discipline Association, which provides certification programs and training for classroom educators as well as parenting classes and training for parent educators. The Positive Discipline Association website is www.positivediscipline.org.

Many schools around the globe have taken the initiative to implement Positive Discipline Tools for Teachers. If you would like to connect with these teachers or learn about other resources, please visit www.positivediscipline.com (where you can find the card deck of 52 Tools for Teachers) and www.positivediscipline.org.

ACKNOWLEDGMENTS

From both of us: We think learning should be fun. That is why we wanted to start with a cartoon. We were so delighted to discover Aaron Bacall's cartoons. Aaron spent many years in education before he became a full-time cartoonist. We discovered his cartoon books written especially for educators. We were deeply saddened to learn of Aaron's death shortly after we signed a contract to use his cartoons and are grateful to his wife, Linda, who helped us fulfill the contract. People also love our illustrations of the icebergs to illustrate the "beliefs" behind behaviors, both generally and for each Mistaken Goal. The iceberg was painted and generously donated by Doug Bartsch of Visalia Unified School District.

We are overwhelmed with gratitude for the many success stories we received for each teacher tool from all over the world. Nothing speaks better for these tools than real-life stories from real teachers about how they work.

We will never tire of acknowledging our roots—the concepts and principles of Alfred Adler and Rudolf Dreikurs. Their philosophy has changed our lives and the lives of millions of parents and teachers who are dedicated to having a positive influence on the children of the world.

You'll notice that many of the teacher tool success stories are from Certified Positive Discipline Trainers who are now traveling all over the world to share Positive Discipline tools. Our thanks go to the Positive Discipline Association (www.positivediscipline.org), a not-for-profit organization that is responsible for the training and quality assurance of these trainers.

If we believed in praise, it would be for our editor, Michele Eniclerico. Since we don't believe in praise, we will be specific. Michele is encouraging. She has a way of making our writing sound better without making us feel bad. She acknowledges our contributions and then makes them better without complaining about the amount of work it takes to reorganize our chapters in a way that makes sense.

From Kelly: I also want to acknowledge all the teachers who have influenced me, and specifically those who introduced me to Adler and Dreikurs. Thank you to Dr. Roy Kern and Dr. Bill Curlette, who first introduced me to Adlerian psychology during my graduate studies at Georgia State University. Thank you for teaching me the importance of empirically studying Adler's and Dreikurs's theory and applied practice. Your guidance shaped my career and lifelong aspirations. Thank you also to Dr. Dana Edwards, who was the first to introduce me to the power of class meetings for solving problems and helping kids feel capable and connected at school.

REFERENCES

1. Kohn, A. (1994). The risk of rewards: ERIC Digest. ERIC Clearinghouse on Elementary and Early Childhood Education, Urbana, IL. ERIC Identifier ED376990.

2. Vitasek, K. (2016). Big business can take a lesson from child psychology. *Forbes,* June 30.

3. Stevens, J. E. (2012). Lincoln High School in Walla Walla, WA, tries new approach to school discipline—suspensions drop 85%. *ACES Too High News,* April 23.

4. Brown, D. (2004). Urban teachers' professed classroom management strategies: Reflections of culturally responsive teaching. *Urban Education* 39, 266–289.

5. Beaty-O'Ferrall, M. E., A. Green, and F. Hanna. (2010). Classroom management strategies for difficult students promoting change through relationships. *Middle School Journal,* March.

6. Blum, R. (2005). School connectedness: Improving the lives of students. Johns Hopkins University, Bloomberg School of Public Health, Baltimore, MD.

7. Dickerson, S., and M. Kemeny. (2004). Acute stressors and cortisol responses: A theoretical integration and synthesis of laboratory research. *Psychological Bulletin* 130, 355–391.

8. Edwards, D., and F. Mullis. (2003). Classroom meetings: Encouraging a climate of cooperation. *Professional School Counseling* 7, 20–29.

9. Browning, L., B. Davis, and V. Resta. (2000). What do you mean "think before I act?": Conflict resolution with choices. *Journal of Research in Childhood Education* 14, 232–238.

10. Gere, J., and G. MacDonald. (2010). An update of the empirical case for the need to belong. *Journal of Individual Psychology* 66, 93–115.

11. Twenge, J. M., R. F. Baumeister, D. Tice, and T. S. Stucke. (2001). If you can't join them, beat them: Effects of social exclusion on aggressive behavior. *Journal of Personality and Social Psychology* 81, 1058–1069.

12. Baumeister, R. F., J. M. Twenge, and C. K. Nuss. (2002). Effects of social exclusion on cognitive processes: Anticipated aloneness reduces intelligent thought. *Journal of Personality and Social Psychology* 83, 817–827.

13. Reyes, M., M. Brackett, S. Rivers, M. White, and P. Salovey. (2012). Classroom emotional climate, student engagement, and academic achievement. *Journal of Educational Psychology* 104, 700–712. DOI: 10.1037/a0027268.

14. Dweck, C. (2006). *Mindset: The New Psychology of Success*. New York: Random House.

15. Mueller, C. M., and C. Dweck. (1998). Praise for intelligence can undermine children's motivation and performance. *Journal of Personality and Social Psychology* 1, 33–52.

16. Dreikurs, R. (2009). *Child Guidance and Education: Collected Papers*. NH: BookSurge Publishing.

17. Nelsen, J., L. Lott, and H. S. Glenn. (2000). *Positive Discipline in the Classroom: Developing Mutual Respect, Cooperation, and Responsibility in Your Classroom*. 3rd ed. New York: Random House.

18. Centers for Disease Control. (2015). School connectedness. September 1. http://www.cdc.gov/healthyyouth/protective/connectedness.htm.

19. Wentzel, K. R. (1998). Social relationships and motivation in middle school: The role of parents, teachers, and peers. *Journal of Educational Psychology* 90, 202–209.

20. Tschannen-Moran, M. (2004). *Trust Matters: Leadership for Successful Schools*. San Francisco: Jossey-Bass.

21. Stronge, J. H., J. M. Checkley, and P. Steinhorn. (2007). *Qualities of Effective Teachers*. 2nd ed. Alexandria, VA: Association for Supervision and Curriculum Development.

22. Ryan, A. M., and H. Patrick. (2001). The classroom social environment and changes in adolescents' motivation and engagement in middle school. *American Education Research Journal* 38, 437–460.

23. Gazzaniga, M. S. (2003). *Psychological Science: Mind, Brain, and Behavior*. New York: W. W. Norton.

24. Belvel, P. S., and M. M. Jordan. (2010). *Rethinking Classroom Management: Strategies for Prevention, Intervention, and Problem Solving*. Thousand Oaks, CA: Corwin Press.

25. Essa, E. L., and M. M. Burnham. (2009). *Informing Our Practice: Useful Research on Young Children's Development.* Washington, DC: National Association for the Education of Young Children.

26. Lewin, K., R. Lippit, and R. White. (1939). Patterns of aggressive behavior in experimentally created "social climates." *Journal of Social Psychology* 10, 271–299.

27. Ferguson, E. D., J. W. Grice, J. Hagaman, and K. Peng. (2006). From leadership to parenthood: The applicability of leadership styles to parenting styles. *Group Dynamics: Theory, Research, and Practice* 10, 43–56. DOI: 10.1037/1089-2699.10.1.43.

28. Emmer, E. T., and L. Stough. (2001). Classroom management: A critical part of educational psychology, with implications for teacher education. *Educational Psychologist* 36, 103–112.

29. Dweck, C. (2006). *Mindset: The New Psychology of Success.* New York: Random House.

30. Kornell, N., M. Hays, and R. Bjork. (2009). Unsuccessful retrieval attempts enhance subsequent learning. *Journal of Experimental Psychology* 35, 989–998. DOI: 10.1037/a0015729.

31. Freiberg, H. J., C. A. Huzinec, and S. M. Templeton. (2009). Classroom management—a pathway to student achievement: A study of fourteen inner-city elementary schools. *Elementary School Journal* 110, 63–80.

32. Nelsen, J., A. Rafael, and S. Foster. (2012). *Positive Discipline for Children with Special Needs.* New York: Three Rivers Press.

33. Resnick, M. D., P. S. Bearman, R. W. Blum, K. E. Buoman, K. M. Harris, J. Jones, J. Tabor, T. Beuhring, R. E. Sieving, M. Shew, M. Ireland, L. H. Bearingere, and J. R. Udry. (1997). Protecting adolescents from harm: Findings from the National Longitudinal Study of Adolescent Health. *Journal of the American Medical Association* 278, 823–832.

34. Loukas, A., L. Roalson, and D. Herrera. (2010). School connectedness buffers the effects of negative family relations and poor effortful control on early adolescent conduct problems. *Journal of Research on Adolescence* 20, 13–22.

35. Wang, T., and R. Holcombe. (2010). Adolescents' perceptions of school environment, engagement, and academic achievement in middle school. *American Educational Research Journal* 47, 633–662.

36. Allday, R. A., and K. Pakurar. (2007). Effects of teacher greetings on student on-task behavior. *Journal of Applied Behavior Analysis* 40, 317–320.

37. Marzano, R. J., and J. S. Marzano. (2003). The key to classroom management. *Educational Leadership* 61, 6–13.

38. Centers for Disease Control. (2015). School connectedness. September 1. http://www.cdc.gov/healthyyouth/protective/connectedness.htm.

39. Siegel, D., and T. Bryson. (2014). *No Drama Discipline: The Whole-Brain Way to Calm the Chaos and Nurture Your Child's Developing Mind.* New York: Penguin Random House.

40. Decker, D., and S. Christenson. (2007). Teacher-student relationships among behaviorally at-risk African American youth from low-income backgrounds: Student perceptions, teacher perceptions, and socioemotional adjustment correlates. *Journal of School Psychology* 45, 83–109.

41. Marzano, R. J., and J. S. Marzano. (2003). The key to classroom management. *Educational Leadership* 61, 6–13.

42. McCombs, B. L., and J. S. Whisler. (1997). *The Learner-Centered Classroom and School: Strategies for Increasing Student Motivation and Achievement.* San Francisco: Jossey-Bass.

43. Adler, A., H. L. Ansbacher, and R. R. Ansbacher. (1956). *The Individual Psychology, a Systematic Presentation in Selections from His Writings.* New York: Basic Books.

44. Hanna, F., C. Hanna, and S. Keys. (1999). Fifty strategies for counseling defiant and aggressive adolescents: Reaching, accepting, and relating. *Journal of Counseling and Development* 77, 395–404.

45. Schmakel, P. O. (2008). Early adolescents' perspectives on motivation and achievement in academics. *Urban Education* 6, 723–749.

46. Ladson-Billings, G. (1994). *The Dreamkeepers: Successful Teachers of African American Children.* San Francisco: Jossey-Bass.

47. Brown, D. (2004). Urban teachers' professed classroom management strategies: Reflections of culturally responsive teaching. *Urban Education* 39, 266–289.

48. Siegel, D., and T. Bryson. (2011). *The Whole Brain Child: 12 Revolutionary Strategies for Nurturing Your Child's Developing Mind.* New York: Random House.

49. Siegel, D., and T. Bryson. (2011). *The Whole Brain Child: 12 Revolutionary Strategies for Nurturing Your Child's Developing Mind.* New York: Random House.

50. Willis, J. (2007). Engaging the whole child: The neuroscience of joyful education. *Educational Leadership Online*, summer, 64.

51. Activities for teaching these skills can be found in Nelsen, J., L. Lott, and H. S. Glenn. (2013). *Positive Discipline in the Classroom*. 4th ed. New York: Three Rivers Press.

52. Sulkowski, M., M. Demaray, and P. Lazarus. (2015). Connecting students to schools to support their emotional well-being and academic success. *Communiqué* 40, no. 7. https://www.nasponline.org/publications/periodicals/communique/issues/volume-40-issue-7/connecting-students-to-schools-to-support-their-emotional-well-being-and-academic-success.

53. Leachman, G., and D. Victor. (2003). Student-led class meetings. *Educational Leadership* 60, no. 6, 64–68.

54. Edwards, D., and F. Mullis. (2003). Classroom meetings: Encouraging a climate of cooperation. *Professional School Counseling Journal* 7, no. 1, 20–29.

55. Edwards, D. (2005). From class lecture notes. Georgia State University, Department of Counseling and Psychological Services.

56. Stronge, J. H., J. M. Checkley, and P. Steinhorn. (2007). *Qualities of Effective Teachers*. 2nd ed. Alexandria, VA: Association for Supervision and Curriculum Development.

57. https://www.facebook.com/Raffi.Cavoukian/photos/a.249846041744561.60969.151883644874135/987679737961184/?type=3&theater.

58. Lasala, T., J. McVittie, and S. Smitha. (2012). *Positive Discipline in the School and Classroom: Teachers' Guide, Activities for Students*. Positive Discipline Association.

59. Sutherland, K., T. Lewis-Palmer, J. Stichter, and P. Morgan. (2008). Examining the influence of teacher behavior and classroom context on the behavioral and academic outcomes for students with emotional or behavioral disorders. *Journal of Special Education* 41, 223–233.

60. Potter, S. (1999) Positive interaction among fifth graders: Is it a possibility? The effects of classroom meetings on fifth-grade student behavior. Master's thesis, Southwest Texas State University, San Marcos, TX.

61. Clifton, D. O., and P. Nelson. (1992). *Soar with Your Strengths*. New York: Dell.

62. Harvard Family Research Project. (2009). Parent-teacher conference tip sheets for principals, teachers, and parents. *FINE Newsletter* 1, no. 1.

63. Henderson, A., and K. Map. (2002). A new wave of evidence: The impact of school, family and community connections on student achievement. Southwest Educational Development Lab, Institute of Education, Austin, TX.

64. Marcon, R. A. (1999). Positive relationships between parent school involvement and public school inner city preschoolers' development and academic performance. *School Psychology Review* 28, no. 3, 395–412.

65. Warneken, F., and M. Tomasella. (2006). Altruistic helping in human infants and young chimpanzees. *Science* 311, 1301–1303.

66. Edwards, D., K. Gfroerer, C. Flowers, and Y. Whitaker. (2004). The relationship between social interest and coping resources in children. *Professional School Counseling* 7, 187–194.

67. Zakrzewski, V. (2014). Just for the joy of it. *Educational Leadership,* June, 22–26.

68. Kohn, A. (1993). *Punished by Rewards: The Trouble with Gold Stars, Incentive Plans, A's, Praise, and Other Bribes.* Boston: Houghton Mifflin.

69. Kohn, A. (1994). The risk of rewards: ERIC Digest. ERIC Clearinghouse on Elementary and Early Childhood Education, Urbana, IL. ERIC Identifier ED376990.

70. Fabes, R. A., J. Fultz, N. Eisenberg, T. May-Plumlee, and F. S. Christopher. (1989). Effects of rewards on children's prosocial motivation: A socialization study. *Developmental Psychology* 25, 509–515.

71. Lepper, M. R., D. Greene, and R. E. Nisbett. (1973). Undermining children's intrinsic interest with extrinsic reward: A test of the "overjustification" hypothesis. *Journal of Personality and Social Psychology* 28, 129–137.

72. Garbarino, J. (1975). The impact of anticipated reward upon cross-age tutoring. *Journal of Personality and Social Psychology* 32, 421–428.

73. Mueller, C. M., and C. Dweck. (1998). Praise for intelligence can undermine children's motivation and performance. *Journal of Personality and Social Psychology* 1, 33–52.

74. Dweck, C. (2006). *Mindset: The New Psychology of Success.* New York: Random House.

75. Marzano, R. (2003). *What Works in Schools.* Alexandria, VA: Association of Supervision and Curriculum Development.

76. Siegel, D., and T. Bryson. (2011). *The Whole Brain Child: 12 Revolutionary Strategies for Nurturing Your Child's Developing Mind.* New York: Random House.

77. Beilock, S. L. (2008). Math performance in stressful situations. *Current Directions in Psychological Science* 17, 339–343.

78. Choudhury, S., S. Blakemore, and T. Charman. (2006). Social cognitive development during adolescence. *Social, Cognitive, and Affective Neuroscience* 1, no. 3, 165–174.

79. Shure, M. B., and G. Spivack. (1982). Interpersonal problem-solving in young children: A cognitive approach to prevention. *American Journal of Community Psychology* 10, 341–356.

80. Browning, L., B. Davis, and V. Resta. (2000). What do you mean "think before I act?": Conflict resolution with choices. *Journal of Research in Childhood Education* 14, 232–238.

81. Siegel, D., and T. Bryson. (2014). *No Drama Discipline: The Whole-Brain Way to Calm the Chaos and Nurture Your Child's Developing Mind*. New York: Penguin Random House.

82. Eisenberger, N. I., M. D. Lieberman, and K. D. Williams. (2003). Does rejection hurt? An fMRI study of social exclusion. *Science* 302, no. 5643, 290–292.

83. Sulkowski, M., M. Demaray, and P. Lazarus. (2015). Connecting students to schools to support their emotional well-being and academic success. *Communiqué* 40, no. 7. https://www.nasponline.org/publications/periodicals/ communique/issues/volume-40-issue-7/connecting-students-to-schools-to -support-their-emotional-well-being-and-academic-success.

84. Garrett, T. (2014). *Classroom Management: The Essentials*. New York: Teachers College Press.

85. Gordon, T. (1974). *Teacher Effectiveness Training*. New York: Wyden.

86. Kubany, E., and D. Richard. (1992). Verbalized anger and accusatory "you" messages as cues for anger and antagonism among adolescents. *Adolescence* 27, 505–516.

87. Cheung, S. K., and S. Y. C. Kwok. (2003). How do Hong Kong children react to maternal I-messages and inductive reasoning? *Hong Kong Journal of Social Work* 37, no. 1, 3–14.

88. Heydenberk, W., and R. Heydenberk. (2007). More than manners: Conflict resolution in primary level classrooms. *Early Childhood Education Journal* 35, 119–126.

89. Shure, M. B., and G. Spivack. (1980). Interpersonal problem solving as a mediator of behavioral adjustment in preschool and kindergarten children. *Journal of Applied Developmental Psychology* 1, 29–44.

90. Shure, M. B., and G. Spivack. (1982). Interpersonal problem-solving in young

children: A cognitive approach to prevention. *American Journal of Community Psychology* 10, 341–356.

91. Durlak, J., R. Weissberg, A. Dymnicki, R. Taylor, and K. Schellinger. (2011). The impact of enhancing students' social and emotional learning: A meta-analysis of school-based universal interventions. *Child Development* 82, 405–432. DOI: 10.1111/j.1467-8624.2010.01564.x.

92. Potter, S. (1999). Positive interaction among fifth graders: Is it a possibility? The effects of classroom meetings on fifth-grade student behavior. Master's thesis, Southwest Texas State University, San Marcos, TX.

93. McLeod, J. (2003). Managing administrative tasks, transitions, and interruptions. In J. McLeod, J. Fisher, and G. Hoover, *The Key Elements of Classroom Management: Managing Time and Space, Student Behavior, and Instructional Strategies*. Alexandria, VA: Association for Supervision and Curriculum Development.

94. Stronge, J. H., J. M. Checkley, and P. Steinhorn. (2007). *Qualities of Effective Teachers*. 2nd ed. Alexandria, VA: Association for Supervision and Curriculum Development.

95. Emmer, E. T., and L. Stough. (2001). Classroom management: A critical part of educational psychology, with implications for teacher education. *Educational Psychologist* 36, 103–112.

96. Kern, L., and K. Parks. (2012). Choice making opportunities for students: Module 4. Virginia Department of Education, Division of Special Education and Student Services.

97. Fox, L., and S. Langhans. (2005). Logical consequences: Brief 18. From *What Works Briefs,* Center on the Social and Emotional Foundations for Early Learning, Vanderbilt University.

98. NASP (2002). Fair and effective discipline for all students: Best practice strategies for educators. Fact sheet. National Association of School Psychologists.

99. Rosenthal, R. (1994). Interpersonal expectancy effects: A 30-year perspective. *Current Directions in Psychological Science* 3, no. 6, 176–179.

100. Yatvin, J. (2009). Rediscovering the "Pygmalion Effect." *Education Week* 29, no. 9, 24–25.

101. Lewin, K., R. Lippit, and R. White. (1939). Patterns of aggressive behavior in experimentally created "social climates." *Journal of Social Psychology* 10, 271–299.

102. Graham, A. M., P. A. Fisher, and J. H. Pfeifer. (2013). What sleeping babies

hear: A functional fMRI study of interparental conflict and infants' emotion processing. *Psychological Science* 24, 782–789.

103. Lynn, S. (accessed Oct. 2016). How do language and tone affect children's behavior? Our Everyday Life website, http://oureverydaylife.com/language-tone-affect-childrens-behavior-16124.html.

104. Wanzer, M. B., A. B. Frymier, A. M. Wojtaszczyk, and T. Smith. (2006). Appropriate and inappropriate uses of humor by teachers. *Communication Education* 55, no. 2, 178–196. DOI: 10.1080/03634520600566132.

105. Stronge, J. H., J. M. Checkley, and P. Steinhorn. (2007). *Qualities of Effective Teachers*. 2nd ed. Alexandria, VA: Association for Supervision and Curriculum Development.

106. Emmer, E. T., and L. Stough. (2000). Classroom management: A critical part of educational psychology, with implications for teacher education. *Educational Psychologist* 36, 103–112.

107. Walker, J. M. (2009). Authoritative classroom management: How control and nurturance work together. *Theory into Practice* 48, 122–129.

108. Chamundeswari, S. (2013). Teacher management styles and their influence on performance and leadership development among students at the secondary level. *International Journal of Academic Research in Progressive Education and Development* 2, no. 1, 367–418.

109. Slate, J. R., M. M. Capraro, and A. J. Onwuegbuzi. (2007). Students' stories of their best and poorest K–5 teachers: A mixed data analysis. *Journal of Educational Research and Policy Studies* 7, 53–77.

110. Bandura, A. (1986). *Social Foundations of Thought and Action: A Social Cognitive Theory*. Englewood Cliffs, NJ: Prentice-Hall.

111. Bandura, A., D. Ross, and S. A. Ross. (1961). Transmission of aggression through imitation of aggressive models. *Journal of Abnormal and Social Psychology* 63, 575–582.

112. Duplass, J. (2006). *Middle and High School Teaching: Methods, Standards, and Best Practices*. Boston: Houghton Mifflin.

113. Harbour, K. E., L. L. Evanovich, C. A. Sweigart, and L. E. Hughes. (2015). A brief review of effective teaching practices that maximize student engagement. *Preventing School Failure* 59, no. 1, 5–13.

114. Blase, J., and J. Blase. (2006). *Teachers Bringing Out the Best in Teachers: A Guide to Peer Consultation for Administrators and Teachers*. Thousand Oaks, CA: Corwin Press.

115. Royal, M., and R. J. Rossi. (1997) Schools as communities. *ERIC Digest* 111.

116. McVittie, J. D. (2003). Research supporting Positive Discipline in homes, schools, and communities. Positive Discipline Association.

117. Yacapsin, M. (2014). Self-care helps student teachers to deal with stress. *Women in Higher Education* 19, no. 10, 34. DOI: 10.1002/whe.10109.

118. Eldar, E., N. Nabel, C. Schechter, R. Talmor, and K. Mazin. (2003). Anatomy of success and failure: The story of three novice teachers. *Educational Research* 45, 29–48.

119. Emmer, E. T., and L. Stough. (2001). Classroom management: A critical part of educational psychology, with implications for teacher education. *Educational Psychologist* 36, 103–112.

120. Brouwers, A., and W. Tomic. (2000). A longitudinal study of teacher burnout and perceived self-efficacy in classroom management. *Teaching and Teacher Education* 16, 239–254.

INDEX

ABOUT THE AUTHORS

JANE NELSEN is the author and coauthor of more than twenty-two books and is a California-licensed family therapist with a doctorate in educational psychology from the University of San Francisco. She finds much of her material as the mother of seven children, twenty-two grandchildren, and ten great-grandchildren (and still counting)—and a very supportive husband. She wrote and self-published the first Positive Discipline book in 1981, which was later picked up by a Penguin Random House publisher. Many books in the Positive Discipline series have followed (including a book written with two of her children) and have now been translated into many languages. Jane has also coauthored training workshops in *Teaching Parenting the Positive Discipline Way* and *Positive Discipline in the Classroom*. Dates and locations for these live workshops (and the DVD training formats for people unable to travel to live workshops) can be found at www.positivediscipline.com, where information also can be found about parenting classes taught by Certified Positive Discipline Parent Educators in the United States and other countries. This book will be published during the year when Jane turns eighty, and she is still traveling the world presenting lectures and workshops.

KELLY GFROERER is the director of Training and Research for the Positive Discipline Association. She has worked as a teacher, school counselor, and educational consultant in the greater Atlanta area for over two decades. She is a Licensed Professional Counselor with a doctorate in counselor education and supervision from Georgia State University. She served as the managing editor for the *Journal of Individual Psychology* from 1995 to 2001. Kelly continues to serve the journal as a contributing editor. Kelly first learned about Positive Discipline in graduate school, where much of her coursework focused on Adlerian psychology. Kelly is a frequent speaker on Positive Discipline and a Positive Discipline Certified Trainer. She lives in Atlanta, Georgia, with her husband, Terry, and three children: Bryce, Riley, and Morgan.

ALSO IN THE POSITIVE DISCIPLINE SERIES

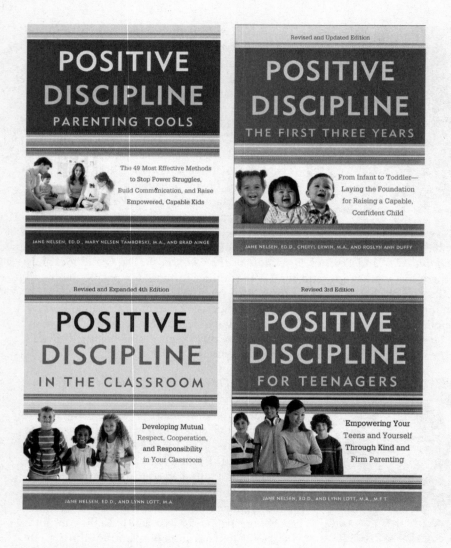

 HARMONY

BOOKS · NEW YORK